CROSS ROADS IN IRELAND

By PADRAIC COLUM

THE ROAD ROUND IRELAND
WILD EARTH AND OTHER POEMS
DRAMATIC LEGENDS AND OTHER POEMS
CASTLE CONQUER
THREE PLAYS
THE KING OF IRELAND'S SON

CROSS ROADS IN IRELAND - - - BY PADRAIC COLUM

6426-D

THE MACMILLAN COMPANY

PUBLISHERS : 1930 : NEW YORK

Printed in the United States of America by
J. J. LITTLE & IVES COMPANY, NEW YORK

The writer gratefully acknowledges his indebtedness to several Irish painters who have given him permission to use reproductions of their pictures—to "A. E." for permission to use his "Strand"; to Paul Henry for his "Cottages," "The Fairy Thorn," and "West of Ireland Scene"; to Sean Keating for "Barney Backed a Winner," "The Tipperary Hurler," and "Night's Candles Are Burnt Out" (picture illustrating the completion of the Shannon hydro-electrical power scheme); to Maurice McGonigal for his "Wicklow Mountain"; to Michael MacLiammoir for his "Galway," and to Leo Whelan for his "Quiet Interior." Thanks are due, too, to Mr. George Gordon Moore, in whose possession "The Tipperary Hurler" is, and to Mrs. John Raskob, the owner of "The Fairy Thorn," for permission to reproduce these paintings. And acknowledgments are made to The Hackett Galleries, New York, through whom these reproductions were procured.

To the Belgian painter, Mdlle. Marie Howet, thanks are given for permission to reproduce three of her pictures of Ireland—"La Montagne d'Achelin," "La Baie de Dooagh," and "Le Seau d'Argent." And to Miss Estella Solomons for her two drawings illustrating the Goldsmith country—"The Busy Mill" and "The Decent Church that Topt the Neighb'ring Hill."

CONTENTS

PART I. MEATH AND CAVAN

PART II. MID-ULSTER

Contents

Contents

PART VI. THE SOUTH

ILLUSTRATIONS

ILLUSTRATIONS

CROSS ROADS IN IRELAND

CROSS ROADS IN IRELAND

PART I

Meath and Cavan

A Road in Meath

THE river flowing towards the old stone bridge of five arches is the Boyne. It is a stream that is better for the fowler than the fisher, a friend of mine tells me: swan, wild duck, heron are upon it. There is no great quantity of fish in it. The Boyne is a peaceful river with meadows and demesnes by its sides. But it has a current stronger than one might think: horses hunting find it hard to ford; reeds grow out from its edges and its mud is deep.

I cross the bridge and fall in with a man who has ten head of cattle before him. He is an old man, and he talks to me about his grandfather who dealt in cattle, driving them from Galway, in the west of Ireland, to Dublin. In those days it would take as long as a fortnight to get from one place to the other, the man trudging along the roads and stopping at fairs on the way. He lived in the Midlands hereabouts; the cattle he brought so far would be left in the yard of his farm-house; his wife would sit up all night, every night the cattle were there, watching them and keeping lighted the spluttering rosin candles that went out so quickly. She had to keep guard over the cattle while the man slept, for those were unsettled times and a man might be robbed of all he had. And indeed my friend's grandfather was robbed in the end—robbed in Dublin of five hundred pounds; he died of a broken heart because of it, for that five hundred pounds was his life's savings—all he had gained by his buying and selling, his tramping and watching along the roads between Galway and Dublin.

The hawthorn hedges that border the road are high and flourishing; the haws are becoming red on them. Cocks of hay are in the fields; they are a sign that the hedges will soon be attended to. Through the last weeks of July and the first weeks of August all effort is put into saving the hay. And then, the hay secured, the hedges are clipped and trimmed. At least, so it is in the County Meath. We meet one or two tramps who quaintly salute us. There are not so many tramps on the Irish roads as there used to be ten or twelve years ago. They were harmless enough, my companion told me. But there are newcomers upon the road who are not harmless. He pointed to a gypsy van which was drawn up by the roadside: the gypsies are coming into the Irish counties now; they'd go to your house and ask you for something, and all the time they'd be spying out for themselves, and a day or two later some of the band would thieve back and steal what the others had marked. They had to be watched, these gypsies, and they would have to be dealt with very soon.

At that moment I saw the very folk who, it seemed to me, might be trusted to deal with the gypsies. Down a side-road was a huddle of asses, carts, children; there were elongated coverings that were not tents—they looked like burrows that had been elevated. A man or a woman could just stretch themselves in one of them. This was a camp of tinkers. The elders might still be asleep upon the hay inside the canvas coverings. But the children and the asses were around, and they were enough to give the impression of an uproarious life. I could see that, if a conflict came, the tinkers would go through the gypsies like hawks through a flock of starlings. . . . While I was standing beside a monument a woman came over from a gypsy van and spoke to me.

Gypsy Sojourners

Since the War the gypsies have been coming into Ireland, and now one sees their vans in many places. Before the War one seldom saw a gypsy on the Irish roads—it might be supposed that the Romany wanderers, like the Roman soldiers, felt that this ultimate island was too remote from their march. Occasionally one saw a gypsy family along a river-bank just outside Dublin, but one never heard of them being anywhere else in the country. Even now the gypsies one sees look tourists rather than sojourners; they are a horse-owning while the vagrants that Ireland knows of are an ass-owning folk.

The woman who spoke to me was, at the back of that town, as noticeable as an exotic flower or bird. Her figure was small and fine; she had on a bright shawl and wore silver ear-rings and brooches. She was young—as yet she had not the sombre eyes and the beaked nose of the elder gypsy women. She carried a basket and a baby, and the name she gave herself was Mrs. Smith.

Mrs. Smith spoke English with unexpected imperfections: her English, I thought, was the English of a Welsh speaker. She had lived in Wales, but she assured me she was pure Romany. Her baby was really a fine little fellow; he slept easily, and wakened only to laugh or crow; he was well cared for and his dress was adorned with scraps of colour. Baby was six months old, Mrs. Smith told me; his name was Patrick; her husband was an Irishman, she said.

Possibly Mrs. Smith was mistaken about the name of her child; she certainly was in error about her husband's race. He may have been a Celt, but he wasn't the sort of Celt that abounds in Ireland. The van they lived in was a new one, and when I called on the family the man was putting finishing touches on it with a pocket-knive. "Pat," the infant, was inside: wrapped in a shawl he slept on the floor of the van as naturally as an April lamb by the side of a furze-bush. "We did have cradle," said Mrs. Smith, "and the cradle got

burn up." There was another child within, a girl with
the more likely name of "Lil."

Mrs. Smith claimed she could teach me Romany.
"Gry" was the word for horse, "drum" was the word
for road, "chavvy" was child, "vada" was van. Or she
would tell me my fortune. I agreed to have her do this,
and I was invited within the gypsy van. Nothing could
be farther from the Blasted Heath or the Delphic Cave
than this homely interior. Little Patrick wakened and
his mother took him up to nurse. The crystal would
cost more than the cards—about a hundred and fifty
per cent more—but I was fascinated by the idea of the
magic glasses and wanted to have my fortune told that
way. So Mrs. Smith took from the bosom of her dress
a crystal composed of three translucent balls joined
together, each about the size of a grape. I lit a candle
and stuck it in the wood of the van, and the séance
opened, the gypsy woman nursing her baby.

It began with a little ritual. "Do you give this with
all your heart?" She crossed the crystal with the coin
I produced and went into the commonplaces of fortune-
telling. Her glances and recurring phrases had a sibyl-
line suggestion, however. "You will cross a mountain
—do you understand me now? You will live to be
fifty—do you understand me now?" I saw no mountain in her magic glasses. I considered the appeal that
fortune-telling makes to our naïf egoism.

Those of us who are only slightly credulous about
other people's power of divination are eager, I suppose,
to know the sort of effect that our personalities pro-

duce. And we can be made satisfied with elementary statements. A little observation, a little knowledge of the world, permits the fortune-teller to make statements that correspond with something in the character, in the course of the life of the person she speaks to. There are passions and spiritual movements that an observer will not be aware of. Fortunately for the seeress, most people are more interested in their external lives than they are in the rare and tragic movements of their real personalities.

I brought away from the gypsy van an impression of a life far removed from what we associate with sibyls and wanderers, an impression that comes with the memory of a shrewd woman nursing her child. They have a civilization of the hearth and the cradle, these gypsies, and a way of living that makes for homely comfort and the assurance that children are well cared for, a tradition that makes for graciousness of manner, for colourfulness in dress. One does not look to find such things amongst the vagrants who are native to the Irish roads.

"The tinkers own Ireland," the man I had walked beside said to me. "They are the real kings of the road. They'll work for you, mending your tins or doing anything that's in their trade, and they'll only steal for their cattle—hay, turnips, and the like. The men will fight in a field with all the others looking on. 'Have you got enough?' one will say to the other, and the fight will go on until one or the other says he has got enough of a beating. And never another blow will

[6]

be struck after that word is said. But one or the other of them will have to say, 'I have enough,' and throw down his shillelagh. They fight in the old-fashioned way, handling their shillelaghs in the middle. They punish each other something cruel, and I have seen them with blood pouring down their heads and faces. But not another blow after a man has said 'I have enough.' The tinkers are not dishonourable men."

Wellington in Meath

The gypsy woman had come to me as I was standing beside a monument. It is a column where the Duke of Wellington in Roman garb stands high above the hedges. I read the inscription:

This column erected in the year MDCCCXVII in honour of the illustrious Duke of Wellington by the grateful contributions of the County Meath.

I reflected that a monument as ill-placed as this one had become appropriate. For Wellington, though born near this place and of a family that had been in Ireland since the fifteenth century, meant nothing to this little town of Trim, nor to the County Meath. He certainly had not caused two potatoes to grow where one had grown before. His name comes into no ballad, no story sung in the streets, or told in the houses near by:

Around and above him Bellona did hover,
And Paris rejoiced the next day.

Cross Roads in Ireland

That song and a hundred songs of its popular kind were made to celebrate Napoleon's marchings through Europe. The people hereabouts did not sing of London's rejoicings after Bellona had hovered over the Duke of Wellington. The victory of Wellington was a victory for the landlords as against the peasants of Europe; the crowbar went under the thresholds of many cabins hereabouts as a consequence of Waterloo.

The house where his father lived, and where, according to accounts, Arthur Wellesley was born, stood near the town of Trim.[1] There is only a wall to mark its site now. And the castle which he had built for himself hereabouts is in ruins—it was burnt down accidentally. Houses which were centuries old when the house he had spent his childhood in and the house he had built for himself were here, are still being lived in, but nothing that belonged to that expert, dutiful, loveless Anglo-Irishman stands intact. This column, then, has become appropriate. Designed, one supposes, for a square in a city, it stands back of this little town; weeds grow around it and a rusty railing shuts people off from it; the boys of the town cannot play ball against it, so useless it is.

The town is Trim. A little way from Trim is Laracor, and Laracor comes into literary history; Jonathan Swift had his parsonage there when he invited Hester Johnson to come to Ireland and be his neighbour.

[1] Arthur Wellesley, it has now been shown, was born in Dublin, not at the family seat in Meath.

Meath and Cavan

At Laracor

I come first to the Protestant church; it is well kept but deserted looking. It is not Swift's church; it was not here he was wont to preach the sermon addressed exclusively to the sexton, and beginning "Dearly beloved Roger," but it is built where that old church was. A mile and a half away was the rectory—a wall stands to mark where Swift lived in Meath. And about two miles from where the rectory was stands a cottage with its gable-end to the road—a cottage that is still lived in—and this is where Hester Johnson had her abode. It is a little higher than the other cottages near by; it is thatched and grey. I enter through a gate and see hens and cocks and ducks; clothes drying on the hedge; two goats, their heads in a sort of scaffolding, trying to climb a ditch. Hester's cottage has been made into two cottages of two rooms each; an agricultural labourer and his family live on each side.

The house has been divided, but it has hardly been altered, and one can sit by the fireside that Swift sat by while Mrs. Dingley got supper ready, and Hetty, the light of the candles showing the darkness of her hair, guessed an answer to a riddle the doctor had made up, or plucked out a needle to mend his frayed bands, or scolded him for letting the laundress return his linen so scorched. He saw Hetty every day (Stella was not the name he had for her then—he named her Stella after the Laracor days). He would lay his hands on her head when she had her terrible headaches; he would bring her the verses he had made, and talk their "little language" to her while she won him from a black mood. Doctor Swift never spent a night under this roof; he never visited Hetty without some third person being in the house.

And while he was here he came to have a better liking for Ireland. "If I love Ireland better than I did," he wrote while he was here, "it is because we are nearer related, for I am deeply allied to its poverty." There was, perhaps, a more human reason for this rise in his liking. At all events he had some peace and happiness while here. In London, afterwards, he met a dean of Westminster, and wrote that he preferred Laracor to those famous cloisters. His Hetty turned herself into an Irishwoman, into something of an Irish nationalist, and this, one can easily suppose, was a token of her being happy in this place.

Two good miles—just five thousand, seven hundred, and forty-eight steps—bring the doctor to the cottage where Mistress Johnson and Madam Dingley are living with Marget, their maid. It is the middle of March. The willows begin to peep and the quicks of the hedges to bud. The cherry-trees are growing along the river-walk; it is not likely the apples have been blasted this year by the frost. Last night, as he will tell Hetty, he dreamt of eating ripe cherries. Now they begin to catch pike, and they will shortly take trout, "if the floods do not get over the holly bank." But if they do, farewell to the pike.

The doctor surveys all as he walks along with his lightning stride. It was he who had planted here the hedges and the apple-trees and the cherry-trees. He congratulates himself on his foresight on having the bottom of the canal cleared a month ago. It was then that he had the willows cut down and new ones planted; it was then that he attended to those quick-sets—to the hedges that now look so well. And Hetty is here, and he can see her every day! And now he goes into the cottage. Dingley is there, but Hetty is still a-bed. Headaches! She comes down, and he lays his hand upon her head. "God help poor, dear Hetty's eyes!" He tells her that she must not read, and when she returns that he is always at her to read more, he tells her he won't have her strain her eyes, and that she has more wit than any woman he has ever known—more by a bar's length, so she has! He will get her a large-print Bible. Hetty does not know the Bible and cannot follow a reference to any personage in it. Dingley has always to explain the references to her.

The doctor stays to breakfast, and Patrick, his man, who has followed him, comes in carrying Madam Dingley's lap-dog. And there is talk with Marget, the maid, who can be awed by long and mysterious words. The doctor recommends the ladies to walk, and tells them how much good he gets out of his walks, or rather out of his runs. They are to walk three miles a day. But out of consideration for Hetty, he would have them stop at every milestone, and would wish that there might be a good inn for them at every stop. To-day is the twenty-fifth of March. A flip on the cheek is given to Dingley and to Hetty to remind them of the date: winter is over to-day; there are to be no more card games and no more fires until September to warm the room where they sit.

And now it is come to April and dear, pretty Hetty's birthday. "Pray God we may never be asunder," he tells her. They talk about the time when they were both domiciled at Sir William Temple's. "In what pain I would be when Sir William would look cold and out of humour for three or four days, and how I would suspect a hundred reasons," he reminds her. What a relief that all that is over, and that they are here together in Laracor. "Well," Doctor Swift says, "I have plucked up my spirit since then; he spoiled a very fine gentleman!" And now visitors come in. Mr. Warburton, the doctor's curate, who makes very little impression on the company. And then Joe Beaumont, "Poet Joe." He is from Trim, a youngish man, but grey-headed, a mathematician and an investigator of longitude. And he is Mistress Johnson's humble servant and has come to pay his respects to her. Later on in the day he will talk to Doctor Swift about the set of sleaing tables he has invented for the improvement of the linen trade, and about the affairs of Trim. The poor town is in danger of losing its franchise. But the doctor offers no help; the townspeople have behaved so ill to him and have so little regarded the advice he gave them, and disagreed so much amongst themselves, that he is resolved never to have more to do with them. But whatever personal kindness he can do for Joe shall be done. And when Joe talks about his calculation and his invention the doctor promises to get him an award from the Government.

Summer comes. Doctor Swift is prevailed upon to visit Raymond, the rector of Trim. Mistress Johnson and Dingley make a visit too. There is eel and trout fishing. Hetty, riding by in the morning, sees the doctor sitting in the rectory garden in his morning gown. And beside him is the night-cap that Dingley made for him—a night-cap trimmed with fur. They call to each other as Joe Beaumont takes her to the Hill of Bree and around by Scurlockstown. The attendant has to get down every few minutes to attend to the lady's saddle-girths. Then evening, and they are together in the rectory, and the doctor drinks coffee or green tea, but not bohea; he is made impatient by Raymond's talk, but he puts up with the parson. Raymond talks of being in London some time when Doctor Swift is there. Later on Presto and his Hetty talk over that matter. "I shall not know what to do with him in town; to be sure I will not present him to any acquaintances of mine, and he will have a delicate life —a parson and a perfect stranger." But Raymond has made himself pleasing to Hetty—he prides himself on his good manners.

Autumn, and a party at Tom Longfield's, four miles from Trim. Such carking, and caring, and scolding from Dingley, as she and Hetty make ready to go.

Hetty is to ride, making a start before the others. But the horses have not come up to the door. The fellow who is to attend her can't find the bridle. Her stirrup is broken. Where did you put the whips, Dingley? Marget, where did you leave Mistress Johnson's riband to tie about her? Hand her her mask. And now she has to take this sup before she starts off. And now she is off! So, so! A gallop, a gallop! And now to ask Dingley whether Hetty has been a good girl. Does she mind her eyes and does she go early to bed? And does she expect to meet the fine-thing man down the road?

It is winter, but not yet very cold. Fires are burning, and the ladies have permission to play cards once more, and Mr. Warburton, the curate, comes and plays with them. Now they hear the riddles that Doctor Swift has been making. He fathers them on others, but they know that they have been made about things that their talk has been around. As Hetty sits idly by the table she makes puns that the doctor laughs at. Mr. Warburton leaves; Dingley reads with her magnifying-glass; Hetty comes over and sits by Presto. His right ear has become more deaf, and she talks to him on his left side. She puts her hands upon his head; her wonderfully clear eyes are shining for him. Dear, dear Hetty, may God Almighty bless her and keep her! There is that maxim of Culpepper's to fix in her mind:

Would you have a settled head? You must go early to bed:
I tell you, and I tell it again, you must be in bed at ten.

Meath and Cavan

They are advised to take their walks; they have to show the ladies of these parts that legs are given them for use.

> Walk fast in snow,
> In frost walk slow,
> And still as you go
> Tread on your toe.
> When frost and snow are both together
> Sit by the fire and spare shoe-leather.

And telling them this, the doctor leaves the ladies.

They go a-frostbiting on his recommendation. But a time comes when Doctor Swift himself, taking his five thousand, seven hundred, and forty-eight steps, comes into the cottage, starving with the cold. He goes into her room and turns Hetty out of her chair by the fire. Uth, uth, uth, uth! is his cry, as he holds out his hands to the fire. He rakes the ashes off; he holds his hands closer to the warmth. No one sees them there, and Hetty puts her arms around his neck, and the hair that is blacker than a raven's wing falls over him. And then they stand at the door of the cottage and see the snow coming on the hedges. All day he stays, and for want of something better to do makes verses on the little house that is beside the churchyard of Castle-knock.

> . . . A traveller, who by did pass,
> Observed the roof behind the grass;
> On tiptoe stood, and rear'd his snout,
> And saw the parson creeping out:
> Was much surprised to see a crow
> Venture to build his nest so low.

Cross Roads in Ireland

A schoolboy ran unto 't, and thought
The crib was down, the blackbird caught.
A third, who lost his way by night,
Was forced for safety to alight,
And, stepping o'er the fabric roof,
His horse had like to spoil his hoof.

Warburton took it in his noddle,
This building was designed a model;
Or of a pigeon-house or oven,
To bake one loaf or keep one dove in.

Then Mistress Johnson gave her verdict
And every one was pleased that heard it;
All that you make this stir about
Is but a still which wants a spout.
The Reverend Doctor Raymond guessed
More probably than all the rest;
He said, but that it wanted room,
It might have been a pigmy's tomb.

The doctor's family came by,
And little miss began to cry,
Give me that house in my own hand!
Then madam bade the chariot stand,
Call'd to the clerk in manner mild,
Pray, reach that thing here to the child;
That thing, I mean, among the kale;
And here's to buy a pot of ale.

The clerk said to her in a heat,
What! sell my master's country seat,
Where he comes every week from town!
He would not sell it for a crown.
Poh! fellow, keep not such a pother;
In half an hour thou'lt make another.

Meath and Cavan

Says Nancy, I can make for miss
A finer house ten times than this;
The dean will give me willow sticks,
And Joe my apron-full of bricks.

A House by the Boyne

I am back again by that reedy river; I mount a
few steps, pass growths of arbutus with their shining
green leaves, and come before the house at which I am
staying. Irish yews, most statuesque of trees, are growing there: a great one stands close to the garden-wall;
it is as wide and as solid as a house—a dark-green
house. These yews go up into turrets: on the turrets
little birds, chaffinchs and red-breasts, are sitting. I go
into a walled garden. Rose-trees and apple-trees are
together; walled by espaliered apple-trees is a sward
on which are beds of roses, red, pink, and white; in
the middle is an apple-tree overgrown with rambler
roses—a tall tree of roses with drooping branches that
are themselves rose-bushes—hanging bushes of roses.
Little birds flit through the garden, but no bird sings
there. Then from the garden to the stable-yard.

Here, sitting astride their horses, two girls in
breeches and with short hair let the reins rest in their
hands while Hugh Lucy talks to them out of his endless interest in horses. The mare has had a chill, but
is getting over it; she is getting to have the stride of
her grand-dam who was first at Punchestown in a memorable race. The black one, to his surprise, for he did

[17]

not think it was in the breed, promises to be a first-class jumper, and should be entered for competition in the Dublin Horse Show. The mounted horses stand on the cobble-stones of the quadrangle, and two others put their heads across the half-doors of their boxes. In the old days thirty horses, most of them hunters, were in these stables: there must have been a great clattering on the cobbles when they were led out and tended before the hunt on an autumn morning. Only four are kept now. But they are as nervous and as powerful as any that were bred here in the old days and are as well attended. And the girls in their knickers and their short hair sit their horses as well as the plumed young ladies with their full skirts who rode out of the quadrangle in the old times. They ride out, down the avenue with the laurel hedges, and out into the flat, green Meath country. We stay to talk with Hugh Lucy.

The quadrangle of the stables is a world to itself: cobble-paved, it has low whitewashed walls with tarred doors and red-tiled roofs. No geese gabble near, no cocks crow; the martens fly up to the nests they have plastered on the walls under the tiles. We are away from the house here. An under-groom brings a pail of water to the horses that put their heads across the half-doors.

There are other charges beside the horses. The Hunt Club has sent two puppies to the house—every house that has hunters is given its quota of puppies to rear. With big head and falling ears, one of them is sniffing at the cobble-stones; the other makes no effort to get around; weak and thin, this puppy is sitting still, and Hugh Lucy judges that it will not survive to hunt the fox in County Meath.

Hugh Lucy acts as steward for the whole place, but his beginning was in this quadrangle thirty years ago, and he still sees the problems of the house, the county, and the country from this quiet and stirring area. All his judgments are, as it were, made from across the saddle. If a man has little spirit, or will take no training, or hasn't much judgment, put him amongst horses and he will soon show himself up. "The fairest court of trial is the battle-field," says an old Irish proverb, and Hugh Lucy could easily be got to say that the fairest court of trial was the race-course or the hunting-field.

Tara

That royal place being near, we go to Tara. It is a deeply grassed plateau with mounds and shallow trenches upon it, and a wide prospect from it. The kings who had primacy amongst the kings of Ireland walked around the seven ramparts of Tara as the sun was rising, and looked on the Plain of Breg. "Beautiful was the colour of that plain, and there was upon it excellent blossom glowing with all the hues that are known." Furze, hawthorn, buttercups, clover, dandelion, foxglove, meadowsweet—there couldn't have been more blossoms than these. Well, as he walked here in the very early morning—for it was *gaessa* for the King of Ireland to be in bed while the sun was rising—he knew that he had a house in which a man could entertain his friends. Yonder mound marks that house—the Banqueting-Hall: our measurements show that it was seven hundred and fifty feet long and ninety wide—the largest building that Ireland has ever had, larger than Saint Patrick's Cathedral. It was built by Cormac MacAirt for the entertainment of a thousand guests. There were other buildings on Tara —the Hall of Synods, the Mansion of the Ladies. All were of timber, and so we can only trace their position and their foundations now. And on the side of the hill is the stone that the Tuatha De Danaan brought with them into Ireland away back in mythological times.

They brought other treasures, too, from those mysteriously named cities of theirs. "From Gorias was brought the spear that Lugh had; no battle was maintained against him who had it in his hand. From Finias was brought the sword of Nuadha; none used to escape who was wounded by it. From Murias was brought the cauldron of the Dagda; none came from it unsatisfied." But first of the treasures was the stone, the Lia Fail, which Lugh the Sun God left on Tara. "This is what used to scream under every king who took the sovereignty of Ireland, from the time of Lugh Lamfhada to the time of the birth of Christ, and it has never screamed thereafter under any king from that out; for it was a demon that had entrance into it, and the powers of every idol ceased in the time of the birth of the Lord." [1] Legend has it that this stone

[1] "Leabhar Gabhala," "The Book of the Invasions."

was brought from Tara into Scotland for the crowning of a king of an Irish dynasty there. From Scotland it was taken to England and it now lies under the Coronation Chair in Westminster Abbey. This is not to be believed. Who would have given permission for its removal? The Lia Fail, the Stone of Destiny, is still at Tara.

I was shown the stone by a Meathean, who, as I discovered when I got into familiar conversation with him, had the same kind of trouble on his mind as was on the mind of many a high-king who walked here between his own hall and the banqueting-hall. It was the old trouble that comes from having marriageable daughters and no husbands in sight for them. My friend had a family of three living in a cottage beside the Boyne. The young men came (or didn't come, I couldn't make out which), but they weren't to be considered. "None of them has as much land as would sod a lark, nor as much stock as you could pull on a cotton thread, nor as much coin as you'd put into a blind man's hat." As was natural to a man who spent his day beside the Stone of Destiny his mind went back to other days and he saw little that was good in the present times. The new type of pigs that the Government was introducing was of no benefit to the people, he told me. "While they're suckers, it's feed, feed, feed. The oul' pigs got nothing to fatten them except the stroke of a stick. The oul' breed of pigs was the best, like the oul' breed of cattle and the oul' breed of men." I think he and the rightful kings that the Lia

Fail screamed under, if they had met and talked here, would have understood each other.

But the kings who walked around the seven ramparts of Tara had a rich domain to look over. Meath, and especially the part of it that is around Tara, is the best pasture-land in Europe; the king who looked from the ramparts could see herds of cattle and droves of horses. Magnificence is always associated with Tara —magnificence and a certain style. When Cormac MacAirt is brought before us we note that "flowing and slightly curling was his golden hair. A red buckler, with stars and animals of gold and fastenings of silver upon him. A crimson cloak in wide descending folds around him, fastened at his neck with precious stones. A rich torque of gold around his neck. A white shirt with a full collar and intertwined with red-gold thread upon him. A girdle of gold inlaid with precious stones was around him. Two wonderful shoes of gold with golden loops upon his feet. Two spears with golden sockets in his hands with many rivets of red bronze. And he was himself besides symmetrical and beautiful of form without blemish or reproach." As splendid as Cormac's was the appearance of a stranger whom King Eochaid saw as he walked on the high ground of Tara one morning. "The tunic that the warrior wore was purple in colour, his hair was of golden yellow, and of such length that it reached to the edge of his shoulders. His eyes were lustrous and grey; in one hand he held a pointed spear, in the other a shield with a white central boss, and with gems of gold upon it." But this stranger was an immortal; he was no other than Midir the Proud, and he had come to win Eochaid's wife, Etain, from him.

This is the loveliest of the stories connected with Tara, the loveliest of the stories, indeed, in Celtic mythology or romance: how King Eochaid married Etain who in another incarnation had been the love of Midir, an immortal; how Midir sang a marvellous song to her, reminding her of the immortal land they both had dwelt in; how he won from the king the right to hold Etain in his arms and obtain a kiss from her, and how, when all this had been granted him, the pair rose in the air, flying from the house of the king to the land where "none speak of 'mine' or 'thine,'" where "eyes flash with many-colored lights and the hue of the foxglove is on every cheek." James Stephens, who in his "Irish Fairy Tales" (but the title is not appropriate; the stories in that book are not fairy tales; they are court romances) has re-told with such skill and poetry stories about kings of Tara and their queens, mortal and immortal, has not yet given us his version of Etain and Midir, nor has he yet re-told the most dramatic of all the happenings on Tara—the story of Grania's elopement from the banqueting-hall with Diarmuid on the night when she, the daughter of Cormac MacAirt, was married to Fionn, the old, unforgiving chief of the Fianna.

In the second quarter of the fifth century, a king, looking along the road that led from the north, saw a fire kindled: it was an evening when all lights were quenched until the Druids gave out lights from their sacred fire. The light had been made by Saint Patrick who was on his way to Tara to defy and overcome the powers of Druidism. He succeeded. But although the successors of King Laoghaire accepted Saint Patrick and his mission, there seems to have been always a conflict between the ecclesiastical power in Ireland and the power represented by Tara. Else why is there a story about Tara being abandoned owing to its being cursed by the saints of Ireland?

Historians do not accept that account of the abandonment. Tara was abandoned because the dynasty divided, or because the place itself could hardly be defended. Still, the story of the cursing of Tara must have some historical significance. As we have it, the story is written in the ecclesiastical interest; still, the saints of Ireland come very badly out of the affair.

The story begins with King Diarmuid who reigned a century after Saint Patrick's arrival—about the middle of the sixth century. Diarmuid seems to have had a real political idea: he wanted, one gathers, to reduce the power and prestige of the under-kings, and to have certain of his rights over them recognized, especially the right to open their fortresses. He sent an envoy through the country, "that his power might be manifested to the men of Erin generally." This envoy carried as a symbol of the high-king's power a spear which "he would carry athwart into the forts and fair cities of kings and other great men." [1] He would not

[1] "Life of Saint Ruadan: Lives of Irish Saints," by Charles Plummer.

enter any dwelling except with the spear of the high-king held athwart—"they made a breach in the city, and admitted Baclam, after breaching the city, with his spear athwart."

This Baclam, the high-king's envoy, was not popular. The writer of the "Life of Saint Ruadan" declares that he was a vile and outrageous person who was never on his guard against the devil, but he and the devil were ever in agreement to do despite to God. Anyway, Baclam was killed by a hot-tempered under-king. Then the killer of the high-king's envoy fled to a sanctuary in the domain of an ecclesiastic named Ruadan. King Diarmuid broke into the sanctuary, seized the culprit, and haled him to Tara.

But the ecclesiastics of the time were not going to let their privileges be over-ridden by any King of Tara. Several of the noted saints of Ireland joined themselves with Ruadan; they appeared before Tara and rang their bells against Diarmuid. "They also sang psalms of cursing and vengeance against him; but they could not obtain their will of the king, and he treated them with great contempt." The saints persisted in their attempt to make the king liberate the slayer of his envoy. He appeared before them and delivered an address; it had no effect on them, but it makes us think highly of the policy of this sixth-century king.

Then spoke Diarmuid: "It is a good work that I am engaged on, striving to uphold order and justice, to maintain right, and enforce respect for law. And I had the certainty of attaining it," said he, "were only peace maintained. But as for you," said he, "ill is your work in attempting to uphold wickedness, overturning right and sovereign rule, bringing law into contempt, and protecting criminals. The vengeance of the Lord will rain upon you therefor," said he.

Ruadan hadn't much to say by way of argument, but he had a good deal to say by way of abuse. "As to the house in which thou shalt die," said Saint Ruadan, "when that house is cleared out after the sheep, it will be on the rubbish-shovel that thou wilt be lifted from the bosom of a dung-heap." Diarmuid was not as persistent as the saints; he delivered his prisoner over to them.

Thereafter, according to the story, Tara was abandoned. On the night after the saints had rung their bells and sang their psalms of cursing and vengeance, the king had a vision that foreboded the ruin of the royal place.

He saw a mighty tree; and it seemed to him that the top of the tree was among the rafters of heaven, and its roots in the earth. He saw further thrice fifty men approach it. A broad-bladed axe was in the hand of every one of them, and they began to hack and hew the tree with them, till they brought it to the ground with them, and the noise of the tree falling roused the king from his troubled and restless sleep. And this is what remained in the windows of his hearing, the sound of the psalmody of Ruadan with his monks, and the ringing of their bells together as they cursed him, so that these sounds continued to fill his ears.

After the sixth century Tara is no longer a power in Ireland, although the high-kings continue to call themselves "Kings of Tara." When Brian Boru made himself high-king in the year 1000 Tara was as it is today, grass-covered and without a building upon it.

A Ruin of To-day

We came to a wrecked mansion on our way back. Once famous in the county as a piece of architecture, it was destroyed during the civil strife. Why was it destroyed? Its destruction was useless from the military point of view, and heavy compensation for it is being paid by the ordinary people in the county. The leaders of the Irregulars claimed that the place was likely to be occupied and used as a base against them. It is much more likely that its destruction was brought about by mere resentment—the resentment that was felt by the people against those in the great houses who took nearly everything from them and gave them neither return nor acknowledgment. I heard that the owner of this particular house was grudging towards the people around and grinding to his servants. The servants, it was said, stored the petrol and explosives that burnt and wrecked the mansion, and gave the signals for the attack.

It stands great and well planned: a double line of exotic trees give, from the steps, a vista to a colonnade around which roses are still growing. The centre and the wings are solidly there; only the doors and the windows show that the house has been devastated. Many are the ruins in the County Meath—castles and abbeys—but this place seems much more abandoned than any of them. There were the gardens without a breach in their walls, flowers and fruits still growing in them; there was the lake with swans upon it; there was the tennis-court with the courts marked, but with grasses growing over the markings. But when we went through the door of the house we found that in the hall rank shrubs were growing with astonishing luxuriance.

No more would the house with its gardens, with its vista to the colonnade, with its lake and its tennis-court, be parts of an integral domain; they were falling apart from each other. An ownerless house with what belonged to it separated and overgrown—lake and tennis-court and gardens—would be there.

And then, as we walk around the place, we hear a clock strike. I had heard in a great cathedral, from a gallery in front of the organ, a clock strike like that. Suddenly, in that deserted place, the strokes come, making a chime of unusual sweetness. We see the clock: its face is high up in the left wing of the house. It is a clock that was not put there just to tell work-hours—its chime is too musical for that. I could think of it as striking only to tell the ladies who were gathering roses in the garden that the carriage was leaving, or to remind one of them to talk to her maid about having her hair arranged another way before it was time to dress for dinner.

The strokes are right by our watches. The clock keeps correct time. But who attends to it? Who, in this forsaken place, can have an interest in keeping it going? Someone speaks of a herdsman who still stays within the gates. A herdsman, I thought, would surely be the last person to have an interest in clocks or to feel any urge to wind one. But Hugh Lucy declares that he knows about the herdsman, and that it is a fact that he goes up to where the clock is and keeps it going.

As we are going through the gate he points out the herdsman to us. He is whittling a stick, a solitary man with a hollow face and very bright eyes. When he moves we see that he has a bent back, either because of rheumatism or some hurt. He does not speak and he watches us unblinkingly. I wonder about him—what interest has he in keeping a sole thing going in that great, empty, ruined mansion?

Into Cavan

We go from that ruin to where we are cheered by bright lake-waters. Boys are fishing and little girls are playing with small stones which they throw up and catch. This is Loch Ramor with its thirty islands. Across the water is County Cavan. Cavan is a county of lakes—indeed, the most famous poem about it begins, "In Cavan of the little lakes." Loch Ramor may be reckoned as the first of its lakes.

We are rowed across it, and a little way up from the landing we come upon a house around which I expected to hear the yelping of whole kennels of dogs. But no such yelping comes to us. The house is a stone one, and had been built, evidently, as a lodge for shooting and fishing parties. There is a gun in the hallway; there is a white grouse in a case, and there are no other trophies. This is not as I expected it would be, for the owner of the house is the breeder and the possessor of a setter that is the last representative of a famous breed.

And when the possessor of the famous setter comes to us we see a man who has the looks of a student of the most earnest kind. He is a student and an earnest enthusiast for the canine race—at least for such of them as have pedigrees. Scratch an Irishman, says a proverb, and you will find a genealogist. We find that our friend carries more genealogies in his head than a Connacht beggar ever did. He is as deep in genealogy as a MacFirbis or an O'Hart. And no one making out a genealogy which would attach him to any of the families of the Five Bloods could have been more single-minded. The subject of the research is Dora, the obedient and alert, but still untrained young setter who is shown to us. Parchments are unrolled; they cover the table, the chairs, and the floor: the descent of Dora from an ancestor who was the first of a famous setter breed is fondly and elaborately traced. But, as often happens in the case of human descent, there is a gap —her descent from the mighty progenitor is a moral certainty, and a document which can be recovered from some archives will make that certainty an historical one. But meanwhile there is the gap. Five gen-

erations back Dora had an ancestor that was fourth in
descent from the founder of the famous line—that her
owner affirms as a credo, and, carried on by that de-
votedness, we are ready to affirm it with him.

And then we are outside, and our friend takes Dora
and her grand-dam, setters showing all good points in
their shapes and having the qualities of modesty, obedience, and alertness, upon leashes. Dora is not conscious that she is making her début, or if she is, her
modesty prevents her showing it. It is afternoon and
a good harvest day. We go through a stretch of furze
that has lost the gold of its blossoms and is now all
dark green; we go through the bracken of a hillside,
and then we come to a stretch of bog. There are snipe
here, and Dora and her grand-dam are unloosed so that
we may note their expertness. The grand-dam ranges
finely, and Dora shows that with training she will be
better than her grand-dam. A solitary snipe rises, then
the whistle sounds, and the two dogs, very obediently,
come back to us. We try a hollow for partridge, we
try a stubble for pheasants, but no more birds rise. We
make progress across the country, not with the swift-
ness of men hunting, but with the steadiness and alertness of men marching who, now and again, have an exciting happening to watch.

We come to a gate, we go out on the roadway, and
there, riding towards us, are the two girls, who, this
morning, had taken their horses out of the quadrangle.
They watch Dora from across the hedge; she is being
left to range by herself, and for every step she takes

forward in the field our friend takes the girls a step backward in her ancestry. She ranges splendidly; indeed it looks as if in the course of the afternoon she had reached complete expertness. A bird rises out of a grassy hollow. It is a corn-crake that had delayed its passage to the south. Dora stands, and the bird makes its low, unsteady flight.

The County Show

I like Ballinagh for many reasons—one of them is that its name means The Mouth of the Ford of Steeds, and that name carries the suggestion of a stirring past. But Ballinagh has not lived up to its name; indeed it has forgotten what its name means. It is a crooked, listless little place; it is a dusty, muddy little place; it is a come-day-go-day-God-send-Sunday sort of a little place. Nothing stirs in it except when a circus comes. And that's not often. And the sort of a circus that comes there is not one to have thirty, or forty, or fifty horses in it. No boy in Ballinagh ever saw fifty circus horses being led down, ten by ten, to drink at the mouth of the ford wherever that ford may be, or helped a black man who was with them to do a score of things. No. The only circus that ever comes to Ballinagh is the sort of one that makes a procession through the town with a single van—clown, acrobats, dare-devil riders all in one van, one beating a drum and all the others blowing into fifes in an effort to stir things up. That is all that ever makes a stir there.

Meath and Cavan

And yet because I know a man who lives near the place
and who once used to play "The Cuckoo's Nest" on the
fiddle who can describe himself coming upon an otter
"in the two lights" in a way that makes me feel that
poets whom nobody has ever heard of have given him
his lines, I'd be glad to be back there.

But I should not have mentioned Ballinagh only
that a bus that goes through Meath passes by it. I
got into that bus on a certain morning and saw a man
there, and the moment I saw him I remembered that
this was the very day of the County Fair and Exhibi-
tion in the town of Cavan.

He had between his knees an ash-plant which had
in it as many wriggles as a serpent: it seemed to be em-
blematical of the crooked roads he had been on. For
this was a cattle-raising, cattle-driving man. His ash-
plant had a head that was about as long as a goose's
beak. On it there was the same sort of gloss as was on
its owner's coat, and stick and coat had got that gloss
from rubbing together. His suit of serge was glossed
and greased, and his half-high hat was tobacco-col-
oured. He was big, with small and intent blue eye; he
gripped his ash-plant with his right hand and held his
pipe in his left and examined the fields of oats and
potatoes as we went by them. I knew him for a man
who would be at the fair that day, taking note of
the stock.

The horses were being led into the show ground as
we got off the bus: they were striking the hard ground
with their hoofs as they were being led along—an ex-

citing clatter. We are a pastoral people and horses and cattle make a very direct appeal to us. The feeling which makes the Dublin Horse Show so vital an event is present in the smallest show in the dullest town in Ireland.

Historians and scribes of the old days have preserved descriptions of fairs when they let other events fall into oblivion. The tellers of the epic stories have put down descriptions of horses that are the most lifelike in any literature. These were the pomps of a life that was mainly pastoral, and so they went into history and poetry. The fairs which have been recorded must have been like the one here to-day: a mixture of horses and bulls and hounds, with strolling musicians and singers, held upon a green on a day of sunlight, with hounds barking, foals whinnying, cocks crowing, cattle lowing, dealers bawling out, rooks cawing in the ash-trees, and trick-o'-the-loop men getting off their patter.

The day is fine; there is sunshine on the ash-trees around the green; there is sunshine on the slopes that go up from the green. And now there is movement as the horses are being led across the green. The various humanity of the Irish countryside move round with them—"squireens" and their womenfolk: some of these young women are going into the jumping contest; they wear riding-breeches and, conscious that they are daring in doing it, they smoke cigarettes; the men smoke cigarettes, wear knickers with high stockings, and carry shooting-sticks on which they can seat themselves. The cattle-raising farmers carry ash-plants, and their sons switches. The sardonic-looking trick-o'-the-loop men are enticing little boys to stake pennies upon their peas. A seller of programs, a sporting youth, is putting down his with a swagger. One cannot help but notice how closely the human types approximate to the stock they are interested in. These straddle-legged men are all for horses. The heavy and slow-moving men, among whom is my friend with the ash-plant, follow the cattle around. The shouting, bearded men have to do with asses—their gait which is to keep beside a trotting ass tells us that.

And now I walk around the fair by myself. The carts which are on show upon the green have red wheels and long red shafts; they have middle boards of blue, and their reds and blues are indeed reds and blues. Green apples are heaped upon stalls which old women keep guard over. Geese, in pairs in cribs, lift up their heads and look at us with goose-grey eyes. Cocks with red enormous combs and with heckles are on roosts. Pigs in their pens have already turned up sods of the green. There are dogs on show—setters and greyhounds—and I hear a man say that it is now more profitable to breed greyhounds for racing than it is to breed pigs or sheep. And near the greyhounds, in hutches, are rabbits which no dog may chase—rabbits with fur that is grey and fleecy like clouds. Asses are here, too. But, groomed and sleek, they are far from being typical of the Irish countryside. Even though on show they are kept in their places: they have got to remember they are asses; their place is beside a ditch full of thistles and nettles.

You can put asses on show and you can put pigs on show, but you cannot put goats on show. You can bring them into the show ground, of course, and leave them in a place by themselves. But wherever they are goats will be goats, insurgent and individual. Here they are tied, but they go on cropping the hedges as if they were still on the ramble.

I thought at first that their owners had not that relation to the goats that the others had to their particular stock. They were boys, mostly, and they stood by their charges in a mixture of pride and shyness. They were proud that they had a place in the gathering of the county, but they knew, too, that other boys had their eyes on them, and were noting that they had been dressed up and sent out by mothers who had faith in the goat they had bred and reared. These boys stood by with a good deal of detachment: the goats they were in charge of were short-horned or hornless, they were sleek and mild-looking, and the native insurgency of the goat seemed not to be in them. And then I saw a particular man in charge of a particular goat. And him I knew to be really representative of all the goat-owners and goat-showers in Ireland for all time.

No boy could go near this particular goat without making some movement of defiance which was answered at once by a movement of offense. She had enormous horns that were curved, she had a great and

BARNEY BACKED A WINNER BY SEAN KEATING

a rank fleece. Her owner had no detachment. No owner of a two-thousand guinea racer ever led up his horse with as much trepidation as he led up his goat to the judges. "Barney," he called her. "Come, Barney," he said, and one could hear him say, "In the name of God," under his breath. He led her up to the judges and stood beside her, the perfect picture of what a goat-owner should be like.

He carried neither a stick nor a switch; he smoked neither a pipe nor a cigarette; he chewed tobacco; he was stunted; he had roving eyes with a ragged cap pulled over them. "Come, Barney," he said, and he turned Barney around so that cool judges might scrutinize her udders. In the way he spoke there was all of the attachment a man might have for a goat.

Barney, scrutinized, was dismissed, and one of the sleek, hornless kind was given the prize.

But this creature was an original and her owner was an original also. This was the native goat, the goat of the ditches and the hedgerows. The asses were not originals; their owners were not originals. They would leave the fair green and walk along crooked roads, driving their asses before them. But not for the goat-owner these roads. He was a mountainy man. For him the whinny hillsides, the weedy fields. He will see the wren fluttering through the holly-bushes and his ear will be cocked for the red-breast's song. A solitary, this man—as solitary as Barney, his goat. Some tumble-down shanty is his shelter, where Barney has a stretch of hedgerow to graze on. All he will get in the town is a glass of porter and a chew of tobacco. He leads his goat, unrewarded, away, his ragged cap pulled down over his roving eyes. Something tells me I shall see this mountainy man again.

An Islet

I came to the lake that is outside Cavan town—one of the lakes through which the river Erne flows. A friend was there who was willing to pull an oar with me; when we were in the boat I pulled in the direction of an islet on which the old keep known as Cloughoughter Castle stands.

When he saw that I was bent for that direction my friend said, "I want you to know that I am the most resolute anti-archeologist in the whole province of Ulster. Not only have I no interest in that keep and whatever it stands for, but I am unwilling to listen to even one word about it."

"It was an O'Reilly stronghold. . . ."

"I suppose you imagine that I'm bound to take an interest in anything that is connected with the O'Reillys."

"Seeing you have that name. Well, this was the last stronghold in Ireland that was taken by the Cromwellians."

"Isn't it wonderful that you can have a mind easy enough to be concerned about such things when there's a squall coming up and neither of us expert in the handling of a boat like this?"

"But don't you know that Eoghan Ruadh O'Neill died on this very islet and inside the walls that we see?"

"And don't you know that you are spoiling the day for me? I hate anything that has to do with Irish or English history."

"But Eoghan Ruadh O'Neill was the finest soldier that Ireland produced. He was trained in the wars of Spain and France; he came to Ireland with the highest hopes of achieving the independence of the country."

"He failed—that's enough for me."

"I see Hardy's poems in your pocket. I expected that you would be interested in a tragedy of circumstance."

"I'd give the island and the keep and whatever interest they may have for anyone to have seen Thomas Hardy in the flesh. I know a boat song. I'll sing it as we pull."

"No, no. We cannot cross this lake without thought or talk of Eoghan Ruadh O'Neill. In spite of dreadful disunion, in spite of the lack of policy on the part of the Council which he served, in spite of its opposition, he made an army, he won a brilliant victory. He was marching to unite his army with Ormond's. But at this time he knew that he was dying."

"Dying! Of what?"

"Tuberculosis or Bright's disease—I don't believe it is known which. You're not pulling very well."

"The fact that Eoghan Ruadh O'Neill had a disease as usual as tuberculosis or Bright's disease makes him a sympathetic character for me. It is the only thing I have heard about him that interests me. It takes him out of the stiff mythological folds that all Irish leaders seem to have been put into."

"Well, he took leave of his army in a place near by. He handed the command over to his nephew, young Hugh O'Neill. The army marched past its leader and its maker, giving the victor of Benburb the last salute. . . ."

"How many in the army?"

"About eight thousand. And eight thousand well-trained men made a considerable army in those days."

"How did you get to know all this?"

"Your cousin told it all to me this morning."

"And so, having avoided hearing it from him, I have to hear it from you now. I suppose you'll tell me that O'Neill's grave is on the islet."

"No. Eoghan Ruadh O'Neill was buried in the chancel of the Franciscan church in Cavan. Of course that church was made over into a Protestant one. The bones of Eoghan Ruadh O'Neill were flung aside to make room for one of a family of newcomers. We don't know where the bones of the best and most chivalrous of Irish soldiers were put."

"And if we did there would be more talk about the place, and I should have more reason than ever for being an anti-archeologist."

"You're going to read me poems about frustration when we get on the islet."

"Yes. But frustration in our own history—I have heard too much of that."

The islet was just beside us now. Three walls stood up; on their tops, at each corner, a bird was standing like a sentinel. Their necks were up and their looks were on us. I thought they were herons. But they looked at us in a wilder way; there was something baleful and fateful about them as they watched with sloping heads and beaks. One, then another, then a third dashed down from the high place when they made sure we were bound for the islet. They disappeared in an instant. And others stood watching our coming. Cormorants! Very proper to the scene were these quick-eyed, baleful watchers! Much more so than the swans that drifted along by the islet.

And then we landed. The islet is just wide enough to hold the walls of the keep: the builders left no room for an enemy to land in force; the keep would have to be reduced before a landing was made. We sat upon bits of fallen walls and read poems about defeats and frustration. The little space held a little wilderness— thorn-bushes with bunches of red haws on them, elder-bushes with cluster of dark berries, hollies and clumps of ivies. The ivy covered the broken walls, big-leaved, dark green, with bunches of buds coming out of its growth.

> If poesy have truth at all,
> If some great lion of the Gael
> Shall rule the lovely land of Fál;
> O yellow mast and roaring sail!

Cross Roads in Ireland

Carry the leadership for me,
Writ in this letter, o'er the sea
To great O'Néill.

The hope that was in this seventeenth-century poem—
James Stephens has translated it—died on this islet,
and nothing afterwards happened on it. We saluted
the images of the cormorants that we had in our memories—the cormorants as they stood on the walls of the
keep, superbly aloof from our interests and history,
their beaks and necks lifted to the sky.

We pulled back in the rain. I realized that I was
on one of the chief water-systems in Ireland. The
river Erne flows through this lake. If we went on (but
we should have to go in a motorboat) we should come
to Enniskillen, and from Enniskillen I might turn towards East Ulster. Or I could go along the winding
course of the river to where it enters the sea at Ballyshannon in Donegal. Two rivers have their rise near
by—the Erne and the great Shannon. The Erne
flows north and west. The Shannon flows south. The
romance of the rivers came to me, and I thought that I
might cross the county to where the Shannon rose,
and follow the river to the south after or before I
had followed the Erne's course.

And thinking on these journeys I went on the lake-
shore with my friend. We landed beside two cottages
that were the nicest I have ever seen in any part of
Ireland. Whoever had built them had taken into account the wood and the lake-water and the remoteness
of neighbourhood, and had put here cottages that had

some relation to the scene. The one that we go into is
built of concrete into which big pebbles, round and
oval, are set. In front are wooden columns whitewashed. Even thatch, now weather-browned, covers
the roof, and before the columns red hollyhocks are
growing. The other cottage is made in the same style
and with the same material, but it has tiles on its roof.
Someone who had an idea of giving some character and
charm to the cottages that he had a chance of building, built these two. It is a pity that his idea did not
spread.

West and North

Like others of the world's noted rivers the Shannon
takes its rise in an out-of-the-way spot, and to get
there would mean something of a journey. I talked
about getting a conveyance. "I'll take you near
where you want to go," said a friend of mine. He
was a man of law, and he was going into that rela-
tively inaccessible district to make inquiries about the
heirs and assignees of an emigrant who had died in
America leaving a small estate which he had to admin-
ister. So I got free transportation and an enlightening
companionship.

We started off not too early in the morning. We
went into Killeshandra, a little town that is a centre
for the farmers' co-operative enterprises; for a while
we watched thousands of eggs being tested and packed
and gallons of milk being separated. We left the place
at noon.

Then I was left for a while before a cabin that looked as if it had been broken off from a more commodious dwelling. I noticed the colour of its door and the sashes of its two little windows—it was an unsightly red—the red you see under the rim of the human eye when some disease has pulled it down. The thatch above the red of door and window-sashes had the blackish brown of very ancient straw. On the window-sills were three jam-pots with a green slip of geranium growing in each of them. A goat lay in the patch of garden before the house with her eyes upon the green of the geraniums and the brown of the thatch, and a man, the householder evidently, was standing beside a fire of furze-roots and briars: he was holding a tin can over the blaze, and I surmised that he was melting the ingredients of bird-lime.

The goat was surprisingly like the goat I had seen on the fair-green the day before. The householder was surprisingly like that goat's owner. Surprisingly like, indeed—they were the same! Here were Barney and Barney's master—I had come upon them in their own habitat! And while the man of law inquired the way of someone down the road I talked with Barney's owner. No, this is a misstatement—I listened to his outgivings. And as I listened I watched Barney whose eyes were upon the green leaf and the brown thatch that was two feet above it: the shaggy, long-horned goat became a symbol of the old folk-Ireland that is being displaced by our new-fangled genteelness and efficiency.

Meath and Cavan

"No premium for a goat of the oul' stock reared by one of the oul' stock—oh, no, none at all," said Barney's owner. "We'll have to have everything the same as the Danes! The Danes, indeed! Why didn't they keep Ireland when they had her? True it is (he said the proverb in Irish) *the green bush gets eaten by the goat!* Too green we are, and we always were, and we ever will be, and why wouldn't someone crop us? Barney, here's a hand-full for you! The Danes give fortunes to their daughters of the land of Ireland, and they needn't give up doing it, either—the land is here for them to take, and there's them that's ready to give it to them! Fellows teaching their grannies to milk the ducks, and paid for doing it! Every patch of hair that's on that goat's worth something—you couldn't make better strainers for milk than out of the hair of a goat like Barney. And many's the thing besides a spoon you could make out of her horns. And meat, too! People who couldn't afford to have beef or mutton would come to you and buy goat's meat of you when you'd kill one. What would they pay? Two pence or three pence, and they'd say 'give me that or give me this'—whatever they'd want to take for the money they had. Barney, here's a hand-full for you. A goat of the oul' stock!"

And here was I listening to a man for whom the admired Danes of our Agricultural Department's bulletins were still a people out of a thousand-year-old tradition, a people to be confounded with the De Danaan folk of our mythology.

Cross Roads in Ireland

My friend came back with the information about the route, and we went away from Barney and Barney's owner. We were going into a glen, the man of law told me, where the people were rougher, hardier, more aboriginal. I could well believe it. We had come out of a countryside where there were horses and pasture-lands. Here there were asses and hillside clearings. Asses were being driven along the road with as much on their backs as would ordinarily fill an ass-cart —peats in one pannier, provisions in another, with a sack of flour laid across the back for good loading. This part of an inland county reminded me of counties that are on the West Atlantic seaboard: we might see asses like these driven by just such old women or barefooted girls in Galway or Mayo. Irish speech, too, may be heard here. A bit of Gaelic Ireland surviving in this mountainous Midland place, I thought. And then I realized that there were more ancient survivals around me. For here is Magh Sleacht, where stood the idol of Pagan Ireland which Saint Patrick overthrew. A living and well-proven tradition could put me upon the actual footsteps of the saint—indeed the friend who was with me could take me to that muddy well with the ash-tree growing over it where Saint Patrick baptized the pagan folk hereabouts fifteen hundred years ago.

Mythology by the Roadside

At the time I had not read Mr. John P. Dalton's "Cromm Cruaich of Magh Sleacht"; if I had, I should have been able to locate the hillside where Cromm and his twelve sub-divinities, imposing in gold, silver, and brass, fronted a congregation that was filled with "the horror of the scare of him." They came to him across a sheet of water that I looked upon. That water keeps in a corrupted form a name that came to it from the cry that went up from the boats as the idols were seen—its name comes from *Guth-ard*, which means "the lifted voice."

The learned and exhaustive brochure which I have since read shows us not only where the idols were positioned, but it solves the riddle regarding the place that Cromm had in the Irish pantheon. Mr. Dalton amends a well-known translation of a poem dealing with the saint's handling of the idol, and gives us this version:

> He was their god
> The faded Sun-deity with many mists,
> The people whom he shook over every field
> The everlasting kingdom they shall not have.

Now there were two Sun Gods in ancient Ireland—one that we hear much about in the epic tales, and one that we hear of in folk traditions and in the poem that tells of the Christian apostle's encounter with him—they were Lug and Cromm. Lug of the Long Arms was a God known to the Continental Celts—he came into Ireland with a late wave of invaders, with the race who became the dynastic people. Cromm was held to by the Sen Tuatha—the older races in Ireland. Until Patrick's time he was worshipped by every folk that had settled in Ireland.

He was obliged, it is true, to divide his empire with Lug, reserving as his own domain the exclusive realm of the thunderbolts; yet there is ample reason to believe that the *Sen Tuatha* never assented to this partial deposition. The depression in rank helped to make Cromm morose, fitful, vindictive. Trusted by none, feared by all, with heartless cruelty he exacted the dearest tribute which the Gaels had to bestow, at one time being placated only by hecatombs of their healthy offspring. His demands were, nevertheless, conceded by all, from the high-king down; and Laegaire himself, sceptic though he apparently was, had not the courage to renounce his religious obligations to Cromm at Magh Sleacht. But the demands of Cromm's officiators having been wrung from his superstitious fears, rather than freely rendered by his faith, it was not so unnatural that Cromm's overthrow by Saint Patrick should have received his royal approval.[1]

Saint Patrick came here from Tara, the seat of the high-king. The wells at which he baptized the folk hereabouts are known and are still venerated. And I looked upon pillar-stones that are the monuments of races that were ancient dwellers in the land when Saint Patrick came—their representatives were the guardians of the old Sun God's sanctuary.

We go through a countryside that is bog-land with fields that have rushes growing up in them. We come to an odd rock-formation that my friend names "Maguire's Chair." When I stand upon the rock I see a

[1] Proceedings of the Royal Irish Academy, Vol. XXXVI, Section C, No. 4. John P. Dalton, "Cromm Cruaich of Magh Sleacht."

stretch of bare country with little patches of tilled land, with great shadows on the bare rises, with flocks of bog larks flying about. This place was also associated with Cromm, as I was to learn when I read Mr. Dalton's brochure.

For although Cromm was overthrown by Saint Patrick, he was still, for many of the folk, the one who had brought wheat into Ireland. He was made over, then, into the servant and helper of Saint Patrick. When Cromm came to die, says a folk-tale, the evil powers tried to carry off his body. "Suddenly Saint Patrick with a host of saints and angels appeared," and assailed the powers of evil with fiery darts, for "it seems that Cromm's charities and good works were more than a balance for his sins." Thereafter, associated with Saint Patrick, Saint Brighid, and Saint Brendan, he had a festival at the beginning of harvest at the places of his old worship. The English-speaking country-people named this festival "Garland Sunday," "from the practice of strewing garlands of flowers on the festive mound on this day." The mound was named "The Altar of the Sun," and those who took part in the festival were "The Congregation of Cromm Dubh." The rock that my friend named "Maguire's Chair" is still a gathering-place for this ancient festival, as I was to learn from Mr. Dalton's brochure. "Its fame is widespread even yet as a 'Domnach Sunday' station, to which people resort, not only from the neighbourhood, but from distant parts of the surrounding country."

Cross Roads in Ireland

The dire aspect of Cromm is recalled in a folk-tale which Mr. Dalton quotes and which Mr. J. H. Lloyd wrote down in Irish. Cromm, in this story, has two hounds whose names are "Hound of Rage" and "Bitch of Wretchedness"—Rage and Affliction. His sons are "Storm-Blast" and "Pillared, Fire-enclosing Clouds." "Cromm Dubh, his sons and his dogs, were noted far and near for their wickedness; and the people were so affrighted by his name, and not his name alone, that they would bury their faces in their breasts when it was mentioned; and if they heard his dogs barking they would hide under the ground to protect themselves from Cromm Dubh and his mastiffs." Saint Patrick, in the story, overthrows Cromm Dubh, his dogs, and his sons. "The people gathered everywhere in crowds paying honour to Saint Patrick; and they felt very sorry when Cromm Dubh was no more."

The Sun deity of the older folk in Ireland, whose festival has been kept up even to our times, has played, according to my friend Roger Loomis of Columbia University, a great but disguised part in Irish literature. The duel between the young and the old Sun Gods is the explanation of many episodes in our epic tales. While Lug incarnates as Cuchullain, Cromm incarnates as Curoi. Curoi has in his power the Flower Maiden whom Cuchullain rescues. This motive goes from Irish into Welsh and Breton story-telling: Mr. Loomis sees Curoi's name in many of the names of enigmatical figures in the Mabinogion. Through Welsh and Breton stories the conflict between Cromm and his

[50]

youthful antagonist gets into the Arthurian romances, and becomes part of the European imagination. At least, that is Mr. Loomis's thesis.[1] And so it was worth while giving thought to Cromm when I stood upon the rock that was a few miles away from where Saint Patrick overthrew the idol that was set up in his name.

Folk-Lore

And in this place, by the gate of a field, we found a quern-stone. It had probably been in use within the last century, but my mind went back to the time when the bond-woman in some ancient household ground the corn with this primitive mill. Hard labour it must have been, for the poet of the Odyssey is moved to compassion over the ancient, wretched woman, covered with the dust of the grain, who puts a malediction upon the suitors who have made her do so much grinding. A woman hereabouts told me a story in which labour at the quern was an incident. It is a story of a well-known type, but the archaic labour at the quern invested it for me with more interest than other versions of the story have.

The house she lived in was the scene of the story, the woman told me. The people of the house used to find the grain left in the haggard ground for them overnight. At first only a little grain was ground, for the work was done while there was light. Then they used

[1] "Celtic Myth and Arthurian Romance," by Roger Loomis. Columbia University Press.

to leave a candle lighted on the ground. They never caught sight of the person who used to work at the quern. They wanted to see the worker, and they made a window that looked into the haggard. One night they saw the person who had been grinding for them: a strange woman was turning the quern, and she was bare-naked. When daylight came the woman went away.

The people of the house were anxious to do something for their helper. The young man went to the town and bought a silk dress. They laid the silk beside the quern. Then they watched through the window. The stranger woman came in and sat by the quern. Then she saw the silk dress and she put it on her. She looked down at herself. Said she: "Silk to my elbow and I grinding a quern!" She stood up then and went out, and she never was seen again.

The woman who told me this story used to say that when the fowl murmured on their roost they were telling where the Danes hid their treasures after their defeat at Clontarf, "for it was the Danes brought the hens to Ireland." In this part of the country a good deal of folk-lore centres around the Danes and their treasures. It was the Danes, they say, who had the secret of making ale out of heather—the Heather Ale. Neil Munro has a fine story in "The Lost Pibroch" about the Heather Ale; in his story the secret of its making is held by a single Gaelic clan, but originally the story must have been told of a people who could be credited with remarkable accomplishments. In the oldest Irish tradition the People of Partholon, who came into Ireland just after the Flood, made "ale of fern." And in this part of the country "the Danes" are connected with the Scandinavians only by pseudo-history. In English-speaking places, "Danes," I think, stand for "De Danaan," the Gods of culture-people of the Irish Celts, owing to the Irish word for the Scandinavians (Lochlannach) being forgotten. This reference to the fowl murmuring on the roost may be the last words of a tradition about some gift-bringing people.

The Cottier

Rain had begun to fall, and when we went into the cottage, the man of law and myself, the household thought we had come in just for the sake of the shelter. The man of law wanted to establish a few relationships before he came out with the most exciting of intimations—that about money from a deceased and distant relative. The man of the house and his wife were present. The man was glum about the falling rain, and the hay and the oats that had not yet been saved. I saw in him the type of the depressed small farmer. He told us he had about twelve acres of land; he had potatoes, oats, and hay in the field, cabbages in his garden; he had two cows, a couple of calves, an ass, and some pigs. On this he lived with his wife and family of five, four of them youngsters. He paid taxes, of course, and a small annuity on his farm. He had so much craft in bringing in matter for complaint that I suspected that a good deal of time went into meditations on such things. His wife, as she stood with a dishclout in her hand, rubbing along the window, looked as if she were more used to being in a neighbour's house than in her own.

There was a clatter and shouting outside; a horse that was being driven up the laneway had fallen down; the man of the house and his wife went outside. Then said the man of law to me:

"This is a house in which there is physical and mental depression, and I don't wonder. They never have any money—they couldn't spend sixpence on something that was out of the way. They never have any variety of food—the same thing every day—bread and tea, potatoes, cabbage and bacon; sometimes potatoes and milk, or porridge and milk. What they have is always prepared in the same way and eaten off the same place—off that old table there. Look out in the garden! Potatoes and cabbages are growing in it— nothing else. They wouldn't dream of growing onions or carrots. Soup with vegetables is something they never have. If I say vegetables to the woman of this house she'll think I mean cabbage—it's the only kind of vegetable she ever thinks of. Look at the poultry they have! They probably get all their ready money for eggs. And yet, in spite of all the efforts of the Government to get them to do it, they haven't improved the breed of fowl. They run all over the place; you couldn't get the people of the house to keep them inside wire-netting and save them all that running about." (But while my friend was speaking the fowl were taking shelter under a hedge in a dispirited manner.)

The man of the house came in with his wife and the son who had been with the horse. The boy worked for neighbouring farmers. He had three shillings a day when he was employed, but the work was intermittent, and he rarely had a full day's work. He sat looking out at the rain while his mother got ready potatoes and cabbage and a little bacon for him. He was subdued, but he had the appearance of a boy who could have been made into a more upstanding young fellow.

And now the man of the house had a lot to say against the Government. The charges against them that he made with the greatest invective was on account of their fining an egg-dealer of the near-by town for sending bad eggs to the English market. They had fined him several hundred pounds. "Where will the poor people get all that money?" He didn't know, and, likely enough, he wouldn't care if he had known that the Government were trying to protect their only market for people like himself.

We went out of the house. The man of law would come back and make the momentous announcement, but he had still to make an inquiry from a relative who lived across a field. And, not suspecting anything of the announcement of good fortune that was soon to be made to him, the man of the house bade us a curt farewell. As we went together the man of law said, "There are scores of such households—probably hundreds in every county in Ireland. The government that is trying to turn a man like the one we have left into some sort of an agriculturist has a tough job on its hands. But even Thomas Purcell (the man we had just left) can't resist the pressure that is being put upon him. In spite of himself he has a surer market than he used to have. The neighbours who kept a bull that was good enough for the cows around here has been forced to get a better one. His fowl will be less of the run-about kind soon, I suppose. But I wish I could believe that some time I'll see something else besides cabbages in his garden. I wonder what he'll do with the money he's going to get. It will be more than all the money he has had in his hands for the past five years!"

A Place to Return to

An outside car, in the shafts of which there was a big-boned grey horse, took me to where I was able to cross fields and come to the river's source. . . . A pool in a field. . . . But in another place I shall write about "The Shannon Pot" and the stream that issues from it. . . . After a while I went back to the road. The big-boned grey horse, going steadily and well, brought me to a little railway-station.

Cavan Story: An Interior

Her mother called her early and confided certain messages to her, and Julia, who was not unused to the mysteries, did everything faithfully and in order. Then the attending women came in. Julia was sent to draw water from the well and the children were drilled to quietness. Like a cadet under orders, loyally but with tension, the little girl did her offices. At the due time she went out to milk the goats, bringing the two children with her. Usually they used to approach the goats nervously, for milking them was something of an adventure.

This evening Julia left the children at a distance and dealt with the wild things firmly. Then the three sat on the grass for a while and talked; little Fardy, who was unused to conversation, brought up enormous things out of his so long inarticulate being. When they went in they found they had the kitchen to themselves. The children were all drawn together and Julia comforted them. Then there was silence for a while. A cow came to the window, and, standing in the half light, put its tongue against the single pane. The children were startled.

Then she began to tell them stories, and the light closed in. A woman came down to tell them that all was well with their mother; she went back to the room and there was tedium again. Julia lit the smoky lamp and hung it against the chimney. Ellie thought up riddles and Fardy considered them profoundly. Afterwards they wanted more stories, and Julia fell back upon an unending description of Heaven. "But could you eat a golden apple?" Ellie asked. "You could," Julia assured her, "and it would taste like a plum." The children went to sleep and Julia was left to vacancy. She got up, swept the floor again, and put more peat upon the fire. Then she went to search on the top of the dresser; many curious things were there, but only on such an occasion as the present had Julia the leisure to explore. There was a ship in a bottle: it was miraculous that it could have been put in there with its masts and everything, and the neck of the bottle so narrow. A one-armed sailor, Julia knew from venerable tradition, had made it and had left it in their house in return for a night's shelter. And this other object he had left too—a shark's tooth it was. While she was handling these wonderful things she heard the cry of the new-born child. Her grandfather came in and sat at the fire opposite her, and then a woman came down and showed her her new care. Then Julia fell asleep sitting by the fire. . . .

"That's Julia," Mickie, her grandfather, was saying, "and I think that Julia had the weight of the day on her."

"My nephew wasn't married when I was in this part before," the strange woman said. That the important personage, her grand-aunt from America, should appear on this night was like a dream to Julia. She opened her eyes to look at her. The bonnet was on her aunt's head, but the strings were unloosed. Her bodice was rusty black and the whalebone in her stays showed itself at her shoulder-blades. She was seated on a folding stool she had brought with her. Julia saw a grey, fleshy face. Her aunt opened a parcel and spread out on her lap a heap of bread and meat.

"I like to come to Ireland now and again," she said. "It does me good."

She took the cork out of a bottle, filled a collapsible cup with the liquid, and drank some off. She filled it again and tendered the cup to Mickie.

"The last time I was here I didn't get whiskey so good," she said, beating the cork back with the palm of her hand. "I brought it with me this time. I always bring whiskey with me on my travels."

She passed the paper of bread and meat to Mickie, ate some herself, and wiped her mouth with the back of her hand.

"I wasn't much bigger than that little girl when I went to the States," she said, "and I was a long time there before I got it into my head to sit up and pay attention. I was no more than a hired girl that time, but I began to put money together. But I was up to forty before I had my first thousand dollars. I had a lodging-house of my own then. There was a strike in the section I lived in, and the men wouldn't draw freight from the railways. I thought of putting wagons upon the street and giving the job of drawing to greenhorns that were boarding with me. I did that, and the next year I had a railway contract. I had twelve wagons out, and I was paying men a pound a day."

"A pound a day! By the mortial!" said Mickie.

Then he added, "I might be your brother, and I hardly ever saw the sight of seven pounds."

"I was giving men a pound a day," said the aunt, "and I was giving it to men from this side too."

"Begob, it was powerful," said Mickie, "and are you in that business now, ma'am?"

"Not now," said the aunt. "I put my money into building and house property. I made good provision for each of my children. I'm living out of investments myself. You must know that I gave over my estate to my eldest son."

The word "estate" had a powerful effect upon Mickie. "It's a high-up lady you are, ma'am," said he. "Estate! Who would think that any of your name could talk of their estate? And isn't this a poor place for you to be spending the night?"

"There's no other place in these parts for me to go to," said the aunt. "I'm tired of travelling on the car, and I can seat myself here until day. I always carry a little stool about with me." She talked of furniture, houses, food, and raiment as Julia talked to the children of the remote material delights of Heaven. "I stay in London, and in Paris, and in Rome," she said, "and I always bring my own sheets with me. When I'm abroad I have tea in what's called the English way. When I was in Rome I was living in a palace."

"And did you see the Pope?" said Mickie.

"I saw him in a procession," said the aunt. Julia thought of the grand golden car of a circus procession, and saw the Holy Father in it with a crown upon his

Courtesy of The Hackett Galleries

COTTAGES BY PAUL HENRY

head. "It's a happy woman you ought to be, ma'am," said Mickie, "and who would think that anyone of your name would see holy Rome?"

"Well, for comfort, I'd rather be in my own flat in Brooklyn, where I could have my own gas stove and hot and cold water." The room door opened and the thin cry of the child was heard. Mrs. Cromer came down. She was a comely woman with grey in her hair. She yawned and continued yawning for a couple of minutes. "I'll have to be going," she said. But when she had put the shawl across her shoulders she sat down again. The aunt produced the bottle, gave the collapsible cup with liquid to Mrs. Cromer and to Mickie, drank herself, and corked the bottle. "I suppose, ma'am," said Mrs. Cromer, "that you're not used to a place where a woman's child is born and the father a hundred miles away?" "Away earning money," said Mickie.

"I'm glad I'm not beginning a woman's life again," said the aunt.

"Well, when we had the youth we had the sport," said Mrs. Cromer. She stood up. "I'll be tossing hay all day, and the boys and girls will be coming into my house for the dance to-night. I don't want to be dropping into a sleep when the music's up. I'll go home now."

She opened the door and the wide light of the morning streamed in. The corn-crakes kept up their revels and were loud in the meadows that were round the house. Mrs. Cromer stood for a while in the doorway

and then went out. Mickie came out of the chimney
recess. On the aunt's lap lay the paper of food, and
her head leaned towards it. The bonnet had slipped
off, and her hair was dishevelled. Mickie took down
the fishing-pole and stood for a while at the open door,
bearing the pole that was so much taller than himself.
The children stirred in the cold of the dawn. Julia put
a coat across their bed, and then fell into a heavy doze.
She dreamt that she was travelling to a place where
her mother was, and beyond that to a place where Mrs.
Cromer was, and beyond that to a place where her aunt
was—"Flat, Brooklyn" she heard somebody say, and
she woke up stiff and dispirited.

PART II

Mid-Ulster

Concerning Station-Masters

THE station-master at an Irish railway-station is generally a most worthy official. Authority gives him dignity, but it does not make him a martinet. He is indulgent as well as commanding, for he knows himself as *primus inter pares*. All under his orders he calls by their full Christian name—"James," "William." He calls by his name, too, the guard who casts out of the van and on the platform the packages that have that particular station for their destination. Of course he does not speak to, and perhaps he does not even know, the engine-driver and fireman who preserve such grim detachment while the train stops—no one never speaks to them: they are as Plutonic arrivals amongst men and divinities. The station-master has a good deal of leisure; he spends it reading the newspaper, and so he is a well-informed man. He talks with the notables of the train-frequenting public ("the subscribers"), and so he is generally something of a conversationalist. It is a little difficult to define his social status. . . . The clergyman, the police-sergeant, the schoolmaster, all more or less regulators of morals, are in the first rank. . . . It was so in pre-revolutionary days, and this hierarchy probably still survives. The station-master, not exercising any social control, was outside this circle. Through his connection with "the line" he had a world of his own, and locally he was not below the schoolmaster. Finally, the station-master is something of an æsthete: he cultivates flowers, and you often see him with a rose or a carnation in the button-hole of his unobtrusive uniform. Such are station-masters everywhere in Ireland. And this station-master who spoke with the Ulster accent I was beginning to be aware of, and who was probably a member of the local Orange lodge, was no different in any essential characteristic from station-masters in Cork or Tipperary. He asked me to join him in his tea. He talked to me about the damage the busses were doing the railways all over the country. He told me about the damage they were doing the little towns. People who had never gone from their village were now making journeys of twenty miles on the buses and doing their marketing at a distance; the little towns were all withering up, he told me. . . . There was no train for Enniskillen for three hours. . . . The distance was about seven or eight miles. I decided not to wait for the train. The road goes by a lake that runs into Loch Erne; it is a nice road, and I decided to walk to Enniskillen.

Into the North

A young man was standing at the doorway of a little farm-house that was by the road. He was a loosely-built young man, dark-eyed, and with good features, and if I had seen him in one of the Western states in America I should have said that he was of the pioneer type. I asked him how far I was from Enniskillen. He told me of a milestone a little farther along the road that would indicate the exact distance. He asked me where I came from. Cavan, I told him. "Are you working in Cavan?" he asked. If I say he put the question suspiciously I over-emphasize an element in his speech. . . . A few miles back, if I spoke to a young man at his doorway, and if he had said, "Are you working in Cavan?" it would have implied, "Come, let us talk of Cavan." But with this young man it meant, "What is your business?" I answered him and went on. He was a young Ulsterman who, I am sure, had small regard for the Pope.

Every country polarizes itself, every country has a North and South. The North and South of a country may be latitudinally with the South and North of other countries, but the North and South will be characterized, not by what makes them akin with what are in their own latitudes, but by what makes them opposites of each other. And the more homogeneous the country is, the more definitely will it polarize itself. At least, this is my notion at the moment. I go on towards Enniskillen: the hills of Fermanagh are before me—hills rising up from lakes and green to their summits. There are stone walls along the roadway and well-clipped hedgerows.

Cross Roads in Ireland

Dynasts in Fermanagh

The little kingdom around Loch Erne belonged in the old days to Me Guidhir Fhearmanach, or, as we should write it now, to the Maguires of Fermanagh. By all accounts it was a prosperous small state. Of one of its rulers, Manus, it is written, "His whole country was so very intimate with him, that there was not in Ulaidh (Ulster) any ruler more beloved or respected by his people, and by everybody than he was in his own reign." For thirty-five years, without strife or discord amongst the laity or clergy, he ruled a kingdom that was made up of seven *tuaths* or cantons.

The tract that we have about Manus's reign purports to tell us about the affairs of this little kingdom in an early part of the thirteenth century. The writer may be putting the time too far back. But, in any case, "Me Guidhir Fhearmanach" gives us a picture of affairs in kingdoms such as were here at a time before the English expansion under the Tudors disrupted Celtic polity. Here was Manus, beloved and respected, but too feeble to emerge from his house on the hill that was named Ninne. The ruler of a Celtic state had to show himself and show himself as a man of vigour, and when Manus did not appear personally, some of his vassals, notably O'Flanagan, decided that this was a good excuse for holding on to a tribute that should be paid. There was a conflict over the collecting of kine, and Manus's stewards slew some of O'Flanagan's people and O'Flanagan himself. The women and youngsters of O'Flanagan's party got the cattle back to their own side of the country.

Then a council was convened by Manus. It consisted of "the clergy of his county and his own territory, his doctors of history and medicine, and the magnates of the county beginning from there." What was to be done in the case of O'Flanagan's recalcitrance? That was the question that Manus put to his council of state.

After it had deliberated apart, the council declared that neither side should pay an *eric*—that is, that O'Flanagan's people should not be fined for their disobedience, nor Manus fined on account of the killing of O'Flanagan and his officers. "Let all that were living, live, and all who were killed to let them be so." The decision was reported by Manus's law-officer, O'Breislein. But Manus was not satisfied. He turned on his law-officer.

"This is not a fair judgment which you report, O'Breislein, but a partiality you have shown towards O'Flanagan, because you yourself and your ancestors before you came from Fanad; and therefore I will arraign you publicly for that you have given a perverse judgment; for it is certain that each vassal is bound to do homage to his liege and to give him what he is lawfully entitled to; and that, therefore, they neither obeyed nor did homage to their liege seeing that they denied me my own right, and that thus they are bound to give me an eric for the death of my people, as they shall do later."

Now although Manus himself was old, and his children of tender age, he was not going to give in to the unruly vassals and the luke-warm magnates of his kingdom. He had a brother or half-brother who was of vigorous age: Giolla Iosa was his name, and at the moment he was staying as a guest with the King of Breffne. Manus had letters written and dispatched to Giolla Iosa.

How I should like to get a full account of the King of Breffne and his household! He was, I suppose, like one of Homer's kings who did not think any the worse of himself for not living in a capital, who counted his own herds of cattle, and instructed his ploughmen and harvesters. An O'Reilly, I could think of him as being like a kingly-looking man of that name I once knew. The tract, however, tells us little about O'Reilly and his household.

The envoys from his brother brought the letters to Giolla Iosa, and when he read them, "his appearance and form underwent a change, and a piercing look came into his eyes and vision so that his grandfather's whole household trembled through terror at the change. . . . He summoned to him his retainers and his escort and directed them to get ready the steeds, and laid his hands on his weapons and put them on without delay." The envoys were entertained, and then:

Giolla Iosa arose and knelt before his grandfather (O'Reilly) and asked his blessing and he gave it to him with good will; and he fared forth by every shortest route, and his doings are not recorded until he reached the regal residence of his own brother. . . . Thereupon the variegated tables of the kingly household were cleansed, and the choicest meat and drink dispensed to them; and when the time came for them to sleep Manus requested that Giolla Iosa's bed be prepared in the same room in which himself was so that they might have a consultation together. This was accordingly done.

Manus counselled his younger brother to get to know the territory. As it was in Ireland until recently, so it was then; every locality had its legend and these legends were looked upon as being relevant to one's daily interest. Ireland itself was the people's Scripture:

"Moreover you ought to seek information often from the person whom you may expect to obtain it, and to get knowledge of the names of the hills and of every local tuath in the county; and besides a knowledge of the old famous names that are current such as that of Sliabh Dha Chon; for it is called Sliabh Dha Chon from two dogs belonging to Fionn which were lost in that mountainous region through devilry or magic; and it was called Gleann Caoin until Fionn gave it that second name after his two dogs had perished there through the magic of the Children of Lir."

Giolla Iosa was to go through this glen on his way to O'Donnell's country as envoy from his brother. O'Donnell, at that time, had his seat where the Erne runs into the sea, at Ballyshannon. In relation to Maguire and O'Reilly, O'Donnell was a dread emperor; he was the greatest military power in West Ulster. But young Giolla Iosa was a kinsman, and when he came before his residence, great O'Donnell went out upon the lawn.

He kissed Giolla Iosa fondly and earnestly and took him with him into his dining-hall and a banquet of delicacies and pleasant drinks was given them; and thus did they pass their time until the hour of the usual meal and then their repast was put in the place where it is taken and they continued to partake of it agreeably, lovingly in each other's company till bed time; and then O'Donnell himself went with Giolla Iosa Me Guidhir to his sleeping couch and the attendants followed them with sweet appetizing ale. So they behaved thus far.

Then, hearing how affairs were with Manus, O'Donnell summoned his constables, O'Boyle, O'Gallagher, and the three MacSweenies. They came forthwith with seven hundred men armed for battle. O'Donnell reviewed their forces and then commanded them to go to the aid of Maguire.

But even when he came with these great forces, Giolla Iosa was told by some vassals that no tribute would be paid until the lord was seen upon his feet. Giolla Iosa had the recalcitrant vassals arrested; they were brought before Manus. Then Manus put the question of the eric that was to be exacted from O'Flanagan's people to the five constables. They deliberated. O'Boyle reported their judgment:

"We have decided on an impost of seven hundred milch cows on O'Flanagan's party as an eric for the fifteen men of your side whom they unlawfully slew." "Brother Giolla Iosa, what do you say to that judgment?" "I say," said Giolla Iosa, "that I will never object to the decision of these kindly chiefs of Tir Chonaill in my own country; and that I would not advise you to object to it; and, moreover," added Giolla Iosa, "I advise you to send for O'Flanagan's party and to bring them here into the presence and to find out whether they are themselves satisfied with the judgment." This was done; and when they had arrived Giolla Iosa asked them whether they were prepared to accept every judgment which the nobles of Tir Chonaill had made in their case concerning every conflict that had taken place between themselves and his brother who was there present. They replied and said that they were. "Well, then," said Giolla Iosa, "take ye the traditional oaths that we have here, namely the Duibheineach, binding your-selves to fulfill everything that has been decreed in your regard in that judgment, in the presence of these nobles and of your own liege lord." They did as Giolla Iosa had told them; and thereupon that judgment was made known to them as we have said; and then they bound themselves in surety and friendship to their liege, and they made friendly, affectionate peace with one another. Then Giolla Iosa seized a golden, decorated goblet and he asked his brother to drink to these nobles in consideration of peace and friendship, who thereupon took the goblet from the hand of Giolla Iosa and drank to O'Flanagan's heir in the chieftaincy and dubbed him O'Flanagan on the spot.

O'Donnell's constables left after a round of banquets and feasts had been given to the high and to the lowly, to the laity and the clergy, to the druids and the ollavs (the doctors of law and medicine). And then a policy was inaugurated to the end that O'Donnell's interven-tion would not again be called for. These great mili-tarists had better be kept out of the affairs of the little kingdoms! We take leave of the dynasts of Fermanagh in an hour of festival.

Then Giolla Iosa ordered the players in general to be as-sembled in their presence in the sleeping chamber. Thereupon there came druids and good players, and those skilled in every composition, and the musicians of the royal household, and they played bouts highly melodious and harmonious on the strings of peaked harps, and they recited the poems and comic songs of their elders and ancestors for them; and they set to drinking and enjoyment in each other's company in remembrance of those good friends who had left them the day before.

All this is taken from "Me Guidhir Fhearmanach, The Maguires of Fermanagh," which has been edited and translated by Father Dineen.

Enniskillen

Enniskillen is a pretty little city—the prettiest in Ireland, I should say. It is a centre for Fermanagh, Cavan, and the southern part of Donegal —a little capital, in fact. It is within the administration of the Northern Government, and so certain superficial things make themselves noted—the red postal-boxes with the monogram of King George instead of the green boxes with the S. A. initials; Constabulary instead of Civic Guards; recruiting posters for the British Army. Enniskillen has always been a military headquarters—its modern history begins as a frontier post—and it has many mementos recalling British military achievement. These mementos do not seem out of place here as they would be likely to in other towns in Ireland. With this military achievement is interwoven the names and the honours of the landowning families hereabouts. There has always been an entente between the town and the landowning families; this, I feel, is what really makes the place different from towns in other parts of Ireland. The landowning families felt an interest in the town, fostered its growth, brought some amenities into it; the townspeople were really proud of these families, rejoiced in whatever honours they were given, and put up monuments to them with a good heart. This, which would be a natural relation in England and Scotland and most places in Europe, is worthy of being noted in Ireland. Enniskillen shows the marks of this fostering. . . . I am at the railway-station; a carriage with horses is waiting there; Lord —— arrives. There is a ripple of interest, of allegiance. The coachman drives off. The house he drives to is still a centre of influence.

In a public ground is a column inscribed to the memory of General the Honourable Sir Galbraith Lowry Cole, G.C.B., Colonel of the Twenty-seventh Regiment, erected by his friends in 1843. I climb the stairway of the column. The keeper of the grounds goes with me, and as we mount shows me the places of interest. The churches, the convent, the row of nice dwellings that the town is building for ex-service men. And then the river Erne, winding away towards Ballyshannon in Donegal. And I am glad that his friends raised this high column to the general, for it gives us who climb to its top a fine view of "the winding banks of Erne." A building in the distance is pointed out to me. "Portero School. A great many of the judges went there. You'd be bound to know their names." He gave me a list of notable judges and doctors who had graduated from Portero. One name he did not mention, but it was the name that was in my mind when I looked at the school he had been in before he went up to Dublin University—Oscar Wilde's.

Next day I would go towards the north and east—Armagh, Derry, and Belfast were before me. Where I stood on the column I looked to the place I had come from—Cavan, along the winding Erne River.

Monaghan

I am in Monaghan; with Cavan and Donegal, it is an Ulster county in the Free State. Like Cavan, Monaghan is a county of little lakes. It is more fertile than Cavan and is better tilled; I think the fields here have a more shining greenness. I pass through a little town that has a name in a rhyme that is recalled to me:

> Castleblaney besoms—
> Better never grew.
> Castleblaney besoms—
> A penny buys the two!

A market-cry, I suppose, that was taken into a children's game. I wondered where they pulled the heather that made the besoms—on what hillside or in what bog hereabouts—and what reason the makers had for feeling so superior about their two-a-penny besoms which, piled upon the backs of asses, they brought into Cavan: two shillings' worth would make a load.

The friends who have invited me to stay with them have a house whose modernity must be an amazement to the county Monaghan. A farm-house which is steam-heated and where one can take a hot bath in the morning! My friends, back from America, have re-built and modernized the house on the farm that belonged to their family. Long ago their father was arrested for his political activities, and was given a long-term sentence. While he was a political prisoner the family was evicted from their land. They went to America. And now, thirty years afterwards, the younger members have returned and have bought back the land that belonged to their father and their forefathers and have built this surprising house. "When they were building the house they should have put up a monument to the landlord who evicted them," a man who had heard of the restoration said to me.

Here I am in this up-to-date house, looking over the improved cattle and improved poultry that my friends are raising, and walking in the sunny fields. But autumn has come. The signs that its coming makes in this particular countryside are here, they suggest verses to me, and I write them down:

Black tassels, black tassels upon the green tree,
The high tree, the ash-tree that tops the round hill—
Black tassels, black tassels, and they are the crows.

Red streamers, red streamers along the hedgeways,
Where roadways are claubered and stubbles are brown—
Red streamers, red streamers, and they are the haws.

A lone song, a high song that comes from the hedge,
That tries for a round and that falls on the turn—
A short song, the robin's, and Samhain's at hand.

In the afternoon we visit the grounds of one of the great houses of the neighbourhood. In my friend's automobile there is a priest who heads the county's Catholic seminary and a Protestant farmer who belongs to the Orange order. I perceive that there is something representative in our group.

I like listening to speech in which the Ulster accent is tonic: always it has seemed to me to be a household speech—a speech for the crooning of lullabies and the telling of household stories. . . . We have come out through the gateway. On the roadway, near the gate of the great house, is a memorial with an inscription, "Erected by his grateful tenants."

"Grateful tenants, indeed!" cries my friend, thinking perhaps of his father's gaol term. "Who ever knew a grateful tenant!"

The Orange farmer is resolved to be tolerant of the violence in my friend's tone. He laughs. "Well, it was the tenants who were grateful that put up yon monument."

"The tenants who weren't grateful could put up a monument four times as high."

"Well, ye see, it takes all kinds to make a world, grateful and ungrateful."

The Orange farmer had a genuine attachment to the "Big House," a genuine regard for the noted family who dwelt in it. But he had to be on his defensive about this predilection. Every onslaught that my friend made he countered with humorous craftiness. The difference between him and my friend, I thought, was part of the difference between "Ulster" considered as a community of Protestant farmers and the rest of Ireland.

For "the Gentry" who, as a class, have passed out of the social life of the rest of Ireland are still part of the social life where Protestants form a community. It was possible for an acute observer watching the anti-Home Rule demonstrations of 1912-13 to write, "The occasion has been used to strengthen the conservatism of Ulster—I do not use the word in a party sense. By disciplining the Ulster democracy and by teaching it to look to them as its natural leaders, the clergy and gentry are providing against the spread of revolutionary doctrine and free thought." This, published in the London *Times* in May 1913, was an observation of a social consciousness that did not exist outside of some of the Ulster counties. And that consciousness still exists and marks a real difference between "Ulster" and the rest of the country.

In general, Protestant tenants accepted landlordism; in general, Catholic tenants did not accept it—at least, in the last century of Irish history. It may be said that the Catholics were the tenants who suffered most under landlordism—they were defenceless—while in the North of Ireland Protestant tenants had some defence through what was called the Ulster Custom—a custom that saved the improvements made by an outgoing tenant from confiscation by the landlord. Then, too, Protestant tenants, like the landlords, felt themselves endangered through a popular movement that was considered likely to leave a Catholic community dominant in Ireland: they wanted the established order to last, even if the established order included landlordism. All this accounts for the attachment that is still felt in "Ulster" for the landowning families. "Besides," said an Ulsterman to me when I talked over these matters with him, "the landowners in the North were a better kind of people; they were not mere adventurers with no interest in the tenants, as so many of them were in other parts of Ireland. They were a better sort of tenants in Ulster, too. They had more education; they were not so down-trodden as in other parts, and for that reason the landlords had to deal with them fairly. In Ulster, they did behave fairly, on the whole, and that is the reason for the attachment between the gentry and the farming people that you notice here."

I am not sure that all that has been set down here explains the difference in attitude between the two men in the car. Once, in America, an historian said to me, "I think that a complete revolution is possible only in a Catholic country." He said this before the Russian revolution had shown itself as successful. By a complete revolution he meant a revolution that ends with a new class having possession of the soil. Such a revolution had happened in France; it had happened in Ireland, and it was completing itself in Poland. In Sweden and Rumania it had quite failed to complete itself. In Scotland the landowners are turning the whole countryside into grouse-moors and deer-forests, and the cottiers have not even a hope of resisting them.

The historian went on to say that he thought there was something in Catholicism which leads to an insistence upon the cultivator's untrammelled possession of the soil. If this judgment is sound it interprets much that has happened in Ireland and it explains the difference in social outlook between two Irish communities.

The Free State has abolished landlordism: the landowners have had to sell their holdings to the farmers, the state making itself responsible for the compensation arranged for. In the Ulster counties landlordism is being more gradually abolished. In spite of the power which they have in the Northern Counties Government, the Ulster landlords are being compelled to sell to their tenants—the example of the Free State is having this effect. Soon landlordism will be a thing of the past in the Ulster counties. Meanwhile I have come upon this item in my *Irish Times:*

The five thousand acre forest in North Tyrone, in which is situated the beautiful home of the Abercorns, resounded last Saturday at midday with the firing of guns and explosives on the occasion of the home-coming of the Marquis and Marchioness of Hamilton for the first time since their marriage a few months ago. The noise of fog-signals marked the arrival of the train at Newtownstewart. The station and pretty little town by the Mourne looked gay with flag and bunting. Arriving at Baroncourt's main entrance gate the car with the young couple had a piper and a navy boat bearing the name "Good Luck" as escort. Flag-decked roadways led to the castle, while large numbers of the people who lived in the demesne joined in the welcome. Across the sky ran Very lights and signal rockets.

Five thousand acres given over to forest in North Tyrone! "By disciplining the Ulster democracy and teaching it to look to them as its natural leaders, the clergy and gentry are providing against the spread of revolutionary doctrine and free thought." Small wonder the notion seemed a good one to the Duke of Abercorn and his associates!

And then we came into the little town of Monaghan. Here was born the statesman who tried to make the agrarian issue a way of uniting the Ulster of the Protestant tenant-farmers with the rest of Ireland. The priest talked to me of Charles Gavan Duffy as the only statesman we had who realized that there was an Ulster problem, and that it was by working for, and with, the men who tilled their lands in Northeastern Ulster that Irish unity could best be brought about.

A Statesman

He was vividly interested in the tangible things out of which the constructive statesman and the able administrator builds the stable state—the peasant's tenure of the land, the wise conciliation of a province, education, the creation of a national art and literature. He wanted to work within a constitution. At the moment when, as he declared, a revolution could hardly be held back, the demand he made for his nation was constitutional—"An Independent Parliament, elected by the widest possible suffrage, a Responsible Ministry, and a Viceroy of Irish birth." He would prefer this, he declared openly, to a Republic won by insurrection, although at the time all the reforming sentiment of Europe favoured a Republic. Charles Gavan Duffy wanted a settlement that should come out of negotiations between two peoples—"not from any unmanly abhorrence of war," he wrote, "which is noble and glorious, waged for one's country, but because insurrection would plant deadly animosities between men of the same Irish race, and because the sudden transition of a people from Provincialism to Republicanism, passing through no intermediate stage, is an experiment for which we are not fit." And yet the man who held these constitutional principles and who acted up to them was imprisoned twice as a political offender and was once put upon trial for his life.

When Charles Gavan Duffy was born the bulk of the people of Ireland were in the state pictured by Davis in his essay on the Irish peasant. "Advancing youth brings him labour, and manhood increases it, but youth and manhood leave his roof rotten, his chimney one hole, his window another, his clothes rags (at best muffled by a holiday cothamore), his furniture a pot, a table, a few hay chairs and rickety stools, his food lumpers (potatoes) and water, his bedding straw and a coverlet—his enemies the landlord, the tax-gatherer and the law—his consolation his wife and the priest." These were the social conditions in broad outline, and the political conditions of the country are fairly pictured for us in the opening of Gavan Duffy's own story, "My Life in Two Hemispheres." In the town of Monaghan there had been a corporation endowed out of confiscated lands, "but the body had long ceased to exist, and its endowment had fallen to the local landlord, Lord Rossmore, who, to keep up the pretense of a corporation, still named a town sergeant and other subordinate officials at his sole pleasure." There was a corps of yeomanry who received arms and uniforms from the Government, and as these arms were left with the corps permanently, every Orange Lodge had a liberal supply of guns and used them freely at their annual festivity. One of Duffy's recollections was having seen a butcher named Hughes shot in the public street before their door by a government gun fired from an Orange procession. "To indict anyone for murder would have been the idlest work of supererogation."

What did Gavan Duffy project for such a society? Catholic emancipation had just been won. Duffy's work, therefore, as he saw it, was to rouse the national sentiment through Ulster, then regarded by the rest of Ireland as an enemy settlement. This was in the outset of his career when he edited in Belfast *The Vindicator*. While he was here he showed his bent towards the formation of a national literature by gathering Anglo-Irish ballads. Then came his association with Davis and the founding of *The Nation*. The work which he did with his beloved colleague for the creation of a national spirit, the making of an instructed public opinion, the fostering of a national literature, and the union of diverse elements in Irish society is known to the most cursory student of Irish history. But it is not known so well how Duffy kept in his mind that great Irish reality, the land, and that great Irish policy of an understanding with Presbyterian Ulster which, as he foresaw, might be reached through a land-reform program. He spoke to Davis about this in their first days together on *The Nation* staff.

He was always waiting for the opportunity to deal with what we have called the great Irish reality, the land. After the break with O'Connell, after the desolating famine, after Mitchel's and O'Brien's failure, after the passing away of the sole Irish national authority, O'Connell, Gavan Duffy had still the courage and the wisdom to plan broadly.

He approached again the question of the land settlement. The Whigs had introduced in the British Parliament a Land Bill which threatened the existence of the Ulster Tenant Right. Duffy seized the moment to create an agrarian movement and to promote an understanding with the Presbyterian farmers of Ulster. Tenant-protection societies had grown up in the country, North and South. He summoned a conference of the representatives of these societies, inviting Catholic priests and Presbyterian clergymen to discuss a Tenant's Charter. A movement spread through the country that anticipated the Land League. The League of the North and South was founded and the conference that came from Duffy's initiative was

[83]

the first responsible body to announce the principles that were afterwards embodied in the historic Land Act of 1881.

A movement that was made sectarian by malicious and by badly-advised men—and, unfortunately, by Cardinal Cullen—ruined the prospects of the League of the North and South and the Independent Irish opposition. The Tenants' Charter, which it seemed possible to gain then, was postponed for over twenty years. Duffy permitted himself to despair. Judge him by this testament: "I could no longer promise the suffering people relief, and to witness injustice without curb, and wrong without remedy would render life too painful. An Ireland where Mr. Keogh typified patriotism, and Dr. Cullen, the Church, was an Ireland where I could not live, but would probably cease to live." He decided to go to Australia. From his first landing on that continent he was a public man. Soon he was permitted to realize in the Antipodes what he had not been permitted to realize in his own country—the career of an administrator.

Charles Gavan Duffy had three careers, and one was spent in Ireland and one in Australia. The third was apart from place. During it he strove for an Irish culture, projecting an Irish Library and founding the Irish Literary Society of London. To this career belongs his most notable book: "My Life in Two Hemispheres." In it one may read of notable projects carried out or marred by national tragedy, in it one may find living and distinct portraits of Irishmen of two historic generations, with intimate glimpses of non-Irish statesmen and poets and notable characters.

In a Court-House

A few cases are before the judge. I stand in a space at the back of the court-room which is for the men and women who do not expect to get seats here, who slouch in, and are prepared to stand here all day watching the proceedings and waiting for decisions. The cases coming before the judge to-day are trivial enough. A man is defending himself against a charge made by a woman, or is bringing a charge against her. "She had a stick about a yard and a half long," he relates in his examination, "and she beat the bridle off the top of my ass's head." He denies a charge that the woman's counsel brings up in examination. "She stoned me at her own gate and abused me with her tongue." And he tells the bench solemnly, "all the filthy names that a human being was ever called by in this world she called me by." For some reason the bench seems to favour the woman; she is waiting to give her testimony.

How rarely do we make decisions even for ourselves! How portentous it is when others make decisions that affect us! For this man trying to stagger the bench with the weight of the stick used upon his ass and the unmeasurable filthiness of the abuse heaped on himself, and for the woman who has a charge of her own to make, the decision of the judge will have the effect of a doom. And how well the word "doom" indicates what a judgment really is, and how well the function of the judge is expressed by the old word "doomster."

It is not only the judge who makes a decision: the witnesses come into the box, and each of them, every few seconds, is under the dire necessity of making a decision. One is asked a question: his reply is not a mere utterance; it is an act of will, a decision. And as we watch the witnesses we come to know how unaccustomed we are—we with our unresolved thoughts—to the making of such decisions. Each witness is constrained in his attitude; the attitudes of all who listen to him are constrained. I think of Chaucer's line:

Such glaring eyen had he as an hare.

Each statement made is a marshalling of the memory; each statement is a decision as well as an utterance. This is what is called testimony. As I listen to it I begin to realize that there is a distinct part of literature that might be called the literature of testimony.

Men have gathered together, in some hall or under some hillside; one rises, and the herald puts a staff into his hands as a sign that what he has to say is worthy of being listened to in the assembly. . . . The assembly and the man testifying before it—how much that is greatest in literature has come out of this!

We who are only too well aware how ephemeral is most of what we say and what we read have no way of knowing how perpetuating are words spoken in this resolved way to men constrained to listen to them. . . . These are not words holding a reverie that is being passed over to us; they are words expressing a fact that we are witnesses to. And we shall remember the fact and tell our children of it in the very words that we are hearing now. . . . We who read books can hardly credit the notion that histories of great deeds were transmitted by word of mouth unbrokenly and accurately and holding the lineaments and the characteristic speech of the men who wrought such deeds. It is so now and it must have been so before. The histories that are in the Gospels, in the stories of Israel's heroes, in the Icelandic sagas, in the Homeric poems, have been spoken in the assembly, have been transmitted by witnesses.

And this literature that has had its rise in the assembly, that has been checked and challenged, that has come out of decision, out of the marshalling of memory before witnesses, has in it no evasions, no reservations. It is plain and authoritative and of public importance. "Beowulf" and "The Song of Roland" are examples of it in poetry. But the virile accent of the literature of the assembly is very rare in modern poetry. I find it in one ballad of our time—in Sir Samuel Ferguson's impressive but unequal "Vengeance of the Welshmen of Tirawley." In prose narrative one finds the accent occasionally in some of Scott's novels. I have felt it in "Lorna Doone." And, of course, it is in "The Pilgrim's Progress." Bunyan's writing is decision as well as utterance; it has its rise in the assembly; it is indeed the literature of testimony.

The proceedings of a court like this have had a powerful effect upon the popular Irish mind, and, naturally, on the poetry that this mind has expressed itself through. Daniel Corkery, in his "Hidden Ireland," tells us that the Gaelic poets of the eighteenth century designated their assembly by the word *Cuirt*. The presiding poet was usually spoken of as sheriff, and sometimes as high sheriff. He explains how it came about that the law-court came to be such an impressive model for the Irish poets of that time.

Their own nobility having vanished, and the ceremonies of their own Church having become despoiled, through fear and poverty, of its native grandeur of ritual, of colour, and music, the only imposing institution with which the people came at all into contact was the law-court: with the law and its forms they then began to associate all ideas of ceremony, judgments, and authority.

He goes on to tell us how a poet writing in Gaelic about the Last Judgment, puts into his verse a line in English, "He's not found guilty, my Lord," to give a full and dread significance to the scene. A word used in legal documents, "whereas," was adopted by the Gaelic poets; it became a word of power for them. The call which brought the poets together came to be named a warrant, and although the rest of the document was in Gaelic, it usually began with this word of power, "whereas."

Mid-Ulster

Poets in Tyrone

I found a poet in a manse, a manse by the roadside in the County Tyrone. The poet was Alice Milligan. When she had given me tea she took me without to show me all that was to be seen from a height near where she lived. As I went with her I thought how little she had changed in the years since I had seen her. She wore a brown waterproof now, and I believed that she had worn a brown waterproof on the last occasion I had been with her. The sandy red was still in her hair and a wisp of it fell over her shoulder. And still she spoke casually of what she did herself and earnestly about what her friends were doing. I had never seen her without something in her hands that was intended for some practical purpose. Now she had a telescope, a long brass telescope such as sea-captains walk about with in their retirement. She could show me, she told me, the stronghold of the Ulster Kings from this—Aileach. She had written a poem about Aileach; it was before she had come to live so close to it.

Ah, woe unbounded! where the harp once sounded
    The wind now sings;
The grey grass shivers where the mead in rivers
    Was outpoured for kings;
The min and the mether are lost together
    With the spoil of spears;
The strong dun only has stood dark and lonely
    Through a thousand years.

Cross Roads in Ireland

But I am not in woe for the wine-cup's flow,
    For the banquet's cheer,
For tall princesses with their trailing tresses
    And their broidered gear;
My grief and my trouble for this palace noble
    With no chief to lead
'Gainst the Saxon stranger on the day of danger
    Out of Aileach Neid.

She examined the long brass instrument before handing it to me. As she did she discovered that there was no glass in it, or if there was glass there was no way of focussing the sight. And so I did not view Aileach through Alice Milligan's glass.

So we talked about poetry on the hillside, and I inveigled her into repeating some of her own. She recited a couple of pieces in the casual way that was characteristic of Alice Milligan in the old days when she would say in the middle of a stanza, "I cannot repeat a poem in the way the Dublin bards have." And as she said her poems I realized what a lucky thing it is that we have a volume of Alice Milligan's "Hero Lays." But only for A.E.'s insistence we should not have it. For this poet is more disinterested than any poet I have ever known: she has only written out of some affection for a comrade or out of some mood of exaltation that she wanted some comrades to share in; never for fame, and certainly never for money. And she, with another woman, Emily Lawless, has written the most heroic poetry that has been written in the Ireland of our day.

Mid-Ulster

The daughter of a Belfast business-man, Alice Milligan writes and speaks as if there was nothing between her and Gaelic Ulster—no plantation, no John Knox, no industrial Belfast. It was probably through Irish traditional music, which her family had a great deal of interest in, that she kept a link with the Tyrone clansmen who were amongst her forbears. A poem of hers tells us that in the midst of Belfast distrust of Irish Nationalism she was a little Nationalist:

When I was a little girl,
In a garden playing,
A thing was often said
To chide us delaying:

When after sunny hours,
At twilight's falling,
Down through the garden walks
Came our old nurse calling.

"Come in! for it's growing late,
And the grass will wet ye!
Come in! or when it's dark
The Fenians will get ye."

Then, at this dreadful news,
All helter-skelter,
The panic-struck little flock
Ran home for shelter.

And round the nursery fire
Sat still to listen,
Fifty bare toes on the hearth,
Ten eyes a-glisten.

Cross Roads in Ireland

To hear of a night in march,
And loyal folk waiting,
To see a great army of men
Come devastating.

An army of Papists grim,
With a green flag o'er them,
Red-coats and black police
Flying before them.

But God (Who our nurse declared
Guards British dominions)
Sent down a deep fall of snow
And scattered the Fenians.

"But somewhere they're lurking yet,
Maybe they're near us,"
Four little hearts pit-a-pat
Thought, "Can they hear us?"

Then the wind-shaken pane
Sounded like drumming;
"Oh," they cried, "tuck us in,
The Fenians are coming!"

Four little pairs of hands
In the cots where she led those,
Over their frightened heads
Pulled up the bedclothes.

But one little rebel there,
Watched all with laughter,
Thought, "When the Fenians come
I'll rise and go after."

Wished she had been a boy
And a good deal older—

Mid-Ulster

Able to walk for miles
With a gun on her shoulder.

Able to lift aloft
The green flag o'er them,
Red-coats and black police
Flying before them.

And, as she dropped asleep,
Was wondering whether
God, if they prayed to Him
Would give fine weather.

The older Ulster Presbyterianism had a core of Republicanism which went to form leaders for the 1798 insurrection—very earnest, very devoted men. Alice Milligan is heir to this Republicanism; it gives earnestness to the lilt that is in her best known poem:

A Song of Freedom

In Cavan of the little lakes,
As I was walking with the mind,
And no one seen beside me there,
There came a song into my mind;
It came as if the whispered voice
Of one, but none of humankind,
Who walked with me in Cavan then,
And he invisible as wind.

In Urris of Inis-Owen,
As I went up the mountain-side,
The brook that came leaping down
Cried to me—for joy it cried;
And when from off the summit far
I looked o'er land and water wide,

Cross Roads in Ireland

I was more joyous than the brook
That met me on the mountain-side.

To Ara of Connacht's isles,
As I went sailing o'er the sea,
The wind's word, the brook's word,
The wave's word, was plain to me—
As we are, though she is not,
As we are, shall Banba be—
There is no king can rule the wind,
There is no fetter for the sea.

I told her of a poet who might claim to be the laureate of County Tyrone. When I mentioned Francis Carlin's name she pressed me to tell her all I knew about him and all the poems of his I remembered. She had read a few of his pieces, but had not seen either of the volumes he had published in America. I told her that when I first knew him Francis Carlin was working in a great department store in New York, and he was then writing the poems that are so redolent of this part of Ulster—the poems he published in "My Ireland" and "A Cairn of Stars."

Sweet are the hills where flowers grow,
As once they grew upon the flax
In Lagacurry, where I go
Through dreams to build the turf in stacks;
But Killydart all pleasure lacks
To one who in those dreams can hear
The music of proud royal packs
Of hounds that chase the foreign deer.

And while he worked in that store he gave a proportion of what he earned for the service of a scribe in

the Academy in Dublin, who copied for him documents
relating to the County Tyrone. It was his intention,
then, to write a history of the county. He had spent
his childhood here; born in America, he had gone back
to this place to live with his mother's people in this
countryside.

One of the best amongst Irish ballads, I said, was
his "Ballad of Douglas Bridge." The place was near
by, and Alice Milligan indicated its direction, and I
repeated the stirring verses:

> On Douglas Bridge I met a man
> Who lived adjacent to Strabane,
> Before the English hanged him high
> For riding with O'Hanlon.

> The eyes of him were just as fresh
> As when they burned within the flesh,
> And his boot-legs were wide apart
> From riding with O'Hanlon.

> "God save you, sir," I said with fear,
> "You seem to be a stranger here."
> "Not I," said he, "nor any man
> Who rides with Count O'Hanlon.

> "I know each glen from North Tyrone
> To Monaghan, and I've been known
> By every clan and parish since
> I rode with Count O'Hanlon.

> "Before that time," said he to me,
> "My fathers owned the land you see;
> But they are now among the moors
> A-riding with O'Hanlon.

"Before that time," said he with pride,
"My fathers rode where now they ride
As Rapparees, before the time
Of trouble and O'Hanlon.

"Good-night to you, and God be with
The Tellers of the tale and myth,
For they are of the spirit-stuff
That rides with Count O'Hanlon."

"Good night to you," I said, "and God
Be with the chargers, fairy-shod,
That bear the Ulster Heroes forth
To ride with Count O'Hanlon."

On Douglas Bridge we parted, but
The Gap o' Dreams is never shut
To one whose saddled soul to-night
Rides out with Count O'Hanlon.

We walked back to the manse, and Alice Milligan told me of a Tyrone beside the one I had been through —the Tyrone where the descendants of O'Neill's clansmen still kept an old way of life with the music of the harpers and their old speech and songs—the Tyrone of the Sperrin Hills.

Tyrone Story: The Lone Man

This time last year, said the man in the smokeroom, I was engaged in a business that kept me some weeks in this very town. I used to go for a walk in the evening, and I was often caught in the throng that loitered about the market house. There is always some itinerant musician there about sunset; I remember a demoralized opera-singer who accompanied himself with a concertina, a tramp who performed on a tin whistle, and a battered ballad-singer who sang in the traditional style. One evening I noticed the person I am going to tell you about. He was playing some fitful, tuneless piece on the fiddle. The man's appearance was remarkable, for he was in his old age, and was tall, gaunt, and emaciated, and with his great figure and his untrimmed beard he suggested the picture of a Russian moujik. I thought he was a passer-by like the rest (this town is on the road from Enniskillen to Derry, and the wanderers going East and North pass through it), but the next day and the day after I saw this strange being roaming along the streets. An acquaintance told me that he had been in the town as long as he could remember.

He used to drift through the town like a withered leaf. Sometimes he would remain still for a while and play on the fiddle, but when he ceased playing he might put the fiddle under his coat and go off without claiming his dues. His wrists hung below his coat-sleeves, showing the whole of his large and nervous hands. He had made a wallet inside the lining of his coat, and it bulged out with the weight of his provision. Generally his coat was buttoned across his fiddle. One evening I spoke to the man. He was standing before a shop-window, and I would say that he was gazing into it intently if I did not feel that his mind was wholly in abeyance. He turned and made some mechanical motion as I passed, and I remember that there was a copper in his hand. "You are not playing to-day," I said to him. His words were difficult to hear. Someone had forbidden him to play, and they had no right to forbid him, but they could move him on from the place where he was playing. Then he said that he would play no more; that he was tired.

I looked into the man's face. There was a spirit in his eyes, but it was a weary spirit. It was not to-day, nor yesterday, nor a year ago that it had become weary. His face was striking. It was noble in its dissociation from what was common, mean, or criminal. Under the brim of his battered hat I saw a brow and nose that were large and prominent. The flesh was soft and clear, and the features were emaciated. He was tired, he repeated. There was, he said, a difference between sitting in a room playing and walking about the streets. Was the fiddle a good one, I asked? He took it from under his coat and sounded it with his fingers, and as he did so some attachment came into his eyes. He had no one belonging to him and he hardly ate; he had no appetite, he said, and what he put into his mouth he could hardly swallow. He said all this in a voice so hollow that it was hardly audible. After a while I asked him what was his name. I was surprised that he answered me, for I thought that he might have forgotten his name. "Mulissa," he said.

I am interested in Irish names and know their distribution with some accuracy. The name he bore belonged to a family that had a place in the old territory

LA MONTAGNE D'ACHELIN BY MARIE HOWET

of Tyrone. I had come across the name "Maelissa" in some Annals and I was surprised to find that it was still in existence. "You are from Tyrone," I said.

"Yes."

"There are not many of your name there now?"

"No one. No one of the name at all."

Speech was difficult with him. He could hardly articulate, and I could hardly hear what he said. Beside, he was far away from our world. I gave him an alms and bid him good-bye.

Afterwards I was in West Tyrone. I went to see some people in a village there. The conversation turned on politics, and it revealed the hopes and tremors of a people who had long lived under the shadow of oppression. "The order of liberty will come out by one door and the order for massacre by the other door; that is the prophecy," said the woman of the house.

"Who made that prophecy?" I asked.

"The Callach Duv—the Black Nun. She lived in the hills a long time ago."

The Penal Days that were only a memory for the rest of Ireland were not very remote to this family that had been long in this place. Their tradition went back to the Gaelic life of the hills and the woman of the house talked about an uncle of hers who knew all the stories of the people there.

"Does he know anything about people named Maelissa?" I asked.

"Mulissa? I heard of the name," she said. "There is a story about the Mulissas."

"What is the story?" I asked.

"I can't tell you rightly. There is no one of the name living there now. But there was a family there thirty years ago. I remember seeing the house they lived in—a long, low house. There was a river before the house and the stepping-stones across the river were forenenst the door. The Mulissas were two brothers and they lived together. Well, the younger wanted to get married, and the girl he was engaged with did not please the elder brother. Well, for a whole day the two quarrelled about the marriage. The younger brother left the house to go to his sweetheart's, and the other followed him outside. They were still quarrelling when the young man was in the middle of the river, crossing by the stepping-stones. The elder brother took a stone in his hand and flung it at him. It struck the other on the forehead. Some said he ran the whole way till he came to his sweetheart's house. She wiped the blood from his face with her apron. They were to be married that night, for it was near Shrove, and a priest had been sent for. Married they were. Then when the young man crossed the threshold he fell down dead. And the bride held him in her arms and keened him all night."

"And what happened to the elder brother?"

"I remember hearing them say he was good with the fiddle. But he went away from the place when the young man died. There's no one of the name living there now."

Well, to-day I saw the fiddler again. His great frame and his untrimmed beard make him noticeable. I met him in an empty street. He stopped to play, and again he drew out the fitful piece that had no music in it. He ceased playing, and with the fiddle in his hands he turned round to me. I came near to hear what he had to say. "The fiddle string—broken," he said. I told him that I would get him another. "Have you had the fiddle long?" I asked. "I wore out four fiddles since I came here," he said. You will see him in the street some day. There is a strangeness about him, and I think it comes from a complete detachment. Those who have not eaten for a length of time are perceptibly less attached to the world of our interests. It may be hunger that makes him so remote from us. But I think there's more than that—I think there is something in the man that an artist or a saint would understand. Anyway, he is a remarkable figure. A painter of mediæval Italy would have given that gaunt frame and that emaciated face to one of the saints.

PART III

East Ulster

Armagh

IN the town a market is being held; there is fruit in
the market and more variety of vegetables than the
usual, or even the unusual, Irish market shows. And
there is an old woman with four ducks in her basket.
I meet with her in every street of the town. As I see
the last of her a man is raising a duck in each of his
hands and telling her how light and meagre they are.

They were hatched in the basket was under her bed,
And on her own floor
They were reared where she'd see them, between hob and
    threshold,
Between hearthstone and door!
And now to a market where prices are harried
Till they're nothing at all, the four ducks are carried!

And the time they'd be gone her heart would be low,
And she'd murn an' murn,
And then they'd be back, and she'd hear in the lane
Their quack, quack of return;
And the cat would be vexed, and cross-eyed her looks
At the old woman's joy when in came her ducks!

At noon they'd be gone, but at dusk they'd be back
From the duck-pond in Urney,

And no hound would chase them that kept the good hours
On their back-and-forth journey;
No weasel nor wood-cat would near them and bite
An old woman's ducks that were lucky and right!

From each end of the basket, too frightened to quack,
A duck sticks a beak,
And frightened is she, the old body who'd sell them,
And hardly will speak:
As she trudges along with her ducks, each as thin
As the water-hen!

I leave the market, and, going out of the town, come to the mound that is the site of the ancient Emain Macha. Here was Conchobar MacNessa's seat when Maeve marched her armies out of Connacht to overthrow him, bringing with her Fergus MacRoig who would avenge the betrayal of Deirdre and the Sons of Uisneach. Around this mound are gathered the greatest of the heroic stories of the Celtic race—the stories of Cuchullain and Deirdre and Maeve—the one cycle of stories out of the early European world that is comparable to the "Iliad."

The same heroic types are in the "Iliad" and the "Táin Bó Cúalnge." Cuchullain, who is fated to die young and who possesses the immortal horses that prophesy his end to him, is the same type as Achilles; Conchobar is the same type as Agamemnon, Conall Cearnach as Diomedes, the great horseman. But while Homer gave the material that came to him supreme form, the Irish *Filid* left theirs with only an approach to form. And while Homer eternalized his action by making it turn upon Helen, the type of beauty and the inspiration of love, the *Filid* cramped their action in an archaic world by making it turn on the possession of a bull.

I go up a grassy slope and stand upon a round mound that is ringed with thorn-bushes and a few ash-trees. As at Tara, as at Cashel, the outlook is over rich grazing lands. The king and his poets standing here, unlike Homer's kings and poets, would look, not towards a sacred city, but out over his herds, his *pecunia*. And because of this difference the tale of their doings is inchoate and barbarous compared to the tale of Troy. Nevertheless, the "Táin Bó Cúalnge" is one of the world's great stories. Oral tradition, scholars tell us, was occupied for five hundred years working over and developing the story, and by the close of the fifth century the saga to which it belonged was substantially the one we have now. The text of the tale must have been completed by the first half of the seventh century; its oldest extant version, the "Book of the Dun Cow," dates from about the year 1100.

The modern town has its name from the ancient Emain Macha. It has its existence from it, too. For from the mound on which I stand I can see the steeples and the turret of two cathedrals—the cathedral of the Catholic and of the Protestant primate. They are there because Saint Patrick made Emain Macha the centre of his mission. Tara had become the seat of political power in his time, and the strength had departed from Emain Macha. But the prestige that was shed on this

place through the saga that spread out from it led
Patrick to place his metropolis here and not in the
middle of Ireland. And Professor MacNeill tells us
that the saint's association with the eclipsed Ultonian
kingdom was the means of preserving the greatest of
the Irish epic tales. Letters were brought here while the
tradition of "the chiefs of Rury's race" was still proud
and vigorous. While it was still living the Ultonian
hero-lore got written down. Then, as the first Irish
written lore, it took on the prestige of a classic. In
spite of its fierce provincialism, in spite of its ignoring
the people who had become the dynastic race in Ireland, the Táin was accepted at every seat of royal
authority. And Professor MacNeill goes on to say:

Thus, the early Christian culture of the Northeast, joined
to the intensely proud tradition of the still unbroken remnant
of the race that ruled in Emain Macha, combined to lay the
foundations of our native literature. The meeting of these two
currents stirred the native mind to its depths. Only a period
of great exaltation could have produced such a work of literature as the "Táin Bó Cúalnge"—the greatest constructive
composition in the ancient Irish language.

And now we are back in the modern town and ready
to look at its public buildings. The Catholic cathedral
is the most conspicuous of them. Like most Catholic
churches in Ireland it is new; also it is rather grandiose.
But, raised upon a height, it is a great monument to
the devotion of the Catholics of Ireland. The Protestant cathedral is more venerable, a brown-stone church
with a square tower. The lawn before it makes it a

place of quietness, and the flags that hang within bring something of the pageant of history into it. Persian lettering on a tablet—alongside the unknown letters I read—"Sacred to the beloved memory of Turner Macan, formerly Captain in the Sixth Hussars, and many years Persian interpreter to the Commanders-in-Chief in India. He was unsurpassed in his knowledge of the language and literature of Persia, and to him is owing the first perfect edition of her great poet Ferdousee." I am glad to know that the poet of heroic Iran had something done for him by a man of Emain Macha.

The library, both as a building and a collection of books, is interesting. The Bronze Age weapons and implements that are housed in it are worth while examining. But what most appealed to me about this library was its flavour of eighteenth-century bookishness. I felt that this was the place to peruse Burke's "On the Sublime and Beautiful." And thinking this I looked out of the window and saw that there was another interesting building across the way. "The observatory," the librarian told me. Then it seemed to me that Armagh, with the evidences of a care for thought that this cluster of buildings shows, and with a tradition that goes back to Saint Patrick, should have been the seat of a Northern university. "Yes," said the librarian when I said something like this to him, "Primate Robinson planned to establish a university here."

Primate Robinson—I had heard about him before, but had taken little interest in what I had heard. Now as I looked on what he had built up here and heard of what he had planned to build up, I recognized that this English ecclesiastic was the real founder of present-day Armagh. He endowed it with such state as made it possible for the town to claim to be an ecclesiastical metropolis. This Primate's achievement has not been overlooked in records of his time. I take Arthur Young's "Tour in Ireland" off a shelf in the library, and I find that that perspicuous traveller met and talked with him on July 23, 1776.

His Grace rode out with me to Armagh, and showed me some of the noble and spirited works by which he has perfectly changed the face of the neighbourhood. The buildings he has erected in seven years, one would suppose, without previous information, to be the work of an active life. A list of them will justify this observation. He has erected a very elegant palace, 90 by 60 feet, and 40 feet high, in which an unadorned simplicity reigns. The barracks were erected under His Grace's directions, and form a large and handsome edifice. The school is a building of considerable extent, and admirably adapted for the purpose: a more convenient or a better contrived one is nowhere to be seen. This edifice was built entirely at the primate's expense. The church is erected of white stone, and having a tall spire makes a very agreeable object in a country where churches and spires do not abound—at least such as are worth looking at. Three other churches the primate has also built, and done considerable reparations to the cathedral. He has been the means also of erecting a public infirmary, which was built by subscription, contributing amply to it himself. A public library he has erected at his own expense, given a large collection of books and endowed it. He has further ornamented the city with a market house and shambles, and been the direct means, by giving leases upon that condition, of almost new building the whole place. He found it a nest of mud cabins, and he will leave it a well-built city of stone and slate. I heard it asserted in common conversation that His Grace, in these noble undertakings, had not expended less than £30,000, besides what he had been the means of doing, though not directly at his own expense.

Armagh should be a centre of public life in the North. If the seat of the Northern Government were here instead of in Belfast, a city with a tradition of animosity to nationalism, a real cantonal arrangement could have been made as regards Ulster: in that case the whole province could have been given a separate government and the way laid down for a federal government. But at the time when it should have been made, no statesman could have taken the risk involved in the making of such a proposal.

Portadown

To-day is market-day in Portadown, and the streets are lively with people. A broad water-way connects the town with an industrial country back to Newry and on to Lough Neagh and Belfast. Transportation is cheap and easy; industries are established; people are employed; Portadown looks a business-like place.

Portadown has its legend—the legend that makes it the ultra-Orange town of Northern Ireland. When a ballad-maker wanted to give a recognizable background to his character he placed him by writing:

I am a loyal Orangeman
From Portadown upon the Bann.

Mothers are said to keep their children out of forbidden places with the warning, "There are wee Popes in it." History joins with legend in giving Portadown this particular eminence: the conspicuous monument of the town is the statue of the champion of Northern Protestantism and the leader of the opposition to Home Rule in the eighteen-nineties, Colonel Saunderson.

Reverting to the legends: there is the tale of the British Government official who stood in a street of Portadown. "My good man," he said to a townsman, "where is the church?" "The Presbyterian church is straight forenenst ye." "No, I don't attend the Presbyterian church." "Well, the Episcopal church is down the street and around to your left." "I want to know where people belonging to other denominations go." "The Methodists go up the town and the Baptists go down the town." "And where do the—er—Catholics go?" "The Papishes, is it? They just go to hell." The tale wrongs the kindliness of Portadown. I am sure the government official said "Cawtholics," and that it was his accent the townsman objected to. I got no such reply. A townsman walked down the street with me to the church of my faith. It is in no obscure place. And the Catholics of Portadown are no unimportant entity. In a population of about ten thousand they number about two thousand.

As I walked through Portadown on an autumn day in 1929, I had a memory of another autumn day on these streets—the 29th September, 1912. The occasion was an historic one, and I was glad I had been present and had some souvenirs of the proceedings. It was "Ulster Day," and I had come to Portadown to be an onlooker while a covenant was being signed that committed the Protestants of Ulster—of the whole of Ulster—to a violent resistance to a Home Rule bill which Mr. Asquith's government was putting through the Westminster Parliament. In those mild pre-bellic days the granting of a measure of self-government to Ireland was considered to be an event of major political importance: the Tory party in England patronized the idea of an insurrectionary movement in Ireland against a constitution that a Liberal government might bring into effect, and the Protestants of Ulster were encouraged to make revolutionary and warlike movements with the object of showing the people of the British Empire that they would enter upon civil war rather than pay taxes to and accept the laws of an Irish parliament. The first movement was to be the signing of the Ulster Covenant.

I was present at the covenant-signing in Portadown. The proceedings began with a service in the First Presbyterian Church. The congregation sang, "God is Our Refuge and Our Strength," and "O God Our Help in Ages Past," and "To Thee, O God, We Fly," with "God Save the King." The young people in the gallery were glancing at the strangers present, and the members of the congregation looked round at every new person who entered. The reader gave out texts from Isaiah and Saint Paul, and prayed to God to enlighten counsels of the British statesmen so that their conscience rather than their party-interest would be clear to them. I expected, I remember, a flow of impassioned eloquence from the preacher, but got from him instead a carefully written statement. Some people pretended to think that clergymen in the North of Ireland were introducing politics into their churches, he told us. But their opposition to Home Rule was not political—it was a question of life and death. What would be their situation if a Home Rule Bill was passed? A prosperous community would be taxed for the upkeep of monasteries and convents, and a tolerant people would be put under the heel of an intolerant Church. Because they wanted to protect their birthright of free citizenship they were going to sign the covenant. They would sign it with the name of Jesus Christ upon their lips, and if they failed to abide by it they would be branded as liars and cowards. He went on to remind the congregation of the signing of the Scottish Covenant, and he told how some men wrote "Till Death" after their signatures, and others drew blood to sign their names. I noted that all this was said to a rather relaxed congregation.

We left the church while a hymn was being sung in which there is this verse:

> Thy best gifts from on high
> In rich abundance pour,
> That we may magnify
> And praise Thee more and more.
> O Lord, stretch forth Thy mighty hand,
> And guard and bless our Fatherland.

Outside there was a streamer across the street, "For God, for King, for Covenant." An old woman was scolding some wondering children at a corner. "We won't let ye have Home Rule. The Protestants will put their foot down."

In the street there were young women in nurses' uniforms standing beside ambulances. There were young men with what seemed to be arms in their hands, and there was what seemed to be cannon at the street-corner. The cannon was wood, painted, the rifles were dummy. But it all meant preparation of a kind, and in those mild days such preparation had a stirring effect. Hundreds of young men marched to where the covenant was being signed—it was a sight that has stayed in my memory. They were well-set-up young fellows with a good swing to their stride. I went into the hall, moved about with the people, and stood at the tables where the Covenanters were signing the roll. Outside "For Union and for King" was being sung; the chorus went:

> Brothers, shall we sever?
> Never! Never! Never!
> But we'll cling for ever
> To Union and to King.
> No Home Rule shall bind us,
> But traitors ever find us
> With thousands more behind us
> For Union and for King.

I thought there was a lack of fervour about the proceedings, but when I said so in Dublin I was mocked at for my lack of discernment.

East Ulster

Ten years later the Union was shattered, and there were two Parliaments in Ireland. The men who signed in Portadown do not have to regard themselves as covenant-breakers: they are not paying taxes to a Dublin Parliament, and, anyway, they have their connection with London. They can be at ease. But there are men in Cavan, Monaghan, and Donegal who have entered into the same covenant, and who are now living under a Dublin government. They are not branded men, however; they have enough philosophy, it seems, to prevent their agonizing over fulfilled or unfulfilled covenants. They celebrate the Orange festival just as publicly as in the years past, and whatever has been lost in neighbourly feeling between them and the Catholics amongst whom they live has been quickly regained. They are not taxed for the upkeep of convents and monasteries, and I can hardly believe that they ever expected they would be.

The Ulster Protestant living in the Free State doesn't see the king's head on the letters he stamps, and he has to drop what he has written into a green instead of into a red letter-box. I am seriously informed that these matters perturb him. There are other matters that might perturb him but probably do not: a moralistic censorship of books and periodicals and a law that forbids divorce. And then there are matters which make for a real contrast in the ordinary life in the Free State and in the Northern Counties. The Ulster Protestant living in the Free State has to send his children to schools in which the Irish language is a compulsory subject. The salaries of the school-teachers are ten per cent lower than in the Northern Counties, although they compare very favourably with salaries paid to teachers in the American countryside. Old Age Pensions are lower and Unemployment Insurance less adequate. The cost of living is two points higher than in the Northern Counties. But the landlords have been compelled to sell their estates to the tenants. The Protestant farmer in Donegal, Cavan, or Monaghan knows that if he were living under the Northern Government he might have to wait a lifetime before he began to pay annuities instead of rents; he hears across the border the yells of the tenant-farmers who cannot induce their landlords to sell to them, and who know that their government is very slow about compelling landlords to do anything. Hearing such yells he probably thinks that living under a Dublin Parliament has its compensations.

When, in 1912, they spoke in such exalted tones about "Ulster," the leaders of the Covenanters knew very well that they were making a claim that they could not substantiate. They kept on saying "Ulster" because they wanted to give the impression that there was a definite and historic territory behind them and for the same reason that they said they paid three-fourths of the revenue of Ireland—because they believed in saying big things in a big way. When it came to setting up a Parliament in Belfast, however, they had to let go of three of the nine counties—Donegal,

Cavan, and Monaghan. But a territory large enough to support a government had to be carved out for them. Two counties which had a majority opposed to separation from the rest of Ireland—a slight majority of Nationalists, it is true, but still a majority, Fermanagh and Tyrone—were forced into the divided area. If there had been a plebiscite by counties, only four of the Ulster counties would have separated themselves from the rest of Ireland. As it is, the Northern Government controls six counties.

According to returns contained in Blue Books for 1926 the six counties have a population of 1,256,561 people.[1] Of these, 420,428 are Catholics. With a majority in two counties the Catholics are one-third of the entire population. Safeguards given to them as a minority have been scrapped by the Northern Government. Proportional representation, which in the Free State gives a chance to minorities, has been suppressed in the six counties. "We have been driven out of control of every County Council in the North," a representative Northern Nationalist declared. "Our large majorities in Fermanagh, Tyrone, South Armagh, and Derry City have been neutralized by a shameless system of gerrymandering local government areas. In Omagh Rural Council twenty-one Unionist Councillors were returned with 4,153 votes, but 4,400 Nationalist votes could only return three councillors. In Fermanagh 36,455 Nationalists can elect only one member to the

[1] The population has declined since, but the proportions remain about the same.

Northern Parliament, but 25,529 Anti-Nationalists can elect two members. In Antrim 38,619 Nationalists get no representation at all." This means repression, and a community that decides on repression has to pay a price. A stranger observes that the Ulster constabulary carry revolvers at their belts—that is one sign of the price that is being paid. Another is in the inability of Belfast to create a municipal government worthy of a great city. An official report declared that Belfast was being run like a village. In the elections in January 1930 "the official Unionists," said the *Irish Statesman*, "were returned unopposed for every ward in which they nominated a candidate, and naturally the reactionaries take the walk-over as a final proof that though rate-payers may talk about reforms, they will not take action to secure them, and so can be safely ignored." They cannot take action without displacing men who secured and uphold the present order. The price that the Northern Counties pay for an illiberal government is a mechanical and unprogressive administration.

The Free State, with its large unemployment, with the dreadful housing conditions in its capital city, with its inability to support a single artist, has not the right, even if it had the will, to cast any reflections upon economic conditions in the Northern Counties. But because an impression has been created that they are not only superior, but immensely superior, in economic condition to the rest of Ireland, and because this alleged superiority has been used to justify the division

[116]

of an ancient land, it is not unfair to test this claim by official figures. Economic prosperity is not consistent with a decline in population, and the Registrar-General's figures for the Northern Counties reveal a decline. In 1926 there were 1,256,561 persons in the Northern Counties. In 1928 the figures were put down as 1,250,000 including military. There were almost 8,000 more births than deaths in the area in a year, so the loss through emigration must have been very considerable. The rate of decrease between 1926 and 1928 suggests that the estimate given by an independent candidate during the recent parliamentary elections is likely to be correct; he stated that since the setting-up of the Northern Government 70,000 people have emigrated from the six counties.

Ireland has now a customs-boundary that marks off the six from the twenty-six counties, and she has two Parliaments. The Parliaments are not of equal status: while the Parliament of the Free State is co-equal with that of Great Britain, the Parliament of Northern Ireland is subordinate. The Free State raises and expends its own revenue, imposes tariffs, enters into treaties with other states, has ministers and consuls in foreign countries, and a representative in the League of Nations. Northern Ireland's taxation is raised and expended by the authority of the Parliament of Great Britain. Her government cannot enter into treaties with other countries nor impose tariffs. But Northern Ireland sends representatives to the Parliament of Great

Britain and has the advantages of British social legislation. Old Age Pensions, Unemployment Insurance, and other social services are not less in the six counties than they are in Great Britain.

This leaves Northern Ireland in the position of a client-state that pays out tribute and gets back doles. Her political leaders are always protesting their satisfaction with the arrangement, and their protestations, no doubt, are sincere. But the arrangement leads to awkward situations. Northern Ireland's political leadership is Tory, and the party that initiates legislation at present at Westminster is Labour. The Northern representatives in their capacity of members of the Westminster Parliament denounce as communistic the measures that their government at home hastens to make the law of the land. Officially Northern Ireland is philosophic about this right-hand and left-hand distinction. "Our friends in the South," said the *Northern Whig* recently, "may smile at our inconsistencies. We have the benefits." The same journal noted that certain measures enacted at Westminster had put the Northern Government "up a tree." "But," it went on to say, "when one is safely up a tree, and all kinds of perils and unknown conditions are at the foot, it is sometimes prudent to stay there."

How high up the tree the Northern Government has got itself through not thinking in terms of its own area's resources has been shown by the well-informed Belfast correspondent of the *Irish Statesman*. Writing on March 15, 1930, he said:

East Ulster

Ten years or so ago the Minister of Finance informed a province ready to believe anything that a Cabinet Minister said to it, and nothing that was said by anybody else, that Northern Ireland could afford to pay £7,000,000 a year as an Imperial contribution and still provide for its own services. He has now informed us that while paying less than one of these seven millions to England, we can spend no more upon ourselves unless we submit to fresh taxation. We can, it seems, have no more money for anything. Not merely the amenities of life, but its necessities, are to be starved. We must, for lack of money, acquiesce in the dreadful figure to which infant mortality in Belfast, and (I suspect) throughout the province generally has climbed, because we have no money for the required palliatives. It is true that the salaries of the private secretaries to our Ministers are to be increased, but this is, of course, inevitable; the people whose political thinking has brought us to this pass must be paid still more if they are to think hard enough to discover how to get us out of it. But our financial policy has brought us to this, that we are faced with one or either of two alternatives, equally distasteful, either to acquiesce in things as they are, or to put our hands in our pockets to get rid of them. Now this extra taxation, if it is resorted to, will be peculiar to Northern Ireland, imposed by the Northern Parliament, which, having no right to remit any taxation imposed by Westminster, has the right to add to it in the area under its own (partial) control. We have either, then, to fall gradually behind England in civilization (the model we have chosen to follow in preference to thinking things out for ourselves), or, in order to keep pace with it, to be taxed more heavily than the English people are whose lead we are following. We are already far behind England in, for instance, education; but we cannot any longer even keep our present distance. If England raises the school-leaving age, more financial stringency will prevent us from following suit. Even at our present rate of expenditure it will be many years before we have primary school buildings in Northern Ireland at which we need not blush; to cope with the additional scholars that would flock in if the age were raised is an impossibility. This is only one instance out of many that might be given of the absurdity of our present policy. We have undertaken, with a total public income of between ten and twelve million pounds, burdens which everyone who reflected upon the matter at all knew could not be discharged with anything like the sum we had at our disposal; and we did so owing to our incurable habit of refusing to think for ourselves, and, instead of thinking, taking the word of people whose only object was to induce us to adopt a certain policy upon grounds of sentiment, without any regard to our material interests. The people who framed our Constitution never thought either of our interests nor even of the natural consequences of their own arrangements. It was enough that a certain party interest should be safeguarded, and we (through our own fault in being too credulous) have to bear the consequences. It may not be a bad thing for us in the long run. We shall have obtained a valuable political education; and even if we have to pay for it more than we like, or than it was necessary to pay, we shall value it (I hope) all the more on that account.

The people who framed the Northern Constitution were not young men. I remember that I got a distinct surprise when I saw some of the Northern Ministers: in the Free State one gets used to the appearance of Ministers who were in their thirties when they entered office, and who have just passed into their forties. The Northern Ministers are men passing from their sixties into their seventies.

When they have to speak in public about relations with the Free State, these Ministers can be counted upon—or could be counted upon until recently—to express horror at the thought of Northern Ireland having any dealings or communications with men who are against the British Empire. It would be hard, I imagine, to get them to consider the notion that the British Empire that exists to-day is not the British Empire that they have in mind. A British Empire has vanished into the past as an Austrian Empire has vanished into the past. "To-day England itself is nothing more than an English-speaking community among others, in which younger ones will soon become dominant in importance," says that shrewdest of European observers, Count Hermann Keyserling. To judge by their public utterance the new dispensation has not been revealed to the members of the Northern Ireland government. This re-casting of a world-power has been made by English, Canadian, South African, Australian statesmen, and (by no means least in contribution of energy and idea) young Irish statesmen like the late Kevin O'Higgins. Northern Ireland politicals, with their attachment to an older Imperial idea, have had no part in this re-construction.

Ireland, a country with an area slightly over thirty-two thousand square miles, and with no physical features to make for division—a poor country, moreover, with two expensive administrations to keep up—must, in time, form a union, no matter how ardently a generation may desire to keep to their own side of a boundary. But the approach to the solution of the difficulties in the way of union will have to be slow and tentative. First of all, the necessity for working together on definite and practical issues will have to be felt—it is being felt now—and then enough good will will have to be generated to get around the real difficulties that are in the way of a union between the two areas.

There are economic difficulties and there are cultural difficulties. Northern people maintain that the Free State has added to these difficulties by making Irish compulsory in the schools, by enacting a law forbidding divorce, and by setting up a protectionist system. Belfast makes linen and ships, and there is no market in Ireland for either ships or linen; moreover, these large-scale industrialists have a fear that an Irish Parliament might do something which would cut them off from their markets or their source of raw material. Then there are the cultural difficulties which arise out of the confrontation of Calvinism and Catholicism, and in connection with these I recollect the state of mind which displayed itself at the services held during the signing of the covenant in 1912. . . . André Siegfried, in his book on America, has shown us that a sense of superiority is essential to Calvinists; it goes with the idea of an Elect. The services that I witnessed then revealed a group who could not bear to think that people who had a different tradition from theirs could take a real part in the government or the industrial life of a country. To work with an Irish government the heads of which might be Catholic would be to acknowledge that Calvinist superiority is not immeasurable— there are people in the North of Ireland who would face anything rather than make such acknowledgment. An editorial in the *Irish Statesman* on March 1, 1930, said:

It is futile sentimentalizing over united Ireland, being oratorical or declamatory over it, if those speaking ignore the division of economic interests, and cultural affections which prevent it being united. Actually what those who work for a united Ireland have to do is to take all these factors into account and try to find a practical solution of the problems. They would have to make inquiries of the Ulster industrialists exactly what economic interests of theirs would be injuriously affected by the application to all Ireland of the economic policy of the Free State. It is not really a hopeless inquiry. There are industries in Northern Ireland which would like for themselves some measure of protection in all Ireland. There would have to be compromise on both sides and guarantees which would not be merely platform protestations that nothing would be done by an All Ireland Parliament to injure any interest. So far as the cultural and religious differences exist we see at present no way out of it but that there should be a provincial Parliament in the North reserving to itself complete control over certain interests they would not trust to a Parliament where the majority would be inspired by different cultural and religious traditions. That is, having accepted for all Ireland the status of a Dominion, each area would put its hand into the bag of powers and decide what powers would be exercised locally. The All Ireland Parliament might have tariffs, agriculture, transport, posts and telegraphs, etc. The best way to start would be to form an All Ireland group with members in both areas who would investigate the problem, meet, discuss, and then tentatively suggest solutions, printing these and sending them to the prominent intelligences and representatives of industry and education in both areas for criticism. Then there should be more meetings to consider these criticisms and new solutions, based on them, sent out again and again until some kind of theoretical agreement is reached.

The probabilities are that it is only through such slow stages that arrangements will be made that can ultimately lead to an Irish unity.

At the moment, on neither side of it, is the boundary a matter of deep concern. What concern there is is shown more in Belfast than in Dublin, for one cannot motor far in any direction in the Northern area without being brought to the boundary, and also because small but once thriving businesses like biscuit-making, shirt-making, tobacco-making have been all but ruined by it. Dublin, with its interests drawn more and more in the direction of Cork and Limerick, is inclined to forget about the border. Meanwhile the relations between Protestant and Catholic in Northern Ireland are becoming settled; that is to say, neighbourly. Between Northern Ireland and the Free State they are no longer disturbed and disturbing, and having reached such a stage they are bound to improve. Cultural relations and sporting relations between Belfast and Dublin have always been good; dramatic companies from Dublin get splendid receptions in Belfast, and sporting teams from the South are always handsomely entertained. "We're entertaining a shooting-club from the Free State," said a stranger to me the other day as I was sitting in the smoking-room of a Belfast hotel. "I know by your accent you're a Dublin man. Will you join us?" I joined in the drinking of a very deep and wide loving-cup. Dublin people know that Irish traditional music has always been better known and cultivated in Belfast than in their own city. A new consciousness is developing in Northern Ireland, friends of mine who are of Ulster Protestant stock assure me, and that consciousness takes account of the Gaelic past of the province. It is true that school-histories still give the impression that the Ulster princes and their clansmen who defeated the Elizabethan generals were savages, and it is also true that for many of the leaders of Northern Ireland European history begins with the preaching of John Knox. But there is a new consciousness, and for evidence of it, there is the speech made by one of the ministers in introducing a bill in the Northern Parliament, a speech which dealt with the Gaelic past so sympathetically that the Nationalist members urged that it should be printed and distributed to every school in the six counties.

Perhaps the Free State in leaving the six counties to their own devices is pursuing the wisest policy under the circumstances. At all events it has had a sobering effect on those enthusiastic Covenanters who maintained before an extended audience that an Irish Government could only exist on the plunder of the prosperous Northeast. President Cosgrave's government has created an administration that is free from the suspicion of graft or corruption; the important municipalities under its jurisdiction, Dublin and Cork, have been modernized and made progressive; a Civil Service Commission has taken appointments out of the hands of elected bodies, thus making for fitness in every branch of the public service. Thoughtful people in Belfast note such developments. They note, too, the efficient handling of industrial apparatus by people whom they had been taught to look on as incapable of any effort except political agitation. Seeing such developments, they are not so easily frightened at the idea of some working arrangements between the separated counties and the Free State.

And perhaps the separation of the two areas has not been an unmixed evil. The absence of Northern Unionist representation made it possible for the Free State to make the Irish language a compulsory subject in the schools and so prepare the way for the Gaelicization of the country; a Northern representation would have defeated this attempt. It would have defeated, too, the attempt to industrialize the southern part of the country—all Irish industries would have been concentrated around Belfast. And the self-exclusion of the unconverted Ulster Unionists has had another effect that is to the good: those unserviceable people who, for some reason known only to themselves, called themselves "Irish Loyalists," backed as they would have been in an Irish unity by the Northern group, would still be encumbering Irish public life: their retirement to the suburbs of London is a moral gain that cannot be overestimated. Irish unity, when it is brought about, will be due to the fact that both areas want it and are prepared to make a sacrifice to attain it. That temper in Ireland—it is bound to be brought about—will be a benefit that will make a temporary division, even a division lasting a generation—not altogether unfortunate. Meanwhile President Cosgrave's ministry should be able to estimate tendencies in the Northern area: two of its members are Ulstermen—Ernest Blythe, the Minister of Finance and Vice-President, is an Ulster Protestant; Patrick McGilligan, the Minister for Industry and Commerce, is an Ulster Catholic.

Derry: A City with Two Traditions

I am standing before the war monument that is in a principal place in Derry. The main figure looks like the cave-man of the cruder ethnologist's fancy dressed up in a modern uniform. He is striving to dig the guts out of someone with a bayonet. Turning from this piece of ready-made ferocity I see two old women walking towards me: shawls are across their heads, and they have stunted figures and worn features. Behind them walks a burly member of the Ulster constabulary, a revolver dangling at his belt.

The Ulster poet whom I had visited said to me, "Derry is half Londonderry and half Doire-Colmcille." She meant that half of the tradition of the place is from the settlement of London merchants and half from Saint Columba whose name is in the Gaelic form of the place-name. And because of that saying the two old women walking by the monument had become noticeable for me. They looked as if they might have approached the little cell that Columba had in the Oak

Grove that gave a name to the place. The sight of the pair gave me hope that I might come on something else that would give me the sense that I was in Doire-Colmcille.

Meanwhile I was certainly in Londonderry. With a friend of mine, a Derry man, I stop to read a placard that announces a celebration in connection with the anniversary of the Shutting of the Gates. My friend says, "I remember when we were neither ashamed nor afraid to lead off on a placard like this with 'The Glorious and Immortal Memory of the Great and Good King William, who saved us from Popery, Slavery, Arbitrary Government, brass money, and wooden shoes. May our City never want Walkers nor Murrays in the hour of danger, and may the flag which undulates so triumphantly over Columbkill's Cathedral never be struck for the gratification of temporisers.' We don't write that on our placards now," he said, "but it's in our minds." "It is all better expressed," I said, "in a song that has a good Irish tune to it:

"Where Foyle his swelling waters rolls northward to the main,
Here, Queen of Erin's daughters, fair Derry, fixed her reign;
A holy temple crowned her, and commerce graced her street,
A rampart wall was round her, the river at her feet;
And here she sat alone, boys, and, looking from the hill,
Vowed the maiden on her throne, boys, would be a maiden still."

Then without saying another word about the song nor the placard we went into the factories where Derry's famous shirts and collars are being made. Business is thriving; between five and six thousand people are employed in this most prosperous branch of Ulster's linen industry. And as we walk through the town I note that the political interest of the townspeople seems to be pretty evenly balanced. Here is an Orange Hall and here is a Nationalist Club. Saint Columba gives his name to a hall. But what is going on in this particular hall is a moving-picture featuring a starry-eyed young Californian. Droves of pigs are going down a street; we hear the bellowing of cattle as they are being loaded on trucks; we see poultry being taken away in crates: like every other town in Ireland that does business at all, Derry is a market-place.

And then we are on the walls thirty feet high that defended the original little town. These must have been the latest built city walls in Europe; I imagine that it was very soon after they were built that rampart-breaking artillery came into use. They are uncrumbled, and they make a promenade for visitors now. Looking from the walls I see the road which I had come along: high, green banks well planted with trees are along the Foyle. These green slopes with cattle grazing on them make a scene that is pastoral enough to recall the Doire, the old Oak Grove.

We walk along the Foyle towards its mouth. On one side are the bleak hills of Donegal; on the other, the cultivated fields of Derry County. Out of Derry, along this highway, Columba with his twelve companions sailed when he went to open his mission to the heathen of Scotland, the mission which made Iona,

Cross Roads in Ireland

"this small and remote isle of the British Ocean," a sacred place, and made his own name known, "not only through the whole of our Ireland and Britain, largest of the islands of the whole world, but to reach even as far as triangular Spain, and the Gauls, and Italy, that lies beyond the Penine Alps, even to the City of Rome itself, which is the head of all cities." [1] He sailed probably in the way that his biographer describes himself as sailing. "The sailors getting the word draw taut the halliards and hoist and square the yards in the form of a cross, and with prosperous and gentle breezes we are wafted without an effort." It may have been so. But the poetry that was to gather round his name was to give him all the sorrow of the exile:

> The seagulls of Loch Foyle,
> They are before me and in my wake;
> In my coracle with me they come not;
> Alas, it is sad, our parting.
>
> I stretch my eye across the brine,
> From firm oaken planks;
> Many the tears of my soft grey eye
> As I look back upon Eirinn.
>
> There is a grey eye
> That will look back upon Eirinn;
> Never again will it see
> The men of Eirinn, or women.
>
> At dawn and at eve I lament;
> Alas for the journey I go!

[1] "The Life of Saint Columba (Colm-cille.) A.D. 521-597," translated from Saint Adamnan's Latin, by Wentworth Huyshe.

[130]

East Ulster

This is my name—I tell a secret—
His-back-to-Eirinn.

The stories told of the Gothic saints, says Spengler, bring over to us the feeling of the springtime of European civilization. The stories told about the Celtic saints bring over this feeling in a fuller measure. And the stories told about Colmcille—Saint Columba—and the poems attributed to him, bring over this feeling of springtime in the fullest measure of all. There is a chapter in his life which his biographer entitles "The holy man's agreeable foreknowledge and prophecy concerning another matter also, which, although of minor importance, is not, I think, one on which there should be silence," and which indicates the springtime of a civilization.

For at another time, when the saint was living in the isle of Iona, calling one of the brethren to him, he thus addressed him: "On the third day from this now dawning, thou must keep a lookout in the western part of the isle, sitting on the sea-shore: for from the northern region of Ireland a certain guest, a crane driven by the winds through long, circling aerial flights, will arrive very weary and fatigued after the ninth hour of the day; and its strength almost exhausted, it will fall and lie before thee on the shore, and thou wilt take care to lift it up kindly and carry it to a neighbouring house, and there wilt hospitably harbour it for three days and three nights, and carefully feed it; at the end of three days, refreshed, and unwilling to sojourn longer with us, it will return with fully regained strength to the sweet region of Ireland whence it originally came. And I thus earnestly commend it to thee for that it came from the place of our own fatherland."

[131]

The brother obeys, and on the third day, after the ninth
hour, as commanded, he awaits the coming of the expected
guest; and, when it comes, he raises it from the shore where it
fell; carries it, weak as it was, to the hospice; feeds it in its
hunger. And to him, on his return to the monastery in the
evening, the saint, not by way of inquiry, but of statement,
says, "God bless thee, my son, because thou hast well attended
our stranger guest; and it will not tarry long in exile, but
after three days will return to its own country." And just as
the saint predicted, the event also proved. For having been
harboured for three days, raising itself on high by flight from
the ground in presence of its ministering host, and considering
for a little while its course in the air, it returned across the
ocean to Ireland in a straight line of flight, on a calm day.

And then there is the episode of Columba bidding
good-bye to the old labouring horse before his own
death, which is one of the most beautiful passages in
the literature of biography. Scholars know that this
episode comes from the epic tradition; they know that
the horse that weeps over the saint is a lowly relative
of the steeds that wept over Achilles and Cuchullain.
But, amongst the saints, it is only Columba that the
episode could be told of:

And after this the saint goes out of the granary, and, returning to the monastery, sits down half-way at the place
where afterwards a cross, fixed in a mill-stone, and standing
to this day, is to be seen at the roadside. And while the saint,
weary with age as I have said, rested there, sitting for a little
while, behold the white horse, a faithful servant, runs up to
him, the one that used to carry the milk-pails to and fro between the byre and the monastery. He, coming up to the saint,
wonderful to tell, lays his head against his breast—inspired,

as I believe, by God, by whose dispensation every animal has
sense to perceive things according as its Creator Himself has
ordained—knowing that his master was soon about to leave
him, and that he would see him no more, began to whinny
and to shed copious tears into the lap of the saint as though
he had been a man, and weeping and foaming at the mouth.
And the attendant, seeing this, began to drive away the weeping mourner, but the saint forbade him, saying, "Let him
alone, let him alone, for he loves me. Let him pour out the
tears of his bitter lamentation into this my bosom. Lo! now,
thou, man as thou art, and possessing a rational soul, couldst
in no wise know anything about my departure hence save what
I myself have just now told thee; but to this brute beast,
devoid of reason, the Creator Himself has clearly in some
way revealed that his master is about to go away from him."
And so saying, he blessed his servant the horse as it sadly
turned to go away from him.

Ireland at the time was influencing the history of
the neighbouring countries, not through force, but
through culture and humane ideas. Columba ordains a
king of the Picts, and the ordination was made on Irish
soil; the relations between the dominant Irish state
and its colony in Scotland were settled by him in a
way honourable to both communities. The biographer
of Saint Columba shows us the Irish of Ulster as the
arbiters of the affairs of the Picts, Gaels, Saxons, and
Britons. We see them constituting themselves the pa-
trons and protectors of civilization in the British
Islands. The springtime of European civilization was
showing itself most promisingly in the Ireland of that
period. But springtime there had no summer, and the

later season brought disaster indeed. "He rode to the north," says Holinshed of an English deputy in Ireland, Lord Grey, "and in his journey he razed Saint Patrick, his church in Down, and burnt the monuments of Patrick, Brigide, and Colme, who are said to have been there interred." Lord Grey was accused "that without any warrant from the King or Council he profaned the Church of Saint Patrick in Down, turning it into a stable; and plucked it down and shipped the notable peal of bells that did hang in the steeple, meaning to have sent them to England."

Through men of this high-handed sort we got Londonderry instead of Doire-Colmcille. I stand with my friend, who is a business man of Derry, outside the Guild Hall. "We are carrying too much lead in our saddles," he says, "but we'll get along." His conversation abounds in military metaphors. Rubicund, stocky, standing with wide-spread legs, he looks, especially when his hand is raised, like one who might direct a battle. I can visualize him on horseback. He is speaking about the business done by the town. The export business is all right. But the Free State boundary cuts Derry off from its hinterland, the County Donegal. Then there is the monopolistic policy of Belfast that wants all the prosperity of the industrial North of Ireland for itself, and cares little about doing anything for the development of other Ulster towns—or so the people of Derry and other towns within the Belfast administration say. The business that Derry does as an emporium is cut into by the boundary that now divides the six Northern Counties from the rest of Ireland.

I offer the suggestion that Derry should have gone into the Free State. Economically that would have been the right policy, but it could never have been thought upon "by me and the like of me," says my friend. And then he points out a man who is coming towards us. "Look at him," he says, "and take your answer. That man had one of the best businesses in the town. He knew that the separation of Derry from the neighbouring counties would leave him without any business. Yet do you think he was for going into a state that you Papishes controlled? No fear. He used all his influence to have the Northern Counties left out of the Free State and to have Derry left with the Northern Counties. Look at him! That little parcel he is carrying is of samples of tea. He has no office now; he is going round selling tea to houses in the by-streets and farmers' cottages. And if you asked him if he would have his business back with Derry in the Free State, you'd get a short answer, I tell you, and that answer would not be in the affirmative. Good-morrow, Mr. MacConnell!" Mr. MacConnell passes, puffing at his pipe, a taciturn salesman. "You see," says my friend, "that we Protestants came here as a garrison, and we still have the feeling that we belong to a garrison. Did you ever see soldiers come into a town, swinging their horses as they turn down a street, looking as if they knew that they were the people that gave the orders and that the other people in the street were there to carry the orders out? Well, that's the way that the Protestants in the North of Ireland have been feeling. You'll say that we have nothing to feel superior about, and maybe I'll have to agree with you, but that's the way we have been feeling anyway, and a mere improvement in our business won't bring us into the Free State." I told him that I fully sympathized with that kind of feeling.

This was Londonderry indeed. I went into the Guild Hall, a new building, and looked at the windows, new, too, which depicted in stained glass the foundation of Londonderry and the later defence made by the townsmen against the enemies of the English Revolution. My heart went out to a group of figures depicted on the glass—schoolboys in their long blue coats; they were being talked to by grave, or rather, by grim-looking merchants. The boys were orphans who were to become the original Derry Prentice Boys. The merchants belonged to some of the twelve London Companies—Fishmongers', Skinners', Grocers', and the like—who were to rebuild a town in the North of Ireland and secure for themselves lands forfeited from the O'Neills and O'Cahans, Irishry who kept no ledgers, and who had been worsted in the wars.

These merchants had a king declare that he "esteemed it a work worthy of a Christian prince to win and recall the same from superstition, rebellion, calamity, and poverty to religion, obedience, sanity, and splendour, which His Majesty conceived could not be effected but by planting the same with British." And

so the London Companies took over the whole county
of Derry, the two towns of Derry and Coleraine, the
fisheries of the Bann and Foyle, the woods of Glencon-
keine. They had free customs and monopolies, and the
king got out of it only a head rent. They re-built Derry,
making "London" and "Derry" one name—the epoch
of transferred and synthetic place-names had begun
and the simplicity which could name a place "The Oak
Grove of Calnach" or "The Meadow of the White
Hazel" was gone out of the world. These Londoners,
men and boys, built a good town here. For the next
sixty or seventy years they were always on the edge of
an attack. They built the walls which still stand—
a carriage could drive along the top of them. And
here, it seems to me, more than in any other place
in England or Scotland, was produced the pioneer
type that was to give such account of itself in remote
America.

In the vestibule of Saint Columbkill's cathedral I
read the inscription:

If stones could speke then London's prayse should sounde
Who built this Church and Cittie from the grounde.

In this cathedral are relics of the beleaguerment that
brought Derry into history—the great padlocks that
closed the gates, weapons, proclamations, news-letters
of the period, the hollow shell in which the demand
for the surrender of the town was flung amongst the
garrison—the demand that brought back the "No Surrender" of the defenders.

Cross Roads in Ireland

A Protestant church in Ireland is always more storied than a Catholic one, which, in general, is newer, barer, less traditional. And, altogether apart from its association with the Derry of history, Saint Columbkill's with its banners commemorating British military victories, its tablets commemorating notable families, is a place of interest and charm. And as I walk amongst the graves that are around the cathedral I come upon names that are well known in early American annals; America must have received a great influx from this territory which already had produced the pioneer.

Their defence was as decisive as any other even that took place in the Three Kingdoms in making for the triumph of the Revolution which English historians used to be so enthusiastic about and which North of Ireland statesmen and publicists still look upon as beginning civilization. . . . Londonderry was about to enter into parley with officers who bore a warrant from King James when "thirteen young apprentices flew to the guard-room, themselves seized the keys of the city, rushed to Ferryquay Gate, closed it in the face of King James' officers, and let down the portcullis." Londonderry became a place of refuge for the Protestants of the Northern Counties as King James' army advanced up North. Then came the attacks upon the city; they were bravely beaten back. Then there was the beleaguerment from April to July when the inhabitants suffered famine and disease. At last a ship broke the bar and brought relief to Londonderry from the sea.

A screen made of casks filled with earth was hastily thrown up to protect the landing-place from the batteries on the other side of the river, and then the work of unloading began. First were rolled on the shore barrels containing 6,000 bushels of meal. Then came great cheeses, flitches of bacon, kegs of butter, sacks of peas and biscuit, ankers of brandy. Not many hours before half a pound of tallow and three-quarters of a pound of salted hide had been weighed out with niggardly care to every fighting man. The rations which each now received were three pounds of flour, two pounds of beef, and a pint of peas. The besiegers' guns continued to roar all night, and all night the bells of the rescued city made answer to the Irish guns with a peal of joyous defiance. Through the whole of the 31st July the batteries of the enemy continued to play, but soon after the sun had again gone down flames were seen arising from the camp, and when the 1st of August dawned a line of smoking ruins marked the site lately occupied by the huts of the besiegers, and the citizens saw far off the long column of pikes and standards retreating up the left bank of the Foyle towards Strabane. The siege had lasted 105 days. The garrison had been reduced from about 7,000 effective men to about 3,000; and the loss of the besiegers, according to Governor Walker, was 8,000.[1]

There is a street in Derry named Longtower Street. It keeps the memory of an ancient round tower that stood there, a round tower that was part of the monastic buildings that were there in Columba's time.

County Derry to County Antrim

Derry has no street named for George Farquhar; it has no memorial of any kind to that vigorous and en-

[1] "Sketches of Olden Days in Northern Ireland," by Rev. Canon Forde.

gaging dramatist who created Sir Harry Wildair, Sargeant Kite and Captain Plume, Mrs. Mandrake and Lady Bountiful, Mrs. Sullen and Cherry, the maid of the inn. Farquhar, the first of the line of Irish writers who re-created the English comedy, was born in Derry —his name shows that he was of Gaelic stock. This very year "The Beaux' Stratagem" is being played in Paris, but Derry would be very much astonished if one expected to find in its streets any memorial of the man who on his death-bed wrote that long-lasting comedy.

But the truth is that I had not thought of Farquhar until I started from Limavady. Limavady has a name that can be very effectively used in light verse. I went down the street of the town hoping to find an inn of the kind in which Thackeray discovered his "Peg of Limavady." I found no such inn. I got into the bus going to a place from which I could get to the Glens of Antrim. And in the bus was a short-legged, round little man whose left eye had acquired the winking habit. He was practising on the Pegs who were in the bus. His vocal communications were in chuckles. And he was being responded to. Who, I wondered, was this congenial companion? And then I learned that he was Limavady's process-server. Now in my part of the country a process-server is a skulking fellow who carries an iron-shod stick because he knows that the dogs of the countryside have been trained to chase him. He dare not show himself in public let alone wink at the girls. In County Derry, evidently, a process-server can go about his business openly. He can hand you the law's reminder that it can collect what you owe while chucking your daughter under the chin. This certainly showed a difference between the two Irish areas. I was fascinated by this chucklesome process-server and watching him I began to think of scenes in inns and market-places in Farquhar's style.

The Glens of Antrim

As I came into the Glens I remembered my first visit to the North. It was back in youthful days. The occasion was a Gaelic festival—the Feis of the Nine Glens.

It was held, I remember, in a little town that the green hills would have folded in only that the sea washed up to it. The hurling matches that belonged to the athletic side of the Feis were played on the sand and by the wash of the tide. Before us, like the flittered nest of a raven, was the MacDonnell Castle that Shane the Proud had plundered; behind was the mound that they call Oisin's Grave. The town had its houses whitewashed for the event: people had come from the farthest of the Glens to sing or play, to show their work or their step-dancing, or to back their fellow-Glensfolk in the contests—they had come from the island of Rathlin, even.

Here I met my contemporary in poetry, Joseph Campbell. Here I met the young composer who had collaborated with Joseph Campbell in the delightful

"Songs of Uladh." Amongst the elders were Roger Casement and Francis Joseph Bigger. There were others, young men and women dear for themselves and for the promise that they had. It was a goodly company, as I remember it, that was at that Feis of the Nine Glens.

But the one I think of now was an old man; he was a piper and lame; he had trudged up from some glen or down from some benn to take part in a competition. He was not one of your hearty old fellows; as I remember him now, he was glum. But his glumness, I imagine, was due to anxiety about his performance. The prize was five pounds. He had probably never had so much money at one time. No wonder he was anxious about a performance that might win him such a sum. We seemed always to be meeting him when he was weighed down with the hopes and fears of gaining this high reward. But we never heard this particular piper play.

We had sleeping quarters in a building that held exhibits in the day-time. For the few nights we were supposed to occupy it we were very little there—there were dances, and walks, and long talks for those of us who were in the twenties. The piper was quartered with us, and he, poor man, would have liked to sleep. And when some of us came in at two A.M., and some at three, he would turn on his bed and say, "Boys-o-boys, but you're the hardy boys!" And when another, after pushing open a door, or making an entrance through a window, would whistle or dance a few steps before

[142]

lying down to snore, "Boys-o-boys, and do yez never sleep at all?" I saw him by the light of a candle when he realized that there could be no sleep for him that night and that the competition was on at noon. He was sitting up in bed, a ragged shirt on him; like Socrates, he was rubbing his leg. He said as we decided to go out into the open air, "Tell me, do yez never sleep at all?"

We saw him no more, for we did not get back for the noon competition. We were going to meet the morning on the hills. The corn-crakes were still being lively in the meadows. One of us began a poem—I don't believe it ever got finished:

> Corn-crake, 'tis often I cursed you
> In the first red shriek of the day,
> I with the sport left behind me,
> And you at the height of your play.

As we went on, and one bird and another stirred and chirruped, the idea of breakfast became more and more grateful to us. Ham and eggs, hot tea and soda-cakes —Herbert Hughes, the musician, kept silence, for he was listening to the first songs of the birds, but the rest of the company talked the subject up. We came to a solitary house on the side of a road. It had the sign of a place of refreshment, but with its closed door and darkened windows, it looked as if it would be hard to bring any stir into the place. I was deputed to make the advances leading up to an early but full breakfast. I knocked at the door. I heard a movement within.

Greatly heartened, I knocked again. There was certainly a stir in the house. How satisfactory to be in a part of the country where householders could be got to rise early! The door opened a little way. I said some words and some words were said to me. Then an object was put into my hands. I held it, and then the door was closed again. And the object left in my hands was a harp! And I was left standing beside my dumbfounded companions with a harp in my hands as dawn broke on the hills around and no more stir was in the house!

I suppose there was a prosaic explanation for the extraordinary happening. No doubt a harpist who was to take part in one of the competitions had left his instrument in this inn, telling the host that he would come for it first thing in the morning. And I suppose the host thought that only a man in want of a harp would make so early a call. We could not get him to the door again —he had yielded up the harp and had gone back to his dreams. We left the instrument against the door and went farther to seek breakfast. We had to go a long way down in to Cushendun or Cushendall or some Glen that Moira O'Neill had put into a song. And for some time afterwards I was known to the literati of the North as the young man who, asking for breakfast, was presented with a harp.

Antrim Countryside

I was not left to my memories and solitary investigations. The Painter and the Singer, friends of mine, whom George Farquhar could have drawn characters

[144]

from, found me, and took me out into the Antrim countryside.

The automobile went on; we came to a place where road-metal was heaped up in the middle of the way so that we could not get across it. Road-menders were about; the Singer went to ask them to make an effort to level the heap.

He got no satisfaction of it. I had seen human beings treated with silent contempt before but never with a silence so contemptuous as the road-menders treated our lively and ready Singer with. Then the burly Painter got off the car to deal with them. He addressed them forcibly. The result was that one of the gang picked up a shovel and held it menacingly. I now realized how smashing a weapon a shovel could be. "Do you want me to break your window and smash your dial?" were the words I heard addressed to the Painter. "I'll do it in a minute." A truculent road-mender! He stood above the Painter looking for all the world like the cave-man soldier of the Derry War Memorial. He declared the law of the road to us: the car was to wait while the gang levelled the heap at their leisure.

Under this duress we waited. The Painter fumed. "You wouldn't see the like of that around Dublin, Papishes and all as they are! So help me, God, I'd rather live where there were Fenians to the right and left of me than have lads the like of these near me. What place do they come out of at all?" And then the heap was levelled and we went from the vicinity of these menacing shovellers. Immediately afterwards we met a red-faced young man carrying a scythe. With him we had an amiable conversation. He was humorous, and what he said was made all the more humorous by his shrewd Antrim dialect. The truculent shoveller was of the city, but this was very evidently our real Antrim countryman. He recommended a public-house down the road to us. There were three young widows there, he told us, all of them sprightly.

There were two young women in the public-house, but I didn't inquire whether or not they were widows. The Singer had much to say to them; he said it in a very spirited way and with what turned out to be the proper gestures. A great lad! He can sing a country song so that you see a blind man standing in the rain singing in the vagrant's mode. He is a master of Irish dialects North and South and East. And he is one of the best of story-tellers. He can tell of a Northern farmer driving a horse with a load of peat, so that his "tch, tch! Go on owre that!" dramatizes the whole life on a country road. The Painter has a feeling for landscape that is different from the studio painter's. As he stands in the open air, and looks around, I get the feeling that he has the huntsman's or the country squire's preoccupation with his terrain.

We were at the stream we were to fish in—a peat-coloured stream running by a boggy field. Men on either side were reaping oats. The Mourne Mountains were across from us. And we could see red carts beside black peat-stacks in a bog.

[146]

East Ulster

As the Painter put his rod together and looked to his flies, the Singer lilted:

"Then stoutly did we cross the Boyne, our enemies to batter,
And valiant Schomberg he was slain as we went over the water,
'Brave boys,' said William, 'no dismay feel for your lost commander,
For God shall be your king to-day, and I'll be general under.' "

And afterwards he sang:

"The lowland fields may roses yield,
Gay heaths the highlands hilly-o,
But high or low, no flower can show,
Like the glorious Orange lily-o,
Then heigh-o, the lily-o,
The royal, loyal lily-o,
Beneath the sky, what flower can vie
With Ireland's Orange lily-o?"

They are good Orange songs, and as my friend sang them he got into the words the rattle of the drums and the fervour of the twelfth of July parade. I contributed the remark that the words were Irish in sentiment, and that they were carried by good Irish tunes. My notion that there was anything remarkable in an Ulster song being Irish aroused the wrath of the Painter and the Singer. "Why shouldn't they be Irish?" cried one. "Man, dear, don't you know that this place was the stronghold of the Gael when Dublin was a Norse settlement?" cried the other.

We started whipping the stream. The three of us caught two little trout. The carts drew out of the bog;

the man went from beside the stocks of oats in the fields; the brown stream ran with a murmur over the stones. . . .

Northern Metropolis

As we neared the city my companion pointed to a line of structures that went striding out into the sea—cranes and gantries and hulks of ships. No more did he regard those hills that almost make a rim for Belfast. "The Island," he said. I could see that that line of structures was what stirred him most. It was where ships were being built. It was Belfast's great work-yards; it was the place where Belfast's energies are gathered up and shown in a form that impresses herself.

I knew something of the significance of "The Island," but I felt that I did not know it as my companion did. I asked him to take me to the place. We crossed over, and we walked alongside great hulks that hammers were beating upon, and I could see that for my companion the meaning of his city was here.

That night, however, I read St. John Ervine's novel, "Mrs. Martin's Man," and out of some chapters in it I got a notion of what "The Island" means to Belfast. The passage that tells of Esther Mahaffy's dreams for that young Belfast man, her nephew, interpreted my companion's feelings, I was sure:

She had heard the regular clanging of hammers on steel as the men in the shipyards beat the sides of ships together, and made them fit for the big adventures of the sea . . . tall, towering vessels that moved from continent to continent and carried a thousand souls as easily as a rowing-boat carries one man; great boilers and shining engines and little twisting wheels that made gigantic energies. . . . Her heart stirred proudly when she recollected that Jamesey had his place in that shipyard where the mightiest boats in the world are made. He had helped to lay the lines of one great vessel and another, and had felt joy surge in him when he saw a ship leave the slips when a little cord was slit, and move slowly into the river with the grace of a royal swan. She, too, would feel that pride. She would have no more sorrows in her heart. She would take her place in this city of hammering men, whose deeds of making and shaping and forming and fashioning are a marvel of the marvels of men. . . .

And there is the passage where James Martin listens to the man who has been driven out of the shipyards of Belfast, but who longs to get back into them:

"Och. A lot of heater-boys started writin' 'To Hell with the Pope' on the side of a ship, an' I checked them for it, an' the whole of them got up a clan again' me, an' I was bate out of the yard. 'You Fenian get, you!' they shouted after me, an' begun cloddin' rivets after me. You would think they were wild savages from the heart of Africa the way they go on. The peelers tried to stop them, but sure, the peelers was afeard of them, an' I was hit over the head with a rivet, an' had me skull cut open. . . . The foreman told me himself to stop away a while. It's easy enough to say stop away, but where's the money comin' from? . . . They're a warm lot in this town. What do you think of lads that writes 'To Hell with the Pope' on a boat that'll sail the world? . . . I wish to my God I was at my work. I come down here to the quay many's a time, an' look across the river at the Yard, an' think to myself it's gran' to be on a boat, puttin' rivets in her side, an' hearin' the hammerin' all round you, and then to see the boat bein' launched. . . ."

"Sure, you can see that on the Tyne or up the Clyde," James interrupted.

"Ah, it's not the same thing. They can't make the boats over there that we can!" He turned sharply to James.

"Will you come across now to the quay an' have a look at the Yard? There's a liner on the stocks now—it'll be the biggest boat in the world when it's afloat. Sure, it'll occupy your mind while the rain's on!"

James turned up the collar of his coat, and he and the stranger ran across the street, and passed through the sheds until they came to a break on the quay where they could see the shipyard lying on the south side of the river.

"Man, it's gran', isn't it?" the stranger exclaimed enthusiastically.

He pointed to the great wooden palisades sunk in the mud of the Lagan and rising to a great height in the air so that they looked like skeletons. Inside the palisades were roughly shaped lines of metal and timber that would soon be ships, and over these little black figures swarmed continually. . . . His voice thickened as he went on. "It near breaks your heart to think that a man can't do his work there in peace without a lot of people thumpin' him for the sake of his religion. I wouldn't care a thrush's mick for no rain or nothin' if I was only over there rivetin' that boat! But I'll have to be goin' to England for a bit, I'm afeard. . . . It'll soon be time for the Island men to be leavin' their work, an' I want to get home before they start comin' over the bridge an' the ferry. I can't bear to see them comin' from the Yard, an' them all dirty an' sweatin' an' me just wanderin' about, not knowin' what the hell to do with myself. . . ."

East Ulster

We saw the same Island men march in their troops across the bridge—not as many, alas! as there used to be in the old days, but even now it was a spectacle worth remembering. That march of the Island men has been celebrated by a Belfast poet, Richard Rowley, in his "City Songs."

> Terrible as an army with banners
> Through the dusk of a winter's eve,
> Over the bridge
> The thousands tramp.

Unless one can share in this exultation, one can never understand Belfast. Belfast has other industries—it was known for its linens before it was known for its ships. But it is its ship-builders, it is the "Island men" who have given the city its character.

They create something gigantic and intricate, and it goes away from them. They see their creation in the scaffolding—as something that has been given perfection only as it slips away from them. All that they have of visible creative power is in the ship that goes away before the city can rejoice in it as in a consummate achievement! One could not wonder if one felt something frustrated in the Belfast mind!

A ship cannot be an assembling of parts like so much that is produced in modern large-scale industry. It is built up visibly, over a length of time; it is built up, not in a factory, but in the open air, with the wind blowing on the builders and the sea sounding near them. It is built up by men who work in gangs and who get a gang-spirit. And the men who build it get the pride of those who make great, visible, ponderable things.

It is the workmen, and especially those who regard themselves as an élite amongst the workmen—the ship-builders—who give its character to Belfast, as it is the professional man—the lawyer, doctor, bureaucrat—who give its character to Dublin. The executives of the great businesses live outside, and hardly anything of their interests shows in the city. More than any other city I have ever been in, Belfast is a city of workmen. The wit and humour of Belfast—and there is much of both in it—is the wit and humour of men turning from a job they have actually in hand to deliver themselves of something as shrewd as a hammer-stroke. And because there is no other than the workman's mentality available, Belfast is a city ruled by very simplified conceptions—the loyalties the people hold to, the aversions they fight against, come out of these very simplified conceptions. The workman's helpfulness, kindliness, friendliness are also in Belfast, that city of hammering men.

The Last Harpers

On a certain day towards the end of the eighteenth century there were two gatherings in Belfast. One was to rejoice over the fall of the Bastille and to congratulate the French people on the Declaration of the Rights of Man. There were bands and speeches at this gathering. Those in the other gathering waited for the bands and speeches to reach their close. They waited to tune their harps.

For, by one of those coincidences that history sometimes provides, the secular and unsecular elements in Irish nationality were manifesting themselves in the same place and at the same time. Here was the democratic state, late product of the European mind, being welcomed, and here was an art in which the national culture had shown itself most appealingly being honoured by people who were very conscious of its decline. The Bastille had fallen, the Rights of Man had been proclaimed, and in a few years a young man who attended both demonstrations, Theobald Wolfe Tone, would sail for France to organize a Franco-Irish army that might help in the creation of an Irish Republic that would be based on the rights that had just been proclaimed. Brave men who heard the enthusiastic speeches and who listened to some of the chords struck upon the harps would go to the gallows for these new and heady ideas. Meanwhile Denis Hempson, "who realized the antique picture drawn by Cambrensis," had begun to play. "He played with long crooked nails and in his performance the tinkling of the small wires under the deep tones of the bass was peculiarly thrilling. . . . He was the only one who played the very old, the aboriginal music of the country, and this he did in a style of such finished excellence as persuaded the editor that the praises of the old Irish harp in Cambrensis, Fuller, and others, instead of being . . . ill-considered and in-

discriminate, were in reality no more than a just tribute
to that admirable instrument and its then professors."
The year of these meetings was 1792. The music that
had been made for the harp was falling into disuse
then; harp-playing had come to its decline; out of the
whole of Ireland only ten harpers could be got together
for this festival, and the professors who were really accomplished amongst them were very old men.

In the Municipal Art Collection here is the bust of
the man who initiated this gathering of harpers, Dr.
Michael MacDonnell. But the man who made the gathering of service to the generations that followed was
Edward Bunting. He wrote down the airs they possessed; he collected other airs; he devoted his long life
to the publication of the music that he went to such
labour to discover and record. . . . Out of the sixteen
airs that Thomas Moore wrote words for in his first
collection of Irish melodies, eleven are from the collection that Edward Bunting had made. The new Irish
poetry was to have its mould in the music that Bunting obtained from the harpers who came to this festival in Belfast. The most distinctive of Samuel Ferguson's poems were written to go with some of these melodies—"The Coolin," "Paisteen Finn," "Cean Duv
Deelish," and "Cashel of Munster." And so this gathering of the harpers in Belfast is at the beginning of
Irish poetry in English. "There were eight men and
one woman all either blind or lame," says a sprightly
letter of the day, "and all old but two men. Figure to
yourself this group, indifferently dressed, sitting on a

stage erected for them in one end of the Exchange Ball-room, and the ladies and gentlemen of the first fashion in Belfast and its vicinity looking on and listening attentively, and you will have some idea of how they looked. . . . The best performers got ten guineas, and the worst two and the rest accordingly. Now how do you like the poor old harpers?"

I look over the collection of Bunting's manuscripts in the Queen's University, the manuscripts that belonged to Bunting's grandchildren, and which have been presented to the university by Mrs. Milligan Fox. And I remember that there is a musician in Belfast who could make what is in these manuscripts living for me.

So I start off to visit Gilbert Hardebeck. I have written that Belfast is a city of workmen, but as I go in search of the street in which the musician lives I am made willing to believe that Belfast is a city of small shop-keepers. Not even in Dublin had I seen such strings of small shops—shops selling cabbages, selling newspapers, selling sugar-sticks, selling sausages, selling cabbages with carrots added to them, selling cabbages with potatoes, selling newspapers with marbles and tops, selling boots, selling stationery with pins and needles; never had I seen before such a monotony of them. At last I came to a little shop in which there were cages and birds for sale. There was a sign there that said "Linnets are cheap to-day" and somehow I felt that I had come near to where the musician lived.

And I found him. I had the privilege of being entertained by this musical scholar in rooms over one of these shops. A harp hung on the wall of the room in which he received his pupils. But the instrument he used to illustrate what he said about Irish music was the German organ that was in the room. A man of great bulk, his eyes were covered by dark-blue glasses. Like the harpers of the eighteenth century, he has only a vestige of sight.

And how should I know anything of what these melodies meant if I had not witnessed the passion of this man, his fury and indignation at the public indifference to this music, and the misconceptions about it that are held by those who are not indifferent to it? He spoke of the harpers of the eighteenth century as if he had gone with Arthur O'Neill from one great house to another, or had talked with Denis Hempson in his cottage, the harper lying in bed with his harp under the bed-clothes. "O'Neill did this, but Hempson had this method." And although this learned man did not take the harp in his hands, he made me understand how incomparable was the art that these men possessed. Geraldus Cambrensis, in the thirteenth century, wrote of the predecessors of these harpers as having "skill beyond comparison superior to that of any nation I have seen." Their distinctive art was in "modulation not slow and solemn, as in the instruments of Britain to which we are accustomed, but the sounds are rapid and precipitate, yet at the same time sweet and pleasing. It is wonderful how in such precipitate rapidity of the fingers the musical proportions are preserved, and, by their art, faultless throughout. In the midst of their complicated modulations and most intricate arrangement of notes, by a rapidity so sweet, a regularity so irregular, a concord so discordant, the melody is rendered harmonious and perfect whether the chords of the *diatessaron* (the fourth) or *diapente* (the fifth) are struck together; yet they always begin in the soft mood and end in the same, that all may be perfected in sweetness of delicious sounds. They enter on, and again leave their modulations with so much subtlety, and the twinklings of the small strings sport with so much freedom under the deep notes of the bass, delight with so much delicacy and soothe so softly that the excellency of their art seems to lie in concealing it."

With the passing of the art of the harper, Irish music became slow, losing that precipitancy that in earlier centuries was its most noted characteristic. Gilbert Hardebeck shows me the effects of the slowing down of the music—the loss of buoyancy. Irish music was made for the harp and cannot be rendered on any other instrument—only when you have heard it on the harp you have heard an Irish melody, he says, speaking like one who is not making an abstract statement, but as one who has passionate feeling for this unique music. Arranged for the piano or even for the violin, Irish music loses what is essential in it. It loses this essential, too, when words in any other language except Irish are set to it. Only those expanding words can accompany it; the definite English words make the music chop and change. And to show me this he plays "Úna Bán" on the little organ, singing the words in Irish. It is a song out of a world in which a man could be lonely and proud to the last desperate degree.

But how can a music that was made to be played upon harps and to go with "Celtic syllables like the rattling of war-chariots" be brought back into the world? I left that learned musician in his little rooms and went out into the street. A phonograph was reiterating something that had once been a tune, and a window showed an announcement of a radio concert that evening. Words that I once heard sung to one of the noble and spirited laments that this musician had played for me came into my mind:

> Where is he now? His sword is in his sheath.
> See where it lies, beside his laurel wreath;
> Helmet and plume hang idle on the wall,
> Hushed is his harp, and desolate his hall.

Lore of Ulster

Memories compel me: as I leave Belfast, and, going along the Antrim road, come in the vicinity of Cave Hill, I open the gate of a house named Ardrie and go into its grounds. I stand and look on the grey waters of Belfast Lough below the garden. The garden itself holds me: the high Lombardy poplars are still here, the deodar, the eucalyptus, and the simple flowers that made such provender for the bees whose skips were all over the ground, still flourish—musk and mint, thyme and tansy, sage, lavender, and marjoram.

East Ulster

But I cannot go into that pleasant house and find Francis Joseph Bigger in his book-room, and talk to him for a night beside his fire—a peat fire it always was in that book-room.

He was a stocky, rubicund man with eyes as brown as old milk-crocks when they are filled with sunlight; it was easy to size him up as a bachelor. By profession he was a man of law, but he seemed to be able to give most of his days to the pursuits of the antiquary. (Did not a writer characterize him as "a bright-faced Old Mortality"?) It was the colour and music of the past that really attracted him; he loved a certain pageantry, the pageantry of a Gaelic chieftain, and he was wont to attend festivals with a piper, whose costume bore some bold and brilliant Celtic design, skirling before him. He it was who designed and arranged the arms of Ireland and her four provinces which I have before me —a golden harp on a green ground, with the Red Hand of Ulster on a white ground above and the Three Crowns of Munster on a blue ground below, the Three Castles of Leinster and the Ship of Connacht on the sides, and with interlacing patterns around. He delighted in such emblazonments.

He felt, I imagine, that the glory of his life rested on his taking over, restoring, and presenting to the people of Ulster a castle of the O'Neills that dated back to Norman times. This—Scan's castle at Ardglass in Down—has been given in rehabilitation our antiquarian's notions of Old World hospitality and liveliness. A fire of peat blazes on the hearth in one of the rooms, a large oak table stands in the centre, a great dresser is against the wall, a bronze candelabra filled with candles hangs from the ceiling. You go up a winding stairway and come out on a roof on which is a garden, and see above the parapets a tower for the pigeons that strut about. Sometimes at night he would have beacon lights blaze here, and young people would dance to the skirling of bagpipes. Above floated the banner of the O'Neills which is the banner of Ulster—a Red Hand on a white ground. When he presented it to the Northern Government, Francis Joseph Bigger made it a condition that no other banner should float above this castle.

He loved to speak of the glories of the O'Neills and the other Ulster princes. But he would own that none of their descendants who managed to hold a portion of their lands after the disastrous "Flight of the Earls" had qualities that gave leadership or protection to the people. In the landowning régime that suceeded the English conquest and the subsequent plantation of the Northeast they fore-showed the pride and folly of later Irish landlordism. Meanwhile, the Elizabethan fighters and intriguers like the Chichesters had possessed themselves of the lands and waters of Ulster; the lordship of Scots fighting clans like the MacDonnells revived in Antrim, and there was another Scots immigration. For James, now on the dual throne, had the wish to advance brither Scots and to turn over rich lands to settlements that would be loyal because dependent on him. Families that had distinct nobility came into Ulster from Scotland—Maxwells and Hamiltons, Boyds and Archdalls. But there came, too, men who were ready to cozen powerless possessors out of their lands, or to squeeze titles out of them. Our antiquary would give me vivid pictures of such doings as with an album of press-cuttings we sat in the book-room and he would read me a sketch he had published in some local journal—illustrations of the times when the Ulster we know was in the making. Perhaps it would be a sketch of one of the survivors of an Irish chieftainship being met by the remnants of his clan, "most of them on foot, many of them on garrans or hack horses, with black breechans for saddles and thorn pricks in the heels of their brogues for spurs, numbers still wearing their hair long . . . presenting to Conn beeves, colpaghs, sheep, fowl, bonny clabber, vessels of butter, measures of meal, marrow, cheese, ample for a long continuous feast, the last perhaps of such festivities held in the grey old walls." And he would tell of some wind-bitten adventurer over from Galloway where the fare was "porridge, kail-brose, and ewe's milk," being made more greedy by what he saw on the oaken table of some surviving O'Neill and more resolute to press an advantage that would make him owner of such productive lands—joints of beeves, firkins of butter, rundlets of fresh milk from the meadow, bannocks in stacks, with the wine of Spain flowing freely. Meanwhile, London companies that had got titles to the confiscated Ulster lands were advertising the lots in the spirit of modern real-estate operators.

Cross Roads in Ireland

Our antiquary would take me through the Antrim and Down countryside, and bring me into the cottages of labourers and small farmers where I would listen to the "cracks" that in Ulster dialect went on between him and the household. Or he would give a lift along the road to some stray character, an old man or woman. "Will ye no sail?" That meant, "Will you not take a lift?" for "sail" means to go in any vehicle. "Will ye sail or travail?" He would tell me that the "travail" of the Ulster dialect is not "travel," but is actually "travail," meaning to strive or labour; one "travails" when one goes afoot.

He knew the origins of this Ulster dialect, for his own forbears had come from the same place as had the forbears of most of the kirk-going folk in these parts. Three hundred years before they had left Scotland for the land across the narrow water. "It was no fear of religious persecution," he wrote, "nor its results that induced them to cross Glenluce Bay and in their open boat to make Donaghadee. Their main inducement was the conviction that they were coming to a freer land, where opportunities were wider and prospects likely to be more satisfying, all of which turned out as was anticipated."

He would tell me that for a hundred years the bulk of the settlers in Ulster came from Ayr, Lanark, and Galloway, and that even at that day, walking through a churchyard in Scotch Nithsdale, one might as well, so far as names were concerned, be at home in Carnmoney or Templepatrick. The immigration into Ulster continued for over a century. A contemporary Presbyterian historian, Stewart, declared that these settlers were the scum of both nations. Our antiquary contradicted that statement. "They were the young bloods, and younger sons and daughters, of people who had larger families than acres, labouring under much local and social restrictions, with, no doubt, a fair percentage of outlaws and free traders on the sea, and ne'er-do-weels; but take them all round they were quite as good as those who settled the United States and Canada. Then again as the century moved on they had amongst them the leaven of a religious persecution in their own land, which went a long way and is still a vital factor on frequent occasions. The large majority of the settlers had, however, no such religious merit to bring about their coming over. Added to the Scotch there were many English settlers and Huguenot refugees, but these were of quite a different mettle to the majority of the Lowlanders who hived out of every port from the Solway to the Clyde in their open boats making for Larne, Carrickfergus, Belfast, Bangor, and Donaghadee." [1]

[1] It must be remembered that there was a Gaelic strain in these immigrants; a large number of them must have adopted Northumbrian English at a date not long before their emigration from Scotland. The element that had Gaelicized Scotland, turning it from a Pictish-speaking into a Gaelic-speaking country, had gone into Scotland from Antrim and Down; it was this element that gave Scotland her dynastic race. There has always been a movement from Northern Ireland to Scotland and from Scotland to Northern Ireland. At present, much to the disturbance of our cousins, the movement is from the Catholic parts of Northern Ireland, from Donegal chiefly, to Scotland. The distinctiveness of character in Northeast Ulster is

Cross Roads in Ireland

Meanwhile, what of the simple people of the old Ulster stock, the men who delved in the fields and paid rents and dues in some shape or form? They had probably seen their Pictish lords go down before the northern and eastern advance of the Gaels a thousand years before "the plantation." When all the battles were over they had remained on, making shift to live in some fashion and holding some corner of the fields for a native stock. "They lingered here and there on hillsides and lough shores," our antiquarian told me, "mingling from time to time with the new order, recording the old names and telling the old tales of the lands and the people who had passed away. Young ones of them were found in the cattle-pens, dog-kennels, and stable-yards, for they had much skill in the field and the chase. Older ones crooned by the big kitchen fires, mumbling in broken words the old traditions, whilst

due, not to difference in race, but to difference in culture of which the seventeenth-century religious element is exceedingly important. I feel sure that the folk of the Glens of Antrim whose lives are reflected in the charming songs of Moira O'Neill, who are often Gaelic-speakers and are accepted as "Irish-Irelanders," have as much of Scotch ancestry as their Presbyterian neighbours: they are, I think, descended from Scots clans who had kept their Catholic faith. Something in the distinction of Northeast Ulster from the rest of Ireland is due, I think, to the fact that the Normans made only a slight dint on Gaelic Ulster. Norman names that are so common in the South, West, and East—Fitzgerald, Burke, Power, Plunkett, for instance—are hardly met with in the North. When Ulster was conquered it was conquered by men who were definitely English or Scotch—men of the seventeenth century. The French-English-Gaelic speaking Norman families of the other parts of Ireland made some sort of liaison between English and Irish, and so the contrast was not as marked as it became in the North of Ireland after the flight of the earls in 1607.

joints of beef and mutton hissed and frizzled in the twirling jacks before the blazing wood and turf fires, piled high upon the hearth under high cross-beams. Boiling cauldrons of the tuber, petatie, bubbled and smiled, for our old friend was never ranked as a mere vegetable, but had a special distinction of its own, which in Ireland, at any rate, it still retains. It was not long in spreading itself over the whole country from Raleigh's garden at Youghal, and soon became as plentiful below the salt as above it, on the Ballinderry oak planks of the big table in the dining hall of Moira as elsewhere, for it was ever esteemed a meal in itself, especially with such condiments as salt and butter, the former being scarcer than the latter."

This was life in the hall. He told me, too, of the life in the farm-house here in the first generations after the plantation when the Galloway reivers had settled down. They had come over in flocks from the arid sheep tracks of Nithsdale to the rich confiscated lands of the O'Neills. "In the middle of the seventeenth century . . . seventy-five acres of good arable land in old Killead was not a bad start for the first adventurer who improved what was good and made better what was never bad. A pleasant lot. Time went on, rents were not screwed up too tight, taxes were fairly easy, and in good seasons there was much comfort about such a holding. A fowl or two on Sundays, boiled beef or mutton through the week, never braxy—oh, no, not never again. There was abundance of good cow's (not ewe's) milk and butter and cheese, and plenty of fresh pork, salted bacon, and ham and vegetables in variety, including potatoes, which a Gallowayman had not tasted for over a hundred years after they were bubbling in every three-legged pot in Ulster. There was some sport, too, and every stout farmer had his gun in his comfortable kitchen. In the evenings it frequently came down for an airing, with its nozzle tilted to the ground, under a sturdy arm."

He would tell of odd incidents out of the local histories that he knew so well. For instance, of a happening in the ranks of the Inniskillings at Waterloo and what ensued from it. "One of the rank fell, heavily wounded by the French, to be carried off the field of slaughter by his wife, for in those days camp-followers often outnumbered the standing army. She, too, was wounded severely by a shell, and both lay helpless in an Antwerp hospital and their little baby girl was born. The poor man lost both his arms, and his wife was lamed for life. It was told that the Duke of York stood godfather to the wee girl, who was born in blood at the famous victory of Waterloo. A sad little wounded family group they would make, with their distressing tale and tottering limbs, begging alms at the high pillars of the parish church of Enniskillen." Francis Joseph Bigger's best bit of writing is concerned with the bridge which I am now approaching, the bridge across the river Quoile in County Down:

The principal gathering place of the swan in Lecale seems to be at the wide inland tidal brackish stretch at Killough, where at times hundreds may be counted, and at rarer intervals a general assembly convened by the booming note of a great aged gander on a gravelly spit. This is often a long sederunt, and there is much talk and wagging of red and black heads on long necks. The discussion, we may safely take it, is not on the future state, but on the present pressing social and sexual questions ripe for determination. There is not much hesitancy, decisions are soon arrived at and adhered to, and then clamorous white wings are spread and the meeting dissolved. It is a fine sight to see the swans breasting the flood at the Quoile Bridge, their only ugly feature strained from toe to body joint, taut and metallic, or to see them gallantly heading down stream out of the deep shadows of Finnebrogue Woods into the sun-tinted currents of the stream. No period passes without the cry of the coot being heard with a following splash amongst the reeds, whilst little coveys of ducks lie low in many a side wash. On a ploughed brae there is a patch of white or rather a dapple of lavender, still and motionless it appears; on close inspection it is seen to be a flock of gulls, pausing and resting from their almost continuous circling. Not a scream escapes them, not a rustle of a feather is observed; calm and placid, mostly on one leg, they stand, their long bills all facing the wind; just a gentle motion of the head can be noticed to give the dark, beady eye a wider and safer outlook. Suddenly one screams and a general clamour ensues, and we see such a picture of crescented air-planing as the ablest and most perfect Japanese artist has failed to copy. At rare times a pair of swans will cross the bridge flying low. Attention is drawn first by the metallic sound of their wings, and then the long graceful pinions are seen scarce moving, yet noticeably strong, swift, and powerful. A gaggle of geese sometimes pass over to the marshes, but they fly high and wedge-shaped, sometimes quite noisy, and generally suspicious towards the close of the year, as if they knew a thing or two as to their likely fate at the festive season. A big glutted geron-crane rises from the shallows on gentle, noiseless wings, flutters like a ghost moth, and then glides away. He is a solitary bird, and makes in flight no metallic noise like the swan; flies low, only rising on his long evening flight to his colony. It is only once in a lifetime that a gathering of herons is seen, and very tall, stately, and solemn they appear in their half-moon-shaped conclave, the silence only broken by a few deep bass guttural notes. . . . There is an old legend that the sweet bells of Down lie embedded in the Quoile not far from the bridge, and that the time will yet come when they will again be heard across "the ransomed hills of Down." In a still eventide at autumn time when the woods shed their brown leaves and the white waves have settled down, like a lace border, on the banks of the Quoile the musical murmur of these bells can be heard by him who has a gentle ear to the earth, the buried bells of Inch out of their reedy bed echo their requiem under the shadow of the woods of Ballyrenan, and far-off Loughinisland gives out one solitary toll like the last note of a thrush as he falls to sleep.[1]

Saint Patrick

A hump-shaped eminence of basalt with scant herbage and scrub upon it—this is Slieve Mis or Slemish, and we come upon it suddenly as we pass from Antrim into Down. It was from the slopes of this eminence that the youthful captive who afterwards took the name of Patrick watched over his master's flocks or droves. Often he prayed up there; his prayers were said in frost and hail and snow, sometimes as many as a hundred in a day. And then he

[1] "In Remembrance: F. J. B.," edited by John S. Crone and E. C. Bigger, Dublin, The Talbot Press.

made an escape from the place. But when he returned to Ireland a bishop and a missionary of Rome he went towards this mount, sailing up the river we see, the river Quoile (another missionary, Duns Scotus, some centuries later sailed down this river, departing from Ireland). The ruler of the territory, believing that his former captive was returning with strange, immense powers and with vengeance in his heart, fired his house and gave himself to the flames. Then another local magnate presented the missionary with a barn: in it he celebrated Christian rites, establishing his first church in Ireland. Years later, an old man, he came back to the place of his first foundation; he died here and was buried near by. Thus the place marked by this basaltic ridge has various memories of Saint Patrick.

Often, as a youthful captive who was swineherd or shepherd, he must have climbed these rugged slopes to look east and south towards the land from which he had been taken. The Roman communities in Britain, although a doom hung over them, to him represented civilization. His dream was to return to the one from which he had been taken by the Irish raiders. Once he heard a directing voice; he made a flight; he discovered a ship about to sail. After he came to the ship he had moments of tragic suspense. He was willing to work his passage to the port to which the vessel was bound. His proposal was entertained by the mariners, but afterwards the ship-master objected, saying sharply, "Nay, in no wise shalt thou come with us."

This disappointment, coming as the end of his captivity seemed to be in sight, was bitter. He turned away from the mariners to seek shelter. As he went he prayed, and before he had finished his prayer he heard one of the crew shouting behind him: "Come quickly, for they are calling you." The ship-master had been persuaded to forego his objections, and Patrick, now about twenty-one years of age, set sail from Ireland in rough company.

The ship, the cargo, and the voyage were as strange as any romance-writer need devise: dogs were part of the cargo—great Irish wolfhounds. The crew wished to enter into a compact of friendship with him, but Patrick refused to be adopted by them. They reached port and then made a journey overland; they wandered through a desert country for eight and twenty days; many of the dogs became exhausted and were left to die on the road. What was the desert land they traversed? Probably Southern Gaul. "It was the last night of the year 406 that the Vandals, Suevi, Alans, and Burgundians burst into Gaul." The picture of the desolation that he gives has helped Professor MacNeill to date Patrick's journey.

Apparently Patrick and his company went into Italy; afterwards he wandered back to the South of France. For a while he stayed at the monastery of Lerens; then, after great labours, he won home again to his friends in Britain.

We know now where his native place was; the researches of Professor MacNeill, published a few

years ago, have cleared up that long-debated matter.[1]
Patrick's native place was Abergavenny, in the country that is now Wales. There was still a Roman organization there in 401, the year, according to Professor MacNeill's conjecture, of Patrick's capture. "From Bath, Aquae Solis, an important Roman town, a Roman road led to the Severn estuary, and was connected by an established ferry (*traiectus*) with the great road which ran from the military station of Venta Silurum northwards to another important military centre, Viriconium, and thence to Deva, now Chester, also a military station of great strategic importance. Not far from Venta, this road reached the Usk at Isca Silurum. Here a western branch traversed the Southern seaboard of Wales as far as Maridunum. The main road, turning northward at Isca, passed through Burrium and Gabannium, Abergavenny, both on the river Usk."

Here, along ways that still communicated with the Roman centre, lived communities loyally Roman, devotedly Christian. Patrick spoke the language of the British Celts as well as the Latin tongue. But at the time he was taken captive—he was fifteen then, it is surmised—he had not been trained in the schools. He speaks in his Confession of his inability to write good Latin, "apologizing that he has not had the double advantage that others (of his calling and station) have had, who, as is most fitting, have been educated in

[1] Proceedings of the Royal Irish Academy, Vol. XXXVII, Section C, No. 6., Eoin MacNeill, The Native Place of Saint Patrick.

sacred literature, and have not lost the Latin speech of their childhood, but have rather constantly acquired a more refined use of it, whereas he, as his style, he says, betrays, was forced in his youth to adopt a strange language in place of Latin." "His style, indeed, suggests," Professor MacNeill remarks acutely, "that, like many a candidate for examination in our time, his conscious weakness in Latin composition caused him to fill out his sentences with phrases taken from other writings, and not always apt to express the intended sense." Well, on this Roman and Christian community that still had communication with the Roman centre, the Irish raiders descended in 401. The raiders were probably under the command of the high-king, Niall. "The object of the raid was to secure a large booty in slaves and other things of value." The household of the decurion Calpurnius hardly survived the raid: its youthful heir was carried off together with its man-servants and maid-servants. Thousands of captives were brought from Britain by these particular raiders. They were sold as slaves, as Patrick tells us, and scattered among many tribes, even to the farthest part of the land.

Roman power, which had long been gradually and steadily decaying, was many stages further on towards its dissolution when Patrick returned to Britain. Irish settlements had succeeded Irish raids, and there were now Irish kingdoms bordering the places in which Patrick had known Roman communities. And a British chieftain holding Roman power irregularly, he whom

LA BAIE DE DOOAGH BY MARIE HOWET

Welsh history knows as Cunedda, was attacking the Irish settlements and organizing a British Celtic kingdom that we now know as Wales. Patrick, now in his forties or towards his forties, feels an impulse to return to the place of his slavery. The impulse becomes a call. In a dream he sees a man standing by his side. He had come from Ireland, and in his hand he held a bundle of letters. "And he gave me one of these, and I read the beginning of the letter which contained the voice of the Irish, and as I read the beginning of it I fancied I heard the voice of the folk who were near the wood of Fochlad, nigh to the Western sea. And this was the cry, 'We pray thee, holy youth, to come and walk amongst us as before.' 'I was pierced to the heart,' says Patrick, 'and could read no more, and thereupon I awoke.'" But years of disappointment and preparation were to go by before he heard again the actual voices of the Irish people. It was twenty-five years after he had taken ship from Ireland, in or about his forty-sixth or forty-seventh year, that Patrick returned to the place where he had spent six years of captivity.

The ancient name of this territory was Dalaraidi; the kingdom was Pictish, and it remained Pictish until the eighth century. At the time the most powerful King in Ireland was Laegaire (Laery), the second in succession from Niall who had carried Patrick off with his hundreds of captives. Laegaire claimed to be Ard-ri, high-king or emperor of the Irish, but it is doubtful if his authority was very real in this outlying kingdom. His seat was at Tara. Patrick went to Tara and preached before the high-king. Laegaire did not adopt the new creed, but he put no obstacles in the way of Patrick's mission.

He sat with three kings to revise the laws of Ireland. That revision was an acknowledgment of the fact that his mission had been successful, for it was to incorporate Christian teachings in the national law. But still Patrick looked on himself as an exile and a man of little account. The world that he felt he belonged to—the world of his father, the decurion—was perishing in his sight: the Roman legions had been withdrawn from Britain, and Germanic pagans with Gaels and apostate Picts were rending what was left of the Roman order. Nay, Christianity itself was no restraint upon men who had knowledge of the Latin language and who claimed some shadow of Roman authority. The soldiers of the King of North Britain massacred Patrick's converts and mocked the envoy whom he had sent to rebuke them. "In hostile guise they are dead while they live, allies of the Scots and apostate Picts, as though wishing to gorge themselves with the blood of innocent Christians whom I in countless numbers begot to God and confirmed in Christ. On that day following that on which the newly baptized in white array were anointed with the chrism—it was still gleaming on their foreheads while they were cruelly butchered and slaughtered—I sent a letter with a holy presbyter, whom I taught from his infancy, with some clerics, to request that they would allow us some of the booty or of the baptized captives whom they had taken. They jeered at him." And then in that epistle comes the bitter cry of the exile—an exile, although perhaps twenty years had been spent in labour in Ireland and he was now an old man. "Did I come to Ireland without God or according to the flesh? Who compelled me—I am bound by the spirit—not to see any of my kinsfolk? Is it from me that I show godly compassion towards that nation who once took me captive and harried the men-servants and maid-servants of my father's house? I was free-born according to the flesh. I am born of a father who was a decurion, but I sold my nobility, I blush not to state it, nor am I sorry for it, for the profit of others."

He did not know it, but he was doing for Roman civilization what soldiers and administrators had been unable to do for it—he was creating for it reserve forces. Later on, when the Christian and the Roman principles were all but destroyed in his Britain, the successors of the men whom he was ordaining were to bring back and reinstate something derived from these principles. Very few men's labour had such fruit as this man's has had. The National Museum in Dublin has the little bell that he held in his hand when he summoned his congregation in the Ireland of fifteen hundred years ago—always and by all visitors it is looked at with special reverence. Beside it is a reliquary made in honour of the saint by one of the Norman lords of the West of Ireland—one of the De Briminghams: it is covered over with the figures of the French saints who were thought most of at the time—one thinks of how present Patrick is in comparison with any of them, and of how deep is the veneration in which he has been held by all comers into Ireland. "I, Patrick, a sinner, the most rustic, and the least of all the faithful, and in the estimation of very many deemed contemptible."

When he died many communities contended for the glory of having his burial in their grounds. Tradition says that leaving it to Providence to resolve their claims, the bier was laid on a wagon to which four white oxen were yoked: from the church that was his first foundation the oxen with their burthen were turned and were permitted to fare on without human direction. On a slope above the river Quoile they stayed and there the body of Patrick was laid in earth. A community grew up around this burial-place, and the round tower that still stands, the depository of its treasures, was raised. The place is Downpatrick, now a good-sized town.

Border Story: Catherine Mulamphy and the Man from the North

My grandfather used to say that more extraordinary things happened in the hamlet of Coney than in any town or village, barony or bailiwick in the whole of Ireland. They were all red-headed people who lived in Coney; they married through each other, and their names were Mulamphy. Now when he wished to illustrate the manifestations of the extraordinary Coney spirit, my grandfather used to tell this story.

Mind you, I knew two of the people concerned, Martin Mulamphy and his wife Catherine. Martin remains on the outskirts of my mind, but Catherine I remember very well. I met her one day on a mountain road; she was riding; her bare legs hung across the donkey and her red hair was loose upon her shoulders. Even after they were married, Martin would not let this red hair be put up. My grandfather used to say that no two beings were ever as fond of each other as Martin and Catherine Mulamphy. Every Christmas, after Mass, the pair would come into our house. They used to sit on the settle, and after some whiskey had been taken, they would sing together, "The first day of Christmas my true-love sent to me one gold ring, one turtle-dove, *and* a pear-tree." The song, with proportional increase in the number of gifts, went on to the twelfth day of Christmas. When it was finished the pair would mount the horse, Martin in front of Catherine, and ride pillion-ways off to their mountain hamlet.

After Christmas comes the fair of Cartron Markey. It takes place at the rise of the year, upon Saint Brighid's Day. Now, our Mulamphys had nothing to sell, but that did not stand in the way of their going to the fair. And for the grandeur of the thing Martin put a pewter chain across his waistcoat. He had no watch to attach to it, but he remedied that defect by taking the lid of a small canister, fastening it to the chain, and putting it into a pocket. Appearance was everything, and Martin Mulamphy gave himself the appearance of a man who could sport a watch and chain.

The pillion was put upon the garron and the pair rode off to Cartron Markey. They put up at Mulvihill's. It was early in the day, and there were only a few people in the shop. Mulvihill himself was behind the counter, and Martin stood and discoursed with him. Catherine sat on a barrel at the far end of the shop. A Connacht man was closing a bargain with a man of the Midlands. "I declare to God," said the Connachtman, "I would divide the gain. *Dar na Muce!* By the pigs, we are as friendly as if we were kissing each other." They were shaking hands when another man came into the shop.

He was an Ulsterman and a horse dealer—a big man with a platter-broad face that fell easily into a grin. "Men, dear," said he, "what are ye havin'? Fill the glasses again," said he to the man behind the counter. "I've a heart as soun' as a prize cabbage."

"Is that so?" said Catherine from where she sat on the barrel, "and is there many in the fair that knows that?"

"Ma'am," said the Ulsterman, "I'd like to be talking wi' ye. Ye look like a fine woman."

"I was intended to be a fine woman," said Catherine, "and what is your name?"

"I'm Neil MacNeece," said the Ulsterman, "an' I'm

a terrible great man. An' will ye take anything, ma'am?"

"A half glass of special," said Catherine.

"Tell us your story, honest man," said Martin, bringing back MacNeece's attention with a tap from a stick he picked up.

"Last year," said MacNeece, "I came into this fair with only three shillings in my pocket. All my money was lost in England. It was early in the mornin' when I came into your town and there was less than a dozen people in the place. There was a farmer with a horse for sale and I went up and spoke to him. 'How much do you want for the beast?' 'Eighty pound,' said he. 'Let me try him,' said I. I jumped up and galloped off, and that was the last the farmer saw of his horse."

"Do you tell us that?" said the man from the Midlands. The three men waited with glasses in their hands. MacNeece brought over the half of special to Catherine. "Good luck to you," said she.

"It's likely you have more to tell,' said the Connachtman.

"I have, and a lot more to tell," said MacNeece. "I came into your gran' town this mornin' an' found my farmer wi' another horse for sale. I stepped up and asked him his price. 'Eighty pound,' said he. 'Let me ride him to the end o' the town,' said I. 'Ye're a bit late, as Paddy said to the ghost,' said he, 'last year a villain asked me to let him try a horse, and I never saw him nor horse again.' 'An' would ye know the man?' said I. 'I would not. I saw him for no more than a minute.' 'I'll buy the horse without trial,' said I. 'Come into such a house and I'll hand ye eighty pound.' Well, I handed him eighty pound and he gave me a luck-penny. 'Would you be satisfied if ye got eighty pound for the horse ye lost last year?' 'I'd be more than satisfied.' 'Well, here's your eighty pound. It was me that took your horse. An' look,' says I, showing my pouch to my farmer, 'I made all that out o' your nag.'"

"You're an extraordinary wonderful man," said Catherine.

"Sowl, but ye're a gran' woman," said MacNeece.

"Do you like me?" said Catherine.

"Ma'am, I like you well," said MacNeece.

It was at this moment, as luck would have it, that the Connachtman asked Martin for the time of day. Martin whipped at the chain. Out flew what was attached to it. It rolled. No wheel of fortune ever rolled as that lid of canister rolled. It rolled behind the counter, the Connachtman pursuing it. It rolled from behind at the upper end of the counter and out upon the middle of the floor. Another man went after it there. It rolled behind the barrel on which Catherine was sitting. As it rolled between his legs MacNeece picked it up.

"And is that what he was going to give us the time of?" said the Connachtman.

"Sowls!" said MacNeece, holding the canister-lid between finger and thumb.

"I thought he had one watch at least," said the man of the Midlands.

"Ye thought wrong, like Paddy's pig," said Mac-Neece with a grin.

Then the Connachtman and the man of the Midlands went out. Martin took the canister-lid from MacNeece and threw it down on Mulvihill's counter. "Are you buying?" said he to MacNeece.

"The one thing I'd like to buy is the red-headed woman yonder."

"Do you make an offer?"

"Do ye own her, now?"

"It was me that put the ring on her finger." Catherine came over to the pair. "What would you give for me?" said she to MacNeece.

"I'd give all I have, ma'am," said MacNeece. "I would, in troth." He took a roll of notes out of the inside pocket of his great-coat and put them on the counter. There were twenty of them. Now there was something of the jackdaw and something of the magpie in Catherine's husband. He was acquisitive and he was vain. He had just put on a new belt. It was a red belt with blue stripes across it, and it had leathern pouches. The notes got inside one of the pouches. Then Martin Mulamphy would let himself be cut across rather than take one of them out.

"Give the man a luck-penny, Martin," said Catherine.

Martin took a crooked ha'penny out of his pocket

and passed it to MacNeece. "Will I be takin' ye to the North?" said MacNeece to Catherine.

"You must give me law," said Catherine.

"What law do you ask?"

"A year and a day."

"An' whaur will I find ye at the end of the year an' the day?"

"In Coney," said Catherine. "Mulamphy is the name. Come," said she to Martin, and then she went into the street. And all that her husband said to Mac-Neece was, "Good-bye to you, honest man."

They went down the street without a word between them, Catherine and Martin. At the corner there was for sale a cart of splendid appearance. The spokes and shafts were freshly painted red, and the body was of a shining blue. Martin priced the cart, and Catherine stood by and watched the proceedings. She had become the onlooker of Martin's motions and movements. The cart went to three pounds, and Martin paid with money out of the pouch on his belt. He put the garron under the yoke, and the pair went home in their new vehicle. But it wasn't like being on the pillion. There was silence between the pair for the length of the road.

Christmas came around, and Martin and Catherine came into our house. They sat down on the settle and took the refreshment provided. They sang together, "The first day of Christmas my true-love sent to me one gold ring, one turtle-dove, *and* a pear-tree." They went out together, and my grandfather watched them from the door. "Believe me," said my grandfather, "I would give that full bottle of whiskey to see Catherine and Martin Mulamphy riding pillion-ways again. Since they came by that cart I see a difference in their nature towards one another."

Martin had told him the episode of Cartron Markey, and my grandfather had given him this sage direction, "Whatever else he'll come for, believe you me, the man of the North will come back for his money. Leave the seventeen pounds in the pouch, roll up the belt, and let me have the keeping of it." Now, upon the next Saint Brighid's Day my grandfather was before the house clipping his hedge into the semblance of a lion, when a stranger strode up to him. "Where is Coney?" asked the man. My grandfather knew him at once for the man from the North. "Maybe you're looking for people of the name of Mulamphy?" "I am," said the man, and he had a wide grin on. "Your name might be MacNeece?" "It is MacNeece," said the man. "We have heard of you," said my grandfather.

He put MacNeece on the way to the hamlet, but he neglected to tell him that everyone in Coney was named Mulamphy. He went into John's with the Two Chimneys, to Michael's with the Running Dog, and to Bartley's the Tailor. Nellie, the tailor's wife, didn't let him leave in a hurry. Well, between one house and another house, Neil MacNeece spent about half his day between doorstep and hob.

My grandfather was playing a game of cards with himself when he saw Catherine upon the road. She had a bundle, and my grandfather thought she was bringing his dinner to Martin. He was trimming a hedge for him that day, but my grandfather had not remembered this when he was speaking with MacNeece. "Good-morrow, Catherine," said my grandfather.

"Good-morrow," said Catherine. My grandfather thought her manner was not effusive at all.

"Your man will be glad of his dinner," said my grandfather.

"I'm not going to provide it," said Catherine.

"But where are you going, then?" said he.

"From the house that he brought me to," said she.

"The man that put the ring on your finger?" said my grandfather.

"There it's for him," said Catherine, throwing the ring—she was holding it in her hand all the time—in the dust of the road. Catherine went her way. My grandfather left his cards and walked up and down. Then he called to me and bid me bring Martin Mulamphy to that spot. "Martin, my poor fellow," said my grandfather, "there's your ring on the ground." Martin took up the ring. "It's Catherine's surely," he said. "I won't keep you in suspense, Martin," said my grandfather, "Catherine threw it there." Martin regarded the ring. "She wasn't great with me for a few days back," said he, "but why should she go off like that?" "With a bundle, Martin," said my grandfather, "as if she was going to work in Scotland or England." "But it's not the season for that," said Martin. "This is only Saint Brighid's Day. By the

Cross of Cong," said he, shearing the top off a hedge with his billhook, "she's gone off with the man from the North."

"Don't say that, Martin," said my grandfather, "don't say that, and give me the billhook out of your hands. But I have to own," said he, when he got the billhook into his own hands, "that Neil MacNeece was round here this morning, and I gave him all directions for finding your place."

"Amn't I the misfortunate man," said Martin, "with my wife gone off with a black-mouthed man from the North?"

"The like never happened in this parish," said my grandfather, "and I'm loath to believe anything of the kind."

"It was a bargain," said Martin.

"Somehow I didn't see what you think in Neil Mac-Neece's eye, anyway, Martin. And Catherine went from this by herself."

"I'm very venomous," said Martin. "When I'm roused up I could puck my weight in fighting-cats. I'll let daylight through MacNeece if he was to have me hanged for it afterwards."

With that he dragged on his coat and made a run of about twenty yards. My grandfather called to him. "Martin," said he, "rash men will do rash deeds I know, but a man oughtn't to show himself to the world worse than his deed makes him. Don't let the name of money come into the dispute, Martin. Give back what you have belonging to him." My grandfather went into the house and brought out the belt. He handed it to Martin Mulamphy. With the belt in his hand he started down the road. He was making for his mother-in-law's. He would borrow a horse and ride into Cartron Markey.

He came to the cross roads and went down by the plantation. Ahead of him he saw a man in a great-coat walking hard. It was Neil MacNeece. Martin caught up on him. "Och, Mister Mulamphy," said the big man, "I hope I see ye soun'."

"I'm sound enough," said Martin, "and I have the use of my hands. Would you try a few rounds with me?"

"Here, is it?"

"Here, on the road."

"Is fightin' your wish?"

"Aye, what have you to say again' it?"

"Nothing again' it. The spirits are that ruz in me that I'll do anything to oblige any man. Fightin', is it? Oh, very well, Mr. Mulamphy."

"Take the belt," said Martin, "your money's in it."

They went down the road a bit. When they came to a ground he knew Martin took up a position. He struck out. MacNeece sparred good-humouredly. Martin was certainly venomous. He manœuvred the fight till he got MacNeece on the ground that dipped to a rotten fence. He struck out; he got his adversary on the mouth and nostrils. Through the fence went MacNeece and into a shough of water. Then Martin turned on his heel and went up to his mother-in-law's.

Catherine's mother was at the door. "Wait a while," said she, "and then go up to her."

"What? Is Catherine here?"

"She's in the room above."

When he opened the room-door he saw Catherine lying in bed. She turned angry eyes on him. "You're as mean as ditch-water," she said, "and I'm glad I saw you to say that to you."

"No matter how mean I may be I've done for the man you were going off with."

"The man I was going off with?" Catherine said. "Who are you talking about at all?"

"Neil MacNeece. I met him and fought him and left him lying in a shough at the Kesh of Keel. That's what your bachelor got this Saint Brighid's Day."

Catherine sat up in bed. "Martin, are you hurted?" she said. She came to him. "Martin, Martin, you're cut and battered. Did he hurt you, Martin? But why did you do badly by me? You said it was a gold ring. After wearing it five years I found you out in a lie. It's a brass ring, after all. Oh, it's badly you treated me! I'd have a right to go off with Neil MacNeece."

"Were you not going with him?"

"Sure, Martin, I clean forgot that this was Saint Brighid's Day. What did he do to you, Martin?"

"I gave him back his belt and fought it out."

"I didn't know he was this side of the world. But I own to you that it makes me proud that he came for me. You didn't give him his twenty pounds back—

oh, no, you didn't, Martin, for you've a mean drop in you. I'll never wear that oul' brass ring again, and I'll make you give the rest of Neil MacNeece's money back to him."

She had just said the words when MacNeece's voice was heard below. She went down the stairs and saw him at the door. And she showed her presence of mind by the way she up and spoke to him. "Mr. MacNeece," said she, "isn't your call too soon? I thought we wouldn't see you for a year and a day?"

"But, ma'am," said he, "it's twins!"

"Oh!" said Catherine. He was shaking hands with her mother and telling about the event.

"Twins. Mrs. MacNeece, ma'am. Two days ago."

Martin was coming down behind them. Catherine turned to him. "It's seldom Mr. MacNeece is in these parts," said she to him, "and we must do our best to pleasure him. Leave everything aside and we'll go off for the day."

Martin put the horse under the cart. When everything was ready he came in and shook hands with MacNeece. Nothing was said about the previous encounter. They went off to Cartron Markey. They had all the fun of the fair. A tramp fiddler entertained them in the room, and MacNeece began to drink with him. But it turned out that the blind musician was pouring the whiskey into a tin behind his wallet so that he might have something after he left Mulvihill's. This unfair competition brought the horse-dealer under; MacNeece was left sleeping in the cart, and

East Ulster

Catherine and Martin rode home pillion-ways. They came into our house on their way back. Just as if it had been Christmas, the pair, sitting together, sang of the ring, the turtle-dove, and the pear-tree.

PART IV

The Vale of the Liffey

Dublin to Kildare

THERE is nothing like a river to give dignity to a town—a river with fine bridges across it. Men as they pass over bridges have a dignity that does not inhere in any of their other peregrinations. They are conscious of it, too; think of the way men and women cross bridges over the Seine! There are no such appearances in Dublin; here the river is nothing in comparison with the Seine or the Thames; there can be no fine bridges across the Liffey.

I walk along the river towards the park. There is no shipping except the steam-driven barges that are laden with barrels from the brewery. There are second-hand bookstalls. There are curiosity-shops of the kind that seldom see a customer. The houses on each side of the unfull river are as listless as any I ever saw. Some day, I imagine, they will be demolished to leave space for boulevards leading to the park. Meanwhile, the most rousing sight on the way is that of the horses—Clydesdales, that draw the long brewery-drays (but they are being displaced by motor-trucks). Big men are with these big horses; they have polished the brasses of the harnesses as sailors polish the fittings of a ship. The

The Vale of the Liffey

brasses sparkle and shine as the immense horses go on, and, big and grave, the men look as if they belonged to a high caste of horse-tamers and barrel-transporters. I come to a bridge at the railway-depot: here up-to-date taxies wait near old-time jaunting-cars on which jarveys sit and wait for the fare that seldom comes to them now. The Dublin jarvey's day is over, and well he knows it and bitterly he resents it.

I go through the park gate, and when I pass the gardens I am in an expanse of country that makes a park that is vast in comparison with Dublin's size—the Phœnix Park. I approach herds of deer. I see the Liffey looking like its natural self as it skirts this pastoral scene, a stream that should never have been asked to go through a city. Here is the Viceregal Lodge, and perhaps Her Excellency will ask us to tea. . . . In the entrance-hall is the portrait of the Viceroy whose design left Dublin so grandiose a park, Philip Dormer Stanhope, Lord Chesterfield, with his livid face and lively eyes. We stand on the lawn and look towards the misty Dublin hills along a line of statuesque Irish yews. The site is a delightful one.

In the old days when one went through this part of the park there were always strollers around who were ready to show one where a murder had been committed —the murder of a Chief Secretary for Ireland and his assistant by a terrorist gang. It was a murder by knives, and it really shocked the country—"The Phœnix Park Murders." The crime was not long before my own time, but it had seemed to me legendary. . . . One day

Cross Roads in Ireland

I found myself sharing a compartment in a train from New York to Washington with a rather noble-looking old gentleman. He took snuff and he read Hebrew, the Book of Job was the text he had in his hands. Although he was vigorous and very intelligent he seemed a survival in some way, perhaps because he had been in service in some out-of-the-way island. Well, this old gentleman was the person who had procured the knives for the Phœnix Park murders. " 'They will have to be surgical knives,' I told them, 'long in the blade.' " Between Philadelphia and Baltimore he told me about the crime and how it had been prepared for, and between Baltimore and Washington he talked to me about Hebrew grammar and literature. He gave a speech that was oratorical, but also witty and sensible. We shared a bedroom in a Washington hotel and he stayed awake quite a long time giving out musty jokes about bedrooms and other men's wives. Then he said some prayers fervently and went to sleep. He spoke very finely, I remember, about some passages in the Book of Job before I got off the train next day, and he said "God bless you" as we parted. I think of him now as I approach the scene of the murder. But I am very glad that no one now seems to have an interest in keeping the memory of it alive.

I come out of the park and walk along where the country goes into little green rises. I come on the river again. From its mouth to its source is a distance of only thirty-five miles, I believe. But the Liffey makes a loop (that is, if a loop can be made with a line that is all

loops) and so manages to get into three counties—
Wicklow, Kildare, and Dublin. I come to a bridge.
Beside the bridge is a public-house, and outside is a
man playing a tin whistle.

He showed me his instrument with great pride. He
had bought it in Henry Street, Dublin, at the shop of
Mr. Smith, tenpence was the price. Every night he said
a prayer for Mr. Smith who had made so perfect an
instrument. I looked at it and found that it had been
made in Germany; if Mr. Smith of Henry Street was
getting the benefit of the nightly prayer he was getting more than was his due. But I said nothing about
this to the instrumentalist. He was so pleased with my
patronage that he stepped outside the public-house and
played for my especial benefit. He played a double tin
whistle, putting two instruments into his mouth. And
he played a tune of his own composition. He knew
someone who was an army bandmaster, he told me, and
he had offered to record the tune. I thought it was stirring; "The Birds That Left the Cage" was the title he
gave it.

And he came with me to the place I was bound for
—"Sarsfield's Demesne" the local guide-book called it.
Patrick Sarsfield, the last military leader of the Irish,
could have had little connection with it, although his
family had owned the land. We went into the demesne
that the Liffey flows by, and came before the house. No
gardens are before it, no peacocks display themselves
in front of it; rough grass is before the house and steps
go up to it.

Cross Roads in Ireland

It is an empty house but not a neglected one. The cicerone had been a groom. He showed us a room in which the decorations were by Angelica Kauffmann. I thought her classical figures had a kind of serious charm. But the instrumentalist was dubious about them. The cicerone did not let himself be disturbed by head-shakings: he visualized, as it were, every objection, rode up to it and went right over, and left it surmounted. He had the instrumentalist with him when he showed us the mantel-pieces in the house. They were inlaid by an Italian who was in Dublin at the period, Bossi. "When he was dying after making this piece, his son, wanting the secret from him, went to where he was lying. But the old man wouldn't tell how work the like of this was done. 'There is only one God and one Bossi,' he said, and he died then, and the secret of putting colours and figures the like of these into the marble died with him." The instrumentalist was impressed with this tale of devotion to craftsmanship.

I liked the drawing-room that had powder-closets in it. The gentlemen stalked into them, and, putting their heads through an opening, had a valet in an ante-room powder their wigs. Then they stepped out to the ladies, fingering snuff-boxes, I daresay. Likely enough Lord Chesterfield would be present: his residence was near by. In this drawing-room his epigrams would surely be retailed—perhaps the one upon the lovely Papist lady who attended his court wearing Orange lilies instead of the white roses of her own cause:

The Vale of the Liffey

Ah, pretty Tory, why this zest
To wear the Orange at your breast,
When that same beauteous breast discloses
The whiteness of the rebel roses!

Chesterfield's idea of governing Ireland by epigram and public works was better than the ideas other Viceroys had, of governing it by hunting, dancing, and bribery.

We went down to the immense kitchen that the cicerone's family inhabited, and ate cakes and drank buttermilk. The Liffey is domestic here; we walked out of the kitchen. And walking along the river-bank we turned up to the demesne.

A friend of mine says that the favourite outdoor sport of the Irish people is walking through demesnes. The Dubliners who were here were getting real enjoyment out of walking through this demesne. Assuming that Patrick Sarsfield had been about the place on the days when he was not in camp or not being besieged, they felt his spirit close to them. Urns, the emblems of the Sarsfield family, are along every walk.

But as I looked upon this classical emblem I thought of how wide was the gap that separated such leaders as Sarsfield from the Irish people. For all this was Versailles, the Europe of the seventeenth century, and the Ireland of the time was in the Europe of a more remote age. From what distance comes the burst of native lament:

Farewell, Patrick Sarsfield, may luck be on your path!
Your camp is broken up, your work is marred for years;

Cross Roads in Ireland

But you go to kindle into flame the King of France his wrath,
Though you leave sick Eire in tears—
Och, ochone!

I parted from my friend here; I went along the riverbank into the County Kildare. I came to another mansion, empty, too, a house that was surely the replica of a French house—a charming house. Here that "ripe-witted young gentlewoman," Esther Vanhomrigh, lived for years after she had followed Doctor Swift to Ireland. She had a pleasant place, not so far from Dublin but that Swift could ride to it. How dreary it must have been for her to look along the Dublin road while she waited for a letter from Cadenus, a letter which, when it came, recommended Vanessa to take exercise and devote more time to her reading, or made covert allusion to coffee-drinking intimacies. "The sweetest ground in Ireland is here," says a man who has cattle grazing between the house and the river, "not a beast that ever tasted a bit of the grass here but would stray back to it." I am glad to think that poor Vanessa's seat keeps such attraction.

I was now in Kildare, that county which has so many memorials of Norman and early English settlements.

The Geraldines

When the small Norman forces were faced with the Irish before Dublin and were affrighted by the possibility of a Norse fleet coming in and joining with these forces, Maurice Fitzgerald exclaimed, "Can we expect aid from our own land? We have no land, and Ireland does not detest us more than England does. To arms, then, Barons!" It was this speech that put heart in the Norman raiders into Ireland. The Battle of the Liffey was fought in 1171, and five Norman barons with a few hundred men overthrew King Roderick O'Connor and prepared the way for Henry the Second's invasion. Of these barons an Irish historian has written, "Fitzgerald, Raymond the Stout, Fitzstephen, De Cogan, now *they* had the blood of nationmakers in them, but they were overborne and betrayed and had to end as barons where they might have reigned as kings." [1] They ended as barons because Strongbow, weaker than his name implied, stepped down when his Plantagenet king bade him do so.

Here is an ivy-covered tower and keep. Part of it is as old as any Norman foundation in Ireland, for the beginning of it was laid by Maurice Fitzgerald. He was given the lordship of Maynooth and Naas. This conquistador was already half-Celtic, for his mother was Nesta, the daughter of a Welsh prince. And already the Fitzgeralds—the Gheraldi of Tuscany —had an ancestry that was carried back to Trojan times.

But while remaining barons in name, the Fitzgeralds became great princes, ruling over these fertile lands of Kildare and taking possession of a royal domain in Desmond. Maynooth was the first and the greatest of

[1] Edmund Curtis: "How Earl Strongbow Took Dublin"; *Dublin Magazine,* October-December, 1929.

their castles. Its fall marked the beginning of a new epoch in Irish history, the epoch that was to end with the extirpation of the great lords. The Fitzgerald of the time was a picturesque and, probably, a chivalrous and romantic young man. He was wont to apparel himself so gorgeously that the Irish knew him as Silken Thomas. He heard that his father had been executed in the Tower of London—the rumour was not true—and forthwith he attempted to set up rule in Ireland in the anti-English interest. But the Irish lords were not ready to give him whole-hearted support in this move. His own uncles were against it. The energetic and resourceful deputy, Skeffington, appeared before Maynooth: Lord Thomas was in the west raising aid, and the castle was betrayed to the deputy by Fitzgerald's foster-brother. Holinshed tells how the traitor received the thanks of the deputy and the great sum of money that he had bargained for; then he was beheaded. No stipulation had been made about sparing his head. Silken Thomas was beheaded at Tyburn. Five of his uncles shared his fate. Henry the Eighth, according to Holinshed, was persuaded "that he should never conquer Ireland as long as any Geraldines breathed in the country."

Eighteen years afterwards the estates, castles, and titles of the Earls of Kildare were given back to the eleventh Earl. Thereafter the Geraldine of Kildare was a great lord, not a semi-independent prince.

Carton, near the old castle, is now the seat of this family; its head is the Duke of Leinster. I go there hoping that I may be permitted to look at the portraits that are in the house. I pass through a gate and see a demesne before me that seems to be as wide as Phœnix Park. I come to a stream that has about a score of water-hens upon it. I never saw so many of these shy creatures together; a flock of them there seemed to be. I crossed the stream and came to another gate and entered another demesne. And then I came to a house that is as big as a wing of Versailles. Here, in the middle of the grass-lands of Kildare, with nothing to lead up to it—no hill, no woods, no other walls—Carton seemed to me about Louis the Fourteenth's size. And before the house, on the grass, were about a thousand of the most rapacious rooks I ever looked on. They had started, I thought, to tear the whole demesne up.

I imagine the house has about one hundredth of the staff of servants and retainers that kept it going in the eighteenth century. I thought that a dozen or else no servant at all would appear. But one old servant came to the door and brought me within.

In a poem which James Stephens has translated, David O'Bruadair, addressing a Geraldine lady, exclaims that it is not possible for one of her princely race "to use a poet less than courteously." Lady Nesta Fitzgerald, I found, is true to the good fame of her line. She took me through the gallery and showed me the portraits of the Geraldines of the old days. She has favourites. There is the Enchanted Earl. I look upon the features of a man of the type that was at Francis the First's or Henry the Eighth's court, and I remember that he has come into many an Irish folk-tale:

> Of Earl Gerald, how he rides abroad,
> His horse's hooves shod with the weighty silver,
> And how he'll ride all roads till those horse's hooves
> Are worn thin—
> As thin as the cat's ears before the fire,
> Upraised in such content before the fire,
> And making little lanterns in the fire-light.

"Yes, when his horse's shoes are worn out he'll come back and destroy the enemies of our country," said the lady. There is another portrait of him, a smaller one that is thought to be by Holbein.

How did Earl Gerald enter into the circle of Fionn and Frederick Barbarossa? His reputation as a learned man, as a wizard came first. He had a library that must have been amongst the best of its time: a catalogue of books that were in it has come down to us, they were in Latin and English, French and Irish. From being a learned man, a wizard, an enchanter, Earl Gerald passed into being one who was enchanted, taking the place of some older hero of the folk.

Alone amongst the nobility of Ireland, the Geraldines produced men who were Irish and who were Europeans. There was, to skip two centuries, Lord Edward Fitzgerald who was like Earl Gerald in his being Irish and European. Here is his portrait with the portrait of his wife, Pamela—Pamela, the daughter of Madame de Genlis and the Duke d'Orleans. She has a little face and long brown eyes, a lovely creature.

The Vale of the Liffey

Lord Edward, with this romantic and enthusiastic face, must have been one of the most fascinating men of his time. I see in the portrait those long, dark lashes that Thomas Moore said was his most noticeable feature.

Lord Edward Fitzgerald was one of the leaders of the United Irishmen, the secret society that tried to prepare the country for a French landing, which would, it was expected, give force enough to create an independent state. "I expressed some doubts to Lord Edward whether the United Men could stand in battle before the king's troops, but he replied to me, 'That would not be altogether necessary, as assistance from France was expected; that then some of the United Men would certainly join in the French lines, and of course would soon become disciplined; but as to the multitude, all they would have to do would be to harass the escorts of ammunition, cut off detachments and foraging parties, and, in fine, make the king's troops feel themselves in every respect in an enemy's country, while the actual battles would be left to the foreign troops.'" Such were the plans he had formed, according to an informer. But before the insurrection broke out, Lord Edward Fitzgerald had died "in a grated room in Newgate," of wounds inflicted on him when his arrest was being made.

Lord Edward, too, has come into the circle of folk-lore. Once, in a Longford cottage, a man told me a story about him, a story that had the simplicity of a folk-tale and some of its charming turns. When he was a young man, Lord Edward heard much of the lewd-ness of London. For a long time he did not credit these stories. He thought they were made up to dis-credit the people of London. But more and more the stories oppressed him, and at last he decided to go in person and find out if London were really depraved. He went over to that city. One night he put on a dis-guise, and went down a very evil street. Now, a lady in Paris had also been oppressed by such tales of wick-edness. She had come to London, bringing her aunt. They had taken lodgings. One night the young lady dis-guised herself and went into the ill street. Like Lord Edward, she was concerned to discover or deny the de-pravity. Its bad report had brought Lord Earl and herself into the same street. The lady was disguised as an old beggar-woman.

Maybe she was wishful to know what sort was the young man who was in the wicked street at an ill hour. "*A mhic*," she said. "My son, would you help an old woman to such a number?" Lord Edward offered his arm. She did not take it. Together they went down the street. Lord Edward was very watchful, being in such a street, and he noticed that the woman kept her hand from him. "Give me your hand," said he. But still she kept her hand away. Then he snatched her hand. It was the hand of a young girl. "Who are you?" said he. The girl ran from him, and let herself into a house. "To-morrow I'm going to Paris with my aunt," she said.

The next day Lord Edward went to Paris. When he

THE FAIRY THORN BY PAUL HENRY

woke up in the hotel he asked what sport there was in the town. He was told there would be a great ball that night in the Royal Palace. Lord Edward went to the ball, and the first one he saw amongst the dancers was the girl who had disguised herself. The moment she saw him she asked a lady to take her place in the dance, and she came over to him. It wasn't one hand she gave him this time. She gave him her two hands.

He used to be out at night drilling the people with Wolfe Tone. She never said, "Edward, where were you last night?" though she knew that it would turn out bad work for him. His mother used to be very fond of her. She was so fond of her that she used to take the young woman to sleep on her lap. But after the death of Lord Edward the mother turned altogether against the young wife. She was very lonesome then. She had three children. She left Ireland, bringing the children with her, and no one had any account of them ever afterwards.

Twilight filled the demesne as I went through it: the road was empty, and I could imagine the men who had become figures in folk-lore riding abroad—Lord Edward riding towards the Curragh, wearing that green cravat that aroused the ire of the British officers; Earl Gerald riding the horse with silver shoes, and that little, strange-looking man whose portrait I had looked at, and who was known as the Fairy Earl. He would be riding a swifter horse than the others rode. And riding like one whose spirit was changing within him, that

Gerald who was Baron of Offaly, son of the eleventh earl, who, turning from gambling and swearing, wrote a Song of Repentance of which this is a verse:

> There is no wight that used it more
> Than he that wrote this verse;
> Who crieth Peccavi, now therefore
> His oaths his heart doth pierce.
> Therefore example take by me,
> That curse the luckless time
> That ever dice mine eyes did see,
> Which bred in me this crime.
> Pardon me for that is past,
> I will offend no more,
> In this most vile and sinful cast
> Which I will still abhor.

Maynooth

In what was once the Deer Park of Maynooth Castle, Saint Patrick's College now stands; the entrance to it is beside the crumbled keep. And this entrance has oddity about it: one goes through gates surmounted by slender sphinxes, the rococo where one expected to find the Gothic.

This is the training-ground for Ireland's priesthood: five hundred students are here, young men mainly from the farmer and merchant classes. For three years they take the National University Arts course. They do not go to Dublin for lectures; their degrees are conferred on them in this college. For four years after they have taken their Arts degree they study theology. And so the candidates for the Irish priesthood for seven years live here; their lives, except for holiday visits to their relatives, are isolated.

Not all the candidates for the Irish priesthood go through Saint Patrick's College: there are other foundations—the Irish College in Rome, the Irish College in Paris, the College of the Irish Nobles in Salamanca; there is also the Dublin diocesan College of Clonliffe. But where these colleges prepare students in dozens, Maynooth prepares them in hundreds. When one remembers that this has been done for over a century, and that there were, and there are, multitudes of ecclesiastics not only in Ireland, but in America and Australia, who look to Maynooth as their Alma Mater, a visitor is surprised to note how very little has been returned to the place. One might expect to find equipment of every kind created out of a spirit of allegiance to the college. But there are no halls, no learned foundations that have come out of such benevolence. Public benevolence in Catholic Ireland is very much wanting; Maynooth with so little endowment from the multitude who have passed through her halls is an example written large of this attitude. Maynooth exists on what was an annual grant made by the British Government and which has been compounded for a sum of four hundred thousand pounds, and on pensions paid by the students. Recently a sum of money has come to the college from a private source, and it is to be expended on an extension of the library. But, I think, this has been the only endowment it has received in the whole course of its history. And so what is here is well-kept, but sparse.

I wish someone would endow a foundation that would help Irish priests towards an appreciation of pictures, statues, architecture. What the bulk of Ireland sees of such things is in the churches, and what is in the churches, generally, is the factory-product of Munich. I suppose that the pictures and statues one sees in the Irish churches are the worst that can be found in any quarter of the world. Maynooth has a church by Pugin that is a fine one, if one can call a church fine that has in it nothing of the locality. I like best its stalls of carved oak in which the choir of students sit and chant vespers.

The corridors have stone flags, the stairways are of stone, and are worn by generations of students' feet. On wet afternoons, when they cannot have their games, the students walk along these corridors, talking together. I think how hardy they must be to go through these corridors and up and down the stairways on December and January mornings. I walk down a gallery and look at portraits of the bishops whom this college gave to the country, amongst them men who have taken great parts in public affairs. All of them are characteristically of the country. One portrait in particular holds me: it is the portrait of Archbishop MacHale. Only the Irish race produces the type that is delineated here —the long upper lip, the wide, mobile mouth, the face that is at once powerful and sensitive, wise, humorous, and austere. The type with the long upper lip, the craggy forehead, the long penetrating gaze, Irish as the lineaments of Lincoln are American, is not as frequently to be met with now as it was in the eighteenth and early nineteenth centuries, judging from the portraits of these periods: Lord Russell of Killowen, in Sargent's portrait, is of this distinctive type. Maynooth is popular—that is the first thing to realize about Saint Patrick's College—what is most general in Irish life is represented in it.

And now the main library of the college. The windows are white and their tops are blue and starred with gold. A monastic table is in the centre of the room. At the end of the room is an altar with a painting above it, a Descent from the Cross. There is striking colour in the picture—the gold of the Magdalen's hair, the blue of the garments, the white of the body of Christ. Projecting to the table are high book-cases—twenty feet high, I guess—with folios with their broods and litters of little books beside them: books with stained-ivory, and blue, and golden-brown bindings. I could never understand the matter, or even the language of most of these books, and so they are curious enough and abstract enough to permit me to think of them as colours that harmonize with the notes of blue and gold that make this library removed from the usual exchanges of learning.

I look on a folio of Peter Lombard's Lectures—Latin —and see pages as magnificent printing; I look on the manuscript known as the Black Book of Limerick, and see it as remarkable scrivenry. And then I look on documents that come like projectiles out of the past. They are licenses that had to be taken out by students who came to Maynooth after its foundation. They show on what suffrance Maynooth existed in the beginning: magistrates declare that the young men who have come before them are well-disposed towards the Government and may be permitted to enter a Roman Catholic seminary.

I look at the successors of these licensed learners. In cubicles formed by the projecting book-cases a few sit at tables, and, in their soutanes, they look like mediæval clerks. One is copying a passage out of the Summa. Here is a life that goes back to scholastic days, and I wonder what possibility there is of these students becoming inspired by the great statements of Saint Thomas, so that they go forth from these halls to bring to their countrymen "a generosity, a noble confidence in human nature, a manner of giving credit to it, and of counting for the rest on Divine goodness" which is the tradition of Thomistic philosophy.

But one has only to think of the pastorals issued by the bishops who hold their synods here to know that this style in scholasticism is not Maynooth's—not yet, at least. "Dreary" is the word that the historian Lecky used of the Irish bishops' pastorals of fifty years ago, and "dreary" is the word that still describes them. A magnanimous philosophy is certainly not their inspiration. And yet an Irish Catholic cannot stand within the halls of Saint Patrick's College and fail to be stirred by what has been accomplished in them. A little over a hundred years ago students began to come here. They came from a people whose cultural life had been brutally broken, and who had amongst them few men of liberal education; they came with licenses which stated that, although Roman Catholics were, strictly speaking, outcasts, a tolerant Government would permit their being educated for their own peculiar priesthood. When they left Maynooth, these men had to be organizers, administrators, church-builders, leaders in political and social movements. They went into a world that was different from the Continental Catholic world inasmuch as there was neither a traditional philosophy nor a traditional art that they could come in contact with. Stress was laid on the practical rather than on the intellectual side of priesthood. But because of the decency of the lives of the men who came out of Maynooth, their helpfulness to their congregations, their understanding of, and sympathy with, the people, Catholicism in Ireland to-day is a living force.

Maynooth is popular and Maynooth is practical. Its heads are giving attention, not to metaphysics, but to conditions. Their first thought is discipline. They have produced no prelate with a philosophical temper or equipment, no one whose utterance has had a ring of universality. But perhaps they have prepared the way for the advent of such men. None of the Irish priests whom I know seem to think of Maynooth as a place where an intellectual life has been shared with others. The professors, it seems to me, do not think of themselves as being part of any corporate life: when they leave the lecture-hall, each goes to his own room and takes up his studies or his own particular private interest. There is never a gathering of professors in each other's rooms. These fine grey buildings on the plain of Kildare have something about them that is like a barracks as well as a hall of learning.

And something about them that is like a great country-house. I am not surprised to see professors on good mounts going riding, and other professors going to shoot in the coverts near by. Meanwhile, what of the students here? I quote from Daniel Corkery's "Threshold of Quiet" a passage that gives us some idea of what they go through:

He spoke of many other incidents, slight in themselves, yet eloquent of the guarded life that goes on day after day in the college. And Finnbarr, realizing that life, longed to be within its walls. But soon Aherne began to tell of the other side—of the fears, the anxieties, the strict rules. He told of students he knew who had got three "cats," that is, he explained, notice to quit the House; and the faults committed seemed to be very venial indeed—breaches of discipline—small things, far different from giving way to such a fit of passion as caused one to do the most dreadful things. From this, Aherne went on to tell of the sense of unworthiness that swoops down on one unexpectedly, overwhelmingly, and just at the moment, perhaps, when an important step is about to be taken. He gave instances of boys who had entered with reputations for brilliancy failing at their examinations.

"Why?" asked Finnbarr.

"Couldn't study; couldn't concentrate their minds on the work owing to conscientious scruples."

Finnbarr's imagination had never pictured such difficulties.

The Vale of the Liffey

"It is not an uncommon thing," Tim went on, "to have their health break down."

Finnbarr nodded; he did not know what to say; the vision of Maynooth as a place full of high spirits and innocent gaiety was gone.

Aherne began to give some idea of the various degrees in the student's career. One ceremony made Finn forget all the rest; the description was graphic, and his mind could seize it. A year before ordination, sometimes only a few days before, at a certain phase in the rites, the students, who are grouped about the altar, are supposed to take a step forward; it is their visible entrance into God's ministry.

"Look, Finn, as that moment draws near, as they wait for the word that calls on them to take that step, they turn all colours, they go as white as chalk, or green, or blaze up like fire; their knees tremble so that they find themselves hardly able to move; and the whole congregation waits in breathless silence, not an eyelid winking. . . .

"They all step forward?"

"No, not all." And here the student stopped; perhaps he had terrified himself as well as Finnbarr, for he himself had yet to take that forward step, or, perhaps, he had begun to doubt whether it was right for him to talk in the free way he had been doing. "Dear!" said Finnbarr; to this simple word he had reduced all his boyish expletives.

Before they come here the students have had a bent given them that makes it easy for them to adjust themselves to the discipline and the studies of Saint Patrick's. They have been selected for candidates for the priesthood from early boyhood, perhaps, and their interests, their studies, their relations with their contemporaries have all been related to this calling. And so the life in a seminary, with its deprivation of feminine society, does not mean a sudden and tragic break with normal interests.

Their lives here are arduous enough to keep their minds well occupied. They rise early; they attend mass, and after breakfast their studies begin. From nine until three they are in the lecture-halls with a short break for refreshment; then dinner. From four to six they have recreation which, for most of the students, means games—football, hurling, tennis. I have known a good many priests who look back on the playing-field as to their best memory of Maynooth.

They read in the library and in their own rooms. But a book that a student takes to his room is supposed to be out of the library or written by an author who is generally approved of. A young priest, a friend of mine, tells me about a severe reprimand he got for reading a book of Tolstoy's in his room. A dean discovered him reading it. A dean may walk into his room and look over a student's reading or writing: this is regarded as the chief of the hardships inflicted on the students, and there is a feeling that the authorities can very well afford to forego this police-power.

By the time he has received orders and has gone out "on the mission," the young priest is well inured to his special discipline and to the prospect of a non-domestic existence. A brilliant priest whom I know thus describes his early experience to me: "A cross roads with a chapel and the priest's house, a neighbour's house across the way from you, and another neighbour's house five miles away—there is where the young priest is likely to find himself. Then he discovers, if he has notions such as I had, that there is no Irish culture but that there is an Irish Episcopacy who are extremely bothered by moral influences coming to their flocks from more sophisticated countries. When I left Maynooth I could think of myself as repeating to my bishop Alice Meynell's 'Christ in the Universe' and announcing to him that all the theology we need know is in the poem, aye, and expecting him to agree with me. Now I know what the Lord Bishop of Kilcluin would say to me if I repeated a poem to him: 'Father MacArt, are your registers written up to date? I noticed an entry of marriage in pencil, and I want you to remember that your predecessor was a good penman.' Oh, yes! I read philosophy still, and I write on philosophical subjects. But I sit here in a village where there isn't a soul to talk with on any intellectual subject, and I make entries of births, deaths, and marriages, visit the school, talk hours to a man whose daughter has got into trouble, talk more hours to the young man's father, and spend a week trying to make an arrangement that will end in a marriage, and do a hundred other things besides the duties of my ministry. I think more sympathetically than I did about the strictness and the orthodoxy of Maynooth. Yes, Maynooth is orthodox indeed! I remember once when our brilliant and unfortunate Dr. MacDonald was lecturing to us, one of our class said to him, 'You should write that down, sir.' 'If I should write down the Lord's Prayer, the bishops here would find a heresy in it.' But don't suppose that there's no intellectual atmosphere in Maynooth! The review published by the college, the *Irish Ecclesiastical Record*, compares favourably indeed with any review published in English by any university. There isn't an issue that has not an article on a social or philosophical subject that isn't first rate."

In the quadrangle that the grey buildings form there is a garden of the kind that I like to see in Ireland; few varieties of flowers are in it, but there are many varieties of evergreens—myrtles, and dark yews, and green Portugal laurels, and laurels with yellowing leaves. These bright and dark greens are in great plenty, making a garden which an Irish autumn can do itself proud in. In this garden is a tree the like of which I have never seen before, a weeping beech.

A Kildare Man, John Devoy

He was born in 1842 and died in 1928, and I can declare that at the age of eighty John Devoy was still a heroic figure. He had a head that should have been put in bronze, a vigorous, positive head that at fore and sides went steeply up, and in the features of which a sculptor would have discovered all sorts of "planes." This head had a good covering of iron-grey hair and a trim beard. His eyes were fading into dimness—pale blue eyes under shaggy brows; deaf, his effort to hear gave his face a look of impatient attention. He went on a platform as if he were mounting a breach in some forlorn hope, and he spoke as if his utterance was to be the opening of a campaign, always he was a campaigner and always he was opening a campaign.

He was nineteen years old when he left Ireland to join the Foreign Legion in France. Then the Civil War broke out in America, and he sailed to join one of the American armies. He did not join. I forgot to ask him why he did not, and the haphazard recollections which he has written have only a few pages about his personal life and these end with his arrival in France. He was back in Dublin after the American Civil War, helping to organize for an insurrection which was to take place in the middle sixties. Officers trained in the American war were to direct operations: John Devoy always said that they had assurances that General Sheridan would give assistance as soon as the Irish Republican Brotherhood had established a provisional government. Well, the Fenian uprising was made abortive; John Devoy was imprisoned, and on his release he went back to America. For forty years afterwards he lived the life of a revolutionary in exile.

No one has written about such a life—at least, not in English—but how odd, how fascinating a Balzac would have made it with its obscure intrigues, its pointless vendettas, its passionate loyalties to certain ideas, its passionate strivings against obscure personalities, the splits within its groups, its hopes, its momentary triumphs, its odd personal associations.

This is not to imply that John Devoy's life in America was ineffective. Its background had the sort of ineffectiveness that belongs to transplanted revolutionary groups. But he himself was a man of political judgment, and he backed the movements in Ireland that were to have results. His interventions were helpful. He went over to Ireland to forward the work of the Land League. He realized the helpfulness of an alliance between Parnell and the Fenian organizations, and he promoted such an alliance. He supported the Irish Volunteers and worked to form an auxiliary in America which was to help them with funds and munitions. He saw the revolutionary movement succeed: it did not bring about everything he had worked for, but he knew that Irish independence had been made possible by the settlement reached. The treaty and the Free State that came out of that treaty he supported; that support meant an alliance that was very valuable for the young state: had John Devoy and his friends stood out for the letter rather than the spirit of Irish freedom the forces opposed to the settlement might have been able to wreck it. So John Devoy's life in America was purposeful and not unsuccessful. He realized that a movement in Ireland that aimed at revolution should have an auxiliary in America to aid it, and he worked to keep such an auxiliary in being in the Clan-na-Gael; he gave the Clan an organ in the *Gaelic American*.

It is difficult for Irish people of later generations to understand the personnel of the group to which young John Devoy attached himself. They were members of the Irish Republican Brotherhood who came to name themselves Fenians or Fianna after the heroic companionship told of in the old stories. We see their pictures in albums—massive, bearded, but mild-looking men who struck attitudes and made orations and originated policies which seem to us to be at the limit of hopefulness and inexperience. "What trained American officers can we get?" John Devoy asked the head of the brotherhood. "Three thousand from Chicago alone," he was told. Under criticism the statement was amended to mean the states that had Chicago for centre. But if the Fenian organization had been able to get three hundred trained officers from the whole American area it would have accomplished an astounding feat. The estimate of the executive shows what a sanguine world these men lived in. Probably they were not politically-minded nor militarily-minded at all, but men of the romantic movement whose expression went into swords and charges and defiance of political powers. Probably theirs was the only way the romantic movement could get into Ireland: their leaders all had connections with a France in which Victor Hugo was still a dominating figure. When O'Donovan Rossa, a Gaelic speaker and one acquainted with the heroic tradition, had them adopt the name of Fenians he characterized them: they were really like men out of a simpler past—simple-minded, unreflective, and, of course, brave and devoted. They came at a period in which Irish public life was at a wretched level; although they failed in their insurrectionary project they gave an example to the country which had an effect, an example of courage and devotion. They won immediate reforms through some terroristic activities, but their single-mindedness and devotion were their real contribution to Irish history.

John Devoy was the last of that companionship. Like several of the others he had remained unmarried, probably because he had been in prison or in strange surroundings at a time when he would have made attachments and entered into intimacies. And like many of the other Irish leaders of that epoch he was prim about sex-topics—shy rather than prim, I should say. He could never assume the air of a man of the world on such subjects. I remember his drawing me into a corner of his office to whisper that a politician we were expecting was a "bye-child." But although he could not assume the air of a man of the world he could adopt a speech that was full of the queer, far-fetched, salty expressions that peasantry use when they are in a Rabelaisian humour—a simple-minded scandalousness was often in his talk. He was no Chesterfield in his way of writing about opponents. His public speaking and his writing belonged to the tradition created by Daniel O'Connell, the tradition of overwhelming abuse. "These Ponsonboys are the curse of my country. Personally and politically they are all prostitutes, from the bedizened hag grinning in the grille above me to the white-livered scoundrel now shivering on the floor before me"—that vituperation characteristic of an earlier period in Irish public life was the style that John Devoy was wont to deliver himself in. I always felt that the fault was not so much in him as in the tradition he spoke and wrote out of. And he got as good as he gave. I remember his showing me letters he had received from people in Irish factions in America who differed from him on some point or another—they were as vituperative as anything I ever heard or read.

In a ramshackle office he conducted the *Gaelic American*, writing a great part of that weekly himself. I have spoken about the odd personal associations that exiled revolutionaries are apt to form. The oddest I ever knew existed in this office, the association between John Devoy and an extraordinary man whose name was George Freeman. George Freeman had been an officer in the British Army in the Crimean War; he had attended the meetings of the Bulgarian Constituent Assembly, and he knew Europe as a military expert might know it. Someone I knew tried to find a limit to his knowledge of political and military Europe. This man had come from an obscure village in Bukowina: he mentioned a hill near his place, and George Freeman told him its height to the metre. He seemed to have correspondents in every town from Canada to India. But at whose disposal did he put his vast fund of information? Could it all have been for the Clan-na-Gael? If so, George Freeman was like the elephant who had taken it upon himself to feed a nest of partridge—he must have brought what would suffice for a great power to this little group. How he came to connect himself with the *Gaelic American* I could never guess, but there he was, and no one in the office ever showed any surprise when they saw him seated at his desk, his head completely bald, giving vent to gleeful chuckles as some political prophecy of his came off, and looking like a great criminal who had become well disposed towards society. He was a fascinating person at a dinner-table, talking with the utmost vividness of people he knew and events he had watched sixty years before. But what had brought about the association between him and John Devoy?

John Devoy told me about his early life and about his birthplace in County Kildare. I was aware that he was writing his recollections, so I made no special effort to hold in my mind what he told me then. It was in August 1915 and I had to see him in his office about some affair. Serious events were happening; the *Arabic* had been sunk by a submarine, and the entrance of America into the war was becoming a possibility. Being tired, I suppose, of thinking about public affairs that day he began to talk personally—about his childhood in Kildare, about his ancestry. His family was not French but Gaelic, he said; his great-grandfather who had lived to be over a hundred was a tenant of the Duke of Leinster. His grandmother had been a waiting-maid to Lord Edward Fitzgerald's favourite sister. His grand-uncle had been a leader of the Kildare men in the insurrection of 1798, and he himself had heard from the men of the next generation the ballads that the rebels had sung on their march and in their camp. He was brought up with brothers and sisters on a farm that was only half an acre; his father had some trouble with the landlord, and the family went to live in Dublin. John spent two years learning Irish. He told me (I cannot find this incident in his haphazard recollections) that the great scholar, Eugene O'Curry, came to the school he attended, put his hand on his head, and said to him, "You will be addressing the hosts of the Gael in the tongue of the Gael." "But I never learned Irish," he said to me, and then he added, "I have never finished anything." He thought he had entered Irish affairs too young, before he had given himself an education. He had, I thought, all the cultivation he needed for what he was, the stormy campaigner for national liberty. However, I was very much surprised to discover that he had read a great deal as a youth; he tells us in his recollections that when John O'Leary asked him what he had read he was able to write down:

Sallust (in English), Gibbon, Hallam's "Middle Ages," Schlegel's "Philosophy of History," Edmund Burke's Speeches, Lecky's "Leaders of Public Opinion in Ireland," The English Poets and Robert Burns, Voltaire's "L'Age de Louis Quatorze," Madame de Staël's "L'Allemagne," Molière's Comedies, Racine, Boileau, many of Balzac's novels, nearly all of Alexandre Dumas, Rancke's "Lives of the Popes," all Sir Walter Scott's work including his life of Napoleon, and most of Dickens.

He was admirable for his single-mindedness and devotion. Throughout his long lifetime in America, Irish independence was the issue that was paramount for him. He went to bed at night thinking of it, and he

[221]

rose up in the morning to carry his thought into action of some kind. He had no home; he had a room in a hotel that was alongside the elevated railway. Perhaps his deafness shut off the noise of the trains which went by every few minutes. He was always devising plots, always exposing plots, always involved in the politics of a secret society. What realization, then, did this violent and devoted man achieve or look forward to? His success, first of all, was in the fact that the politics of Irish revolution were not utterly quelled and defeated upon the American scene. The Clan-na-Gael was kept in being, and it was kept in being mainly through his effort, his influence. And then he saw a revolutionary movement in Ireland succeed. Distrust of English authority was in nearly everything he wrote, everything he said. And yet I never heard him speak except with sympathy of the English people. I remember his telling me how he made some sort of ornament out of the seals that were on his order for release so that he might have something to present to the governor of the prison, an Englishman of whom he used to speak with affection and admiration. John Devoy was not an embittered man. And once I saw him looking as a man might whose dream had been realized. It was in Dublin where he was the guest of the Free State Government. He was back after an absence of thirty years; he saw the flag of an Irish state, he watched the march of an Irish army. And as the soldiers went past they saluted John Devoy. He stood inside the grounds of the Leinster Lawn, grasping the railing and looking at the men, the horses, and the guns go by. There was a look of intentness and raptness on the veteran's face that I shall remember.

The Hunt

Men in red coats, women in black riding-habits stay on their horses around the market-place. Dogs come slipping amongst them; they put their forefeet delicately down on the ground, their raised tails curve backwards, they have falling ears. As the horses whinny, as the dogs pad around, as the men and women address, soothe, or encourage the creatures, one senses the old comradeship between man and the beasts he hunts with, perhaps with the beasts he hunts. There is tenseness in the market-place; the horses are restive, the hounds patient but anxious, the men and women expectant. At last a start is made. Along the road by the river horses and hounds go. The field-beasts become excited as they pass by. An old horse gallops down to the fence; donkeys gaze over gates; cows raise their heads; sheep bunch themselves together and look sheepishly at the procession; pigs snort and scurry round. All are excited by this passing of horses and men. All except the goats. The goats give it a glance but refuse to take an interest, and go on cropping the hedges. And now one sees riders coming down laneways and showing their red coats under brown-leaved trees. The dogs become encouraged as the horses break into gallop; they lift their heads and one hears their deep-sounding, bell-like cries.

Cross Roads in Ireland

I went beyond the fields and came to the plain that is called the Curragh of Kildare. Ten thousand sheep were on it, grazing in many great flocks. This part of Kildare is like part of England—the downlands and Salisbury Plain. Sheep in flocks as large as these cannot be seen in any other part of Ireland—the Gael is a herdsman, not a shepherd. And I was reminded by the English look of the country hereabouts that poetry in Early English was written in Kildare:

> This song wrought a friar
> Jesus Christ be his succour,
> Lord, bring him to the tower,
> Friar Michael Kildare;
> Shield him from helle bower
> When he shall from hence fare!
> Lady, flower of all honour,
> Cast away his care;
> From the schour of paines sure
> Thou shield him here and there! Amen.[1]

I thought of writing a story about Kildare. The plain with its sheep came before me, and with it a memory of this poetry. What I wrote was based on an English Nativity Play. The speech I used was that of the country people here.

Kildare Story: The Shepherds

"Boys, O boys," said the First Shepherd, "this season is very severe! I'm in dread to stand on my

[1] "Anglo-Irish Literature, 1200 to 1582," by St. John D. Seymour.

feet," said he, "for my two legs might break under me, they're that stiff with the cold. And my hands are perished too! Well them that's born to it know the hardship! We're abroad east and west, day and dark, without rest or comfort, and for all our striving we're near out of the door with the poverty."

"No wonder we're that way," said the Second Shepherd, "for them that are above us are keeping us down; we have to be doing this and that for them, and our own fields, little as they are, have to be left as fallow as the mud floor at home. 'Give us a day's work here,' says the landlord. 'Send a yoke and a horse there,' says the steward, and if we refused either of them, we'd be between the mill-stones. It would be a miracle, I say, if we could thrive at all. I wonder when I see the people dressed up, for I wouldn't know when Sundays or holidays come around, I'm that bent to the hardship."

"The man that's married is the worst off," said the Third Shepherd. "He's in the shackles in earnest. 'As sharp as a thistle, as rough as a briar!' Could you tell me the meaning of that riddle, honest men? It means a wife. I wish I had run until I had lost my woman!"

They were talking like this, three shepherds out in the plain in the middle of winter, as they kept watch over the flocks that were around them. It was then that their serving-boy came to them, and he whinging for his supper. "High hanging to you," said the First Shepherd to him, "you're thinking of your stomach early in the night."

"The bit to eat is always late in coming to the serving-boy," said the lad. "He sweats and strives while his masters take their ease. His hire is late in coming to him, and there's a good hole made in it if he makes a slip at all."

"When it's ready you'll get your supper with the rest of us," said the shepherds.

They were making it ready when Mac, the vagabond, came to where they were, all wrapped up in his old cloak. "Storm and wind and rain," he was saying, "I never saw the like of it! Since Noah there were never such floods. If the prophecies don't come to pass now they'll never come to pass. No wonder that I heard a shepherd say: 'We that are watching at night may well see strange sights.'"

It was then that the shepherds saw him, and they called out to him, asking him who he was. "I'm a man going on a journey," said Mac, the vagabond.

"It's Mac, I declare," said the Second Shepherd. "Come here, Mac, and tell us your news."

"It's Mac, is it?" said the Third Shepherd. "Then anyone who wants to keep his own had better look after it."

"I'm a man sent on a journey by a great gentleman," said Mac. "Be civil-spoken to me. If I made a complaint I'd get every one of you gaol."

"It's the stroke of my crook I'll give him," said the Third Shepherd. "It's Mac. Look at the devil in his eyes."

And when that was said to him he came near them.

The Vale of the Liffey

"I know you now," said Mac. "You're good companions. God save the three of you."

"You have a name for something, Mac," said the Third Shepherd, "and if you travel so late people will say that you're for stealing a sheep."

"I'm a man that has to keep moving," said Mac.

"How is your wife?" said the First Shepherd.

"She's by the fire at home, poorly enough, amongst a houseful of children."

So then the shepherds asked him to their fire, and he came and sat with them by it, and they gave him a share of what they had, and he ate his supper with them. After that the shepherds asked the boy to sing a ballad to them, and after he had sung one ballad and another, the First Shepherd said:

"I could sleep on a furze-bush. Before anyone in the parish I was out of my sleep this morning."

"I'll sleep if I was to lose fourpence by it," said the Second Shepherd. "I'm harassed with walking the grounds."

"I tell you that if there was a harrow under me I wouldn't find it hurting me," said the Third Shepherd; and he lay down. The boy kept watch.

"Come and sit by the fire with me, Mac," said the boy. And after a while he said: "I'm as good a man's son as any of them. I'll lie down too. And you, Mac," said he, "lie down beside me and put your cloak over the two of us."

So the shepherds and their boy slept, and after a while Mac, the vagabond, rose up, saying to himself,

"A man that's in want might take something now. He might go into the fold yonder and steal a sheep." He stood up, and he looked to the fold and he looked on the shepherds and their boy who were lying there. "I'll work a spell on them first," said he.

So he went over to them, and he made a circle round them with his staff, saying the spell he made up:

"Let there be round you a circle, as round as the moon—
Let you lie stone-still till it be done.
Over your heads my hands I lift,
Out go your eyes, your sight I shift.
Manus tuas commando
Pontio Pilato."

"I was never a shepherd," said he, "but now I'll learn the trade."

He went to the fold and opened the hurdle and a sheep came out to him. "I'm obliged to you for drawing near to me," he said; and he put the sheep across his shoulder. "You'll take our house out of sorrow to-night," said he.

When Mac went into his house, Gill, his wife, was spinning by the fire, and the children were crowding hungrily around her. They were in dread and they were in gladness when they saw the sheep that he carried in with him.

"Before the night is over we'll have meat on the coals," said Mac. "This twelvemonth I hadn't such a taste for mutton as I have now."

"If you kill it they'll hear the sheep bleat," said Gill, his wife. "You're not so far from them now."

"Aye, and then they'd come here and take me," said Mac. "What will we do about it?"

"Mac, here's a plan," said Gill. "We'll tie it up and hide the live sheep in the child's cradle."

"A good plan, good woman," said Mac; and he and his wife went and tied the sheep up. Then they put it in the child's cradle and covered it over.

"I don't care who spies now," said Gill, Mac's wife. "Go out again, you," said she, "and keep near them, so that they won't think you had any hand in carrying away their sheep."

"It's a good plan," said Mac, "and a woman's advice helps in the end." So he went back to where the shepherds were, and he lay down beside the boy.

"My foot's asleep," said the First Shepherd, wakening up.

"Lord, I've slept well," said the Second Shepherd. "I feel as light as the leaf on the tree."

"We were four," said the Third Shepherd, jumping up. "Do you see Mac? I dreamt that he came before us in a wolf's skin."

"Your dreams make you wild. There's Mac lying down by the boy. Waken up, Mac."

"Catch hold of my hand, someone," said Mac when they came to him. "I can't stand up. My neck's lain wrong. Oh, and I had a dream that's worse than all. I dreamt that there was another youngster in our house since the cock-crow. God help me that has so many children and such little earning. I must go home. But watch me now so that I won't have the name of stealing anything on you."

So he went from them then, leaving the shepherds talking together, one saying that he would go before the other to the pasture with his sheep, and that they all should meet before evening at The Crooked Thorn.

Mac came to his door and knocked at it. "Who's making that stir?" said Gill, his wife.

"Gill, it's Mac," said he, and she opened the door, and he came in and stood on the floor of the house.

"However the game goes they'll blame me," said he. "I believe they'll come after me here and that soon. We'll have to take them cunningly."

"Then," said Gill, "we'll put more wrapping around the sheep and keep it in the cradle. You rock it and sing lullaby. And I'll lie by the wall and cry out as if in my pains, and if we don't baffle them that way never trust to me again."

All day then they kept the stolen sheep in the child's cradle, and the knife to kill it wasn't taken into Mac's hand; night came down; the rush-candle was lighted, and the children gathered around the fire. But still Gill lay by the wall, and still Mac sat by the cradle and sang lullaby into it. The night was wearing on when a clatter came to the door.

"Mac, open the door," said one outside.

"Who's there? Tell me that first," said the man of the house.

"Open."

"Will ye not speak soft over a sick woman's head?" said he. But he went and opened the door.

The shepherds were there, but Mac stood between them and the threshold.

"God save ye," said he. "My wife's brought another one home to me. God knows we had enough in the house, but then we must eat as we bake. Come in," said he to them then, seeing that they were for pushing by him. "Is there anything on ye that isn't good?" said Mac.

"There is, in troth," said the First Shepherd. "Our good sheep that's stolen."

"Stolen, did you say?" said Mac. "A sheep stolen! Well," said he, "if I had been there I'll engage I'd have been blamed for something."

"There are some that think you were there," said the Second Shepherd.

"Come. Rip up the house then," said Mac. "My wife wasn't up since she laid down there. I wasn't out of the house since the time you saw me. But come and look around you. If you find sheep, goat, or cow here I'll let you put me under a harrow."

"Out, thieves, out!" said Gill.

"Do ye hear how she goes on?" said Mac. "Your heart would melt if you had to be listening to her groans."

"If ever I wronged ye," said Gill, turning round to the shepherds, "I pray that I may eat what lies there in the cradle."

"Peace, woman," said Mac to her. "My brain will

jump off me listening to my poor woman's complaints,"
said he to the shepherds. "Easy, easy, Gill. You'll
split my heart with your moaning."

"Our sheep is stolen," said the Third Shepherd,
"and it's our business to look about it."

"Our labour's lost," said the First Shepherd, "and
we may as well go home. Hard or soft, salt or fresh,
there's no flesh here except the child in the cradle."

"God save my child from the hands and eyes of ill-
wishers," said Gill.

"We've missed the mark," said the Second Shepherd. "Our respects to you, ma'am," said he to Gill,
"and our blessing on what's in the cradle. Is the child
a boy?"

"A boy he is," said Mac, "and a lord might be proud
to have him for a son. When he wakens up he skips in
a way that would delight you."

"May his steps be happy," said the First Shepherd.
"Who stood for him?"

"Two honest men that we are known to."

"You should have asked one of us," said the Third
Shepherd. "We're friends and neighbours, you know."

"I'm glad I'm not in any way beholden to your
friendship," said Mac. "Good-bye to ye," said he as
they stepped across the threshold, "we won't be lonesome for you when you're gone."

He hadn't closed the door before one of the shepherds said: "Did you leave anything for the child in
the cradle?"

"It never came into my mind to put as much as a

farthen in his hand," said the First Shepherd. "Wait for me," said he, "I'll leave sixpence in the cradle." He went back into the house then, and he said: "Mac, don't take it badly that I've come back."

"I take it badly enough. You brought an ill mind into my house," said Mac.

"By your leave, I'll leave something with the child," said the First Shepherd; and before Mac could stop him, he was at the cradle. But Mac said to him:

"Go away. The child is sleeping."

"I see him looking out at us," said the First Shepherd. "What the devil is this?" said he then. "Mac, your child has got a snout on him."

"He's marked amiss, God between us and harm," said the Second Shepherd.

"What's ill-spun comes out badly," said the Third Shepherd. "In troth, this is our sheep. Do ye see how they've swaddled his four feet in the middle?"

It was then that Gill sprang out of the bed and came to them. "The child was changed by the fairies," said she. "I saw it done myself as I was sitting there by the fire."

"This is false work," said the First Shepherd. "Get your weapons, men."

"If I've done any trespass, you may strike me down," said Mac.

"We'll strike you down, and we'll leave you for dead," said the First Shepherd. "Lay on him, men."

"And these are the men that were spoken of in the

prophecies," said Mac, "and now they'd beat a poor man in his own house."

"What prophecies do you speak of, Mac?" said the First Shepherd.

"They that watch at night may well see strange sights!"

"And maybe it were better that we were watching at night," said the First Shepherd, "instead of being here."

But they had raised their hands against him when they heard the hymn that we now call Gloria in Excelsis. The cabin they stood in was all filled with light, and they saw an angel of the Lord outside.

"O hired men," said the angel, "be gentle with each other, for God is your friend. To-night is born a Child that will free Adam's race."

Gill spoke. "Where is the Child?" said she.

"In Bethlehem, between two beasts. I bid ye go there," said the angel. Then he passed on, singing:

> "Hail, comely and clean; hail, young Child
> That is born this night of a maiden mild."

They laid down their staves and they went outside. "He spoke of a Child that is lying in Bethlehem," said the First Shepherd.

"Of God's Son in Heaven he spoke the word," said the Second Shepherd.

"The star shines above Him. Let us go seek Him," said the Third Shepherd.

They went from that house and towards Bethlehem.

The Vale of the Liffey

"It is as true as steel what the prophets spoke," said one to the other. "As poor as we are, and as simple as we are, we the shepherds," they said, "would be the first to find Him when He appeared in the world."

PART V

East and South

The Slaney

FROM Kildare I went into Carlow, littlest of Irish counties, and following the Slaney's course, went into Wexford. Below Enniscorthy the Slaney becomes a river that is wide, full and swift-flowing; a river that makes the Liffey and the Boyne seem unabundant. And as I walk by the river-side I have the constant and ever-changing music that the wind makes in the tops of the reeds, for the river here has sedgy sides. Water-hens are feeding in pairs on the open margins, and grey herons lift themselves out of the reeds. And where the river makes a bend I come on a sight that I shall long remember—a hundred swans on the ground, moving their wings. On the river are white birds—swans or sea-gulls, I cannot make out which, for the rain has begun to come down, and what I look towards is blurred. I wonder what a grouping of swans as big as the one I saw would be called—they speak of "a muster of peacocks," "a stand of partridge," "a gaggle of geese." But how is a great company of swans named?

I knew I had come into the barony of Shelmalier, the place in Wexford known for its fowlers. "The

WICKLOW MOUNTAIN BY MAURICE MCGONIGAL

bold Shelmalierer" is noted in the Wexford songs of
the 1798 insurrection: the other Wexfordmen fought
with the pike, but he had a gun, a long fowling-piece.
The Shelmalierers were good marksmen, for they had
shot along these banks and from cots on the river—
there must be quantities of wild duck here.

I could not see across the water at this point. The
rain had begun to fall, and in all my life I had never
looked into such greyness. The clouds were undefined
because the sky was a single cloud that dropped and
dripped; the clumps of trees were black, and the fields
were patches of wistful green; the grey of the sky was
identical with the grey of the wide river, and the flats
by the river were grey also. It was greyness so complete that one could not help but get some satisfaction
out of it. It was like a poem of Verhaeren's in which
one is won to a crepuscular mood through insistence
and monotony. But I should not have given that com-
fortless day such credit if I had not seen the hundred
swans.

Wexford: The Town

In a little eating-house that I went into two men
were before the fire. One was on the single chair that
was there and the other knelt on one knee before the
blaze. I sat at the table and ate my mutton and potatoes. The man who knelt by the fire was young; his
look was intent, and he held an ash-plant in his hand
in a way that gave him the appearance of the bronze
pike-holder of the monument in the market-place.

The other had a light switch in his hand. I knew them for cattle-drovers who had brought their beasts to the fair that day.

The younger man who knelt by the fire—it was his position that gave him that look of intentness—did not speak at all. I liked his looks. His eyes were grey, and his face, I thought, showed that there was some music in him. The other had a toughened, thickened face with protruding lips. He was garrulous. He told me about his day—up at six in the morning, standing about the fair all day, eating a sandwich at twelve o'clock, coming in here for his tea now that the beasts had been put upon the train. He talked about adventures he had had in towns in Carlow, Kildare, and Wexford, none of them of much interest. He was from the Midlands, and the young man was of Wexford.

I asked the talkative man to sing to us. "I'd like to do something to oblige you," he said. He was urged a little by his kneeling companion. Then he began to make ready to sing. His preparations were unusual. He took off his hat and showed a closely cropped head. He made a lot of movements towards pulling himself together. Then he opened his mouth. Vocables came forth in a distinguishable rhythm. The rhythm had the irregularity and the gustiness of wind upon the hillside and the vocables were few and far between and formed no intelligible order of speech. He made gestures that added to the mystery of his chant. At what I conceived to be the significant part of his utterance he darted a finger towards me. His manner was solemn.

I thought of a Lapland sorcerer uttering an incantation while he handed to a mariner a bag containing the winds. The vocables came like the rain emptying from the gutters on the roof; the breath behind them was gusty. And then I heard sounds that seemed to make familiar words. Were they Irish? Were they that "ould English" that was spoken in some of the Wexford baronies until recently? I could not make out. The singer became more enthusiastic. He seized my hand and he sang straight at me. I heard words. They were "Beau—ty's . . . home . . . Kil—a—ar—n'y. . . . Heav'—n's re—flex . . . Kil—a—ar—ny'y." And so the vocables which I could have believed were an invocation to a boreal Æolus were derivatives from the most banal of concert-room songs. Having finished, the singer put his hand in mine; I shook it. The young man who still knelt by the fire nodded his appreciation of the singer's accomplishment and my acknowledgment of it. Then the singer swung back to his seat by the fire. Often, I imagined, the young man had heard "Killarney" sung as the two tramped after their herds. He must have got something very stirring and solemn out of it.

The streets of Wexford have the narrowness that belongs to a town that was once walled. But except the house that Cromwell lodged in when the Ironsides were here it has no ancient building. Selskar Abbey where, as I was told, Henry the Second secluded himself one Easter in penance for the murder of Becket, is beside the town—a ruin, of course. In the narrow main street the rain was running off the roofs of the houses and clattering down the gutters. I went through the town. I looked at the Ninety-eight monument that is the work of my friend Oliver Shepherd—a young Wexford man advancing, an insurrectionist's pike in his hand. It is in bronze; the best monument, I suppose, that any Irish country town has (except, perhaps, Shepherd's monument to the novelist, Charles Kickham, in the town of Tipperary). I went down to the water-side and looked on the beached boats with sea-gulls resting on them and on the fishing-boats in the harbour with bare masts. Everything seemed very patient of the rain. Now Wexford is not a rainy county, but on two occasions when I have been in the town it rained very insistently. It is a county full of interesting places. But nothing memorable ever happened to me in any of them. So if I wrote about them I should be merely descriptive. (And yet the Slaney at Ferrycarrig with the Norman keep on the height above it and Rosslare with sands that remind one of a picture by A. E. are enchanting places.)

When his Stella went on a visit to Wexford County Swift wrote her that she should observe the people she went amongst: they were the descendants of the original English in Ireland, speaking an English that was centuries out of date. She would see magpies, too, her mentor told her: the magpie had been brought into Ireland from England, and he seemed to think that these birds would mostly be found where the Englishry had old establishments—a simple-minded notion

for a great dean to entertain! Wexford at its southern
end was the landing-place of the first Norman invaders
—Fitzstephen's little band: there is the point of Bag-
inbun, where, as the old bit of doggerel has it, "Ireland
was lost and won." The first English towns were in
this county—Bannow, whose site is now covered by
the sea, and New Ross, which was founded by Strongbow's daughter.

In the days when there was possibility of English
speech vanishing out of Ireland, the Anglo-Irish looked
to Wexford County as the seat of the remnant who
had preserved the "ould English." In Elizabethan
times a great deal of interest was aroused by the discovery that the farmers of Forth and Bargy spoke the
English of Chaucer's time. They spoke it into the nineteenth century, and words and terms out of this language still linger in Wexford dialect. But this did not
prevent the men of Forth and Bargy from using their
pikes against King George's men in 1798.

Wexford County has had plenty of political history.
It already had a name from a Norse settlement (Waes-
fjord) when the Normans made their incursion. Dermot MacMurrough, King of Leinster, had his seat
here, and it was he who called upon them to cross the
Irish Sea and give him aid in his quarrel with the
high-king of Ireland—the unending quarrel between
the kings of Leinster and the high-kings. The Normans
would have come into Ireland in any case, and perhaps we should try to remember Dermot as the king
who had made the compilation that contains a version

of our great epic tale, the "Book of Leinster." The second English invasion of Ireland, Cromwell's, also left its mark on the county: Wexford was taken after Drogheda; there is a tale of a subsequent massacre around the Market Cross. But I leave Wexford without being harrowed in any way by this probable happening. I remember once hearing from an old priest whom I used to visit when I was young (he was more or less retired at the time because of his unconventional views of Irish politics and his outspoken distrust of the compromises that were being suggested) these memorable words: "As for the men and women who knelt around the Market Cross in Wexford and begged Cromwell for mercy, Cromwell didn't massacre half enough of them. He spared too many to leave descendants amongst us." A good saying, and if it had been posted up on the site of every massacre in Ireland there would have been a good deal less failure in Irish history. At Clonmel where the defence under young Hugh O'Neill was a great and resourceful one, there was no massacre, and Oliver, who had borne great losses, behaved like a real soldier. And anyway he had to bear the rain round here. "It being so terrible a day as ever I marched in all my life," he wrote when he had to abandon his attempt on Waterford.

A Performance

And so I came to the Barrow River and the town of New Ross. In early Norman days New Ross must have been a good town. We have a thirteenth-century poem about the entrenching of it that shows its inhabitants as numerous, well organized, and lively.

Outside a broken gateway, The Bishop's Gate, I think, there was a huddle of sightseers. They were watching a performance. Ass-carts belonging to folk going into or out of the town were drawn up by the side of the road, and men and women, boys and girls, were watching the gyrations of a tumbler. He had laid a strip of carpet on the ground: now, with his head between his legs, he was running on all fours towards us. The crowd were excited; they seemed to be amused, too, for there was a good deal of laughter. The man unfolded himself, stood up, and made grave acknowledgments of the applause. He was in tunic and pants, and across his chest were a row of medals which had been presented to him, no doubt, by the crowned heads of Europe before whom he had given the same surprising performance. He had a heavy Roman head which was quite bald. A few pennies were thrown on his carpet, and he began a simpler performance—somersaults which delighted the youngsters, and, I imagine, aroused active ambitions in them. I did not wait for the completion of the performance, but went away meditating on the lives of travelling tumblers. They have always seemed to me to be the loneliest, the most tragic of roadside performers. I suppose they have to be very absorbed in their mystery—that would account for the aloofness that one feels around them. And practising such a perilous mystery they must scorn association with unaccomplished fellows whom they meet on the roads, ballad-singers and mere tramps. Anyway, they go aloof and alone. No one ever saw a company, a troupe, or even two or three tumblers going together. They go on their ways more alien than the communicative fortune-tellers. I have often thought of a particular tumbler that he must have a grand name, "Theodore" or the like.

Waterford

From New Ross I go down the Barrow to Waterford. The Nore had joined the Barrow, then the Suir, flowing down from Tipperary County, meets this river. The confluence gives Waterford a water-front. But the shipping I saw on it was not worthy of the grand bend of river. Still, there was shipping enough to give the town the look of an emporium. I look across the river, to round, green hills.

Along the quay I go, and at one end I come to a round, squat tower. I go within. Men were once imprisoned here: they must have felt themselves jailed; the movement of the town was close to them, but, muffled by this thickness of wall, how far away it would have seemed! More than a hundred years before Strongbow and his Normans came to Waterford Reginald the Dane planted this tower here! I go to its top. Looking across its parapet I see the sloping city, and the river flowing towards the channel that divides Ireland from Wales. Strongbow came here with a force that converted the Norman landing from an incursion to an invasion; Henry the Second arrived afterwards with a great force; Prince John, Richard the Second, and Prince Hal came here, not to speak of Perkin Warbeck (but the gate was closed on that weak impostor), and yet there is hardly a relic of Plantagenet times to be seen here, except the names of people and the racial strains the names reveal. Prendergast and Power (le Poer), names common in the town, show that the lines of the first conquistadores are in existence still. But they have not displaced the older names. O'Faelain, or O'Phelan, or Whelan, names belonging to the Desi Gael, still flourish. And the name of the city with this tower that is the oldest and strongest structure in it make us know that the Danish strain here must be a strong one.

The barber in the shop near it talked to me about the tower when I sat in his chair. "Did you ever hear Percy French, sir?" he began.

I said I had heard him tell his stories and sing his songs.

"Did you ever hear him tell about how Strongbow came to Waterford? 'Dick,' says Strongbow, 'put a shovel of slack on the fire and leave the kettle on the hob till I get back. I'm going over to take Waterford.'"

"Dick?"

"The king who was in it at the time."

"I thought his name was Henry."

"Then he'd have said 'Hal,' wouldn't he?"

"I expect he would."

". . . Till I get back from taking Waterford. Strongbow married the King of Leinster's daughter here, Eva."

"In the tower, wasn't it?"

"No, along the river here. Do you remember the picture in the National Gallery, Dublin, 'The Marriage of Eva and Strongbow'?"

I asked in a strained voice when he had seen that picture.

"It's thirty-five years since I left the capital, and I'm in Waterford ever since. It's above that time since I saw it. But I remember that picture well."

So did I. I tried to replace it in my memory with some other picture—a Rembrandt, a Goya—but I couldn't. "The Marriage of Eva and Strongbow" came before me as immovably as Reginald's Tower. It was an enormous canvas and it was filled with figures and objects. Every detail of it was buried in my unconsciousness and it only needed the barber's reminiscence to bring it all before me. In the foreground were the nuptial pair—a grim, sworded earl grasping the hands of an innocent whose eyes were modestly and fearfully cast down. In the background was a round tower and a stormed wall. There were heaps of slain along the sides, weak women and great-thewed men, and there was a monk whose eyes were raised in direful prophecy. There was an ancient harper bending over his harp, the strings of which were broken. The painter, Daniel Maclise, had combined the allegorical with the historical; the picture had once taken up the whole

[246]

end of a room in the National Gallery—perhaps it had been a warning to those who would have painted pictures on historical subjects.

"Waterford is a very historical place," said the barber. "The picture we were talking about, sir, did you see it lately?"

I told him that "The Marriage of Eva and Strongbow" had been retired. He looked as if he thought that the National Gallery had got rid of its prime attraction.

I walked towards the other end of the quay. As in all places to which rivers flow and roads run and new routes open from, in Waterford there are many vagrom men. I like talking with such. The river Mississippi came into a conversation with one. We were both looking down into the water, and I gave him a cigarette.

"Yes," I said, "I have been at the Mississippi."

"Tell me," said he earnestly, "is it known at all, the place where they pushed him in?"

"Whom?" I asked.

"The general," he said. "He had won all the wars he was in, and he was on his way to beat the English— he would have done it—and they knew what he was up to, and when the boat he was on came to a certain place on the Mississippi—it was a dark night and the place was a lonesome place—they pushed him in, and from that day to this, tale or tidings of him has been none. I'd have thought they'd show you the place where Thomas Francis Meagher was last seen and heard tell of."

Cross Roads in Ireland

To my friend the course of the Mississippi was no longer than that of the Barrow, the Suir, or the Nore, and Thomas Francis Meagher's personality and career were as much noted abroad as at home. He was arrested in his house beside the quay after he had made a speech in reply to O'Connell's foolish statement that the winning of national freedom was not worth the spilling of human blood. The church bells of Waterford were rung in alarm at his arrest; the mob surrounded the coach that was bearing him away and cut the traces of the horses that were drawing it. But he was taken from Waterford. Then he escaped and went to America and became a commandant in the Irish regiments in the Civil War. After the war he lost his life somewhere in the waters of the Mississippi. "It's a wonder they never showed you the place," said my friend.

A Ballad-Singer

He belonged to that declining race, the ballad-singers of the Irish streets and roads. These ballad-singers are—or, rather, they were—companionable men. Their way of living brings them into pleasant relations with the world; consequently they are more amiable than tramps, tinkers, race-card vendors, or roulette practitioners. Then, they have not taken to the roads because of any artistry in their natures, and consequently they have none of the reticences of men with the gift—pipers, fiddlers, and the like; they are, moreover, genuine idlers, and, as such, are fond of company. Notice a pair meeting; they go down the road chatting together like two young girls. Of what do they speak? Of someone on the quays of Waterford who sells tobacco cheap because he buys it off the sailors, of the sergeants of the Civic Guard who have been shifted to another town, how such a person in Bally-this or Cahir-that died, and why the public-house he had has been closed, and how such a tinker has become a dangerous fellow since he got a stroke on the head with a bottle. Being more idle than any of us have the chance of being, they can talk with infinite zest and endless detail. They hardly allude to the bleakness of the roads, the rheumatics that winter brings, the un-broken fasts, the casual shelters, and the deaths by the wayside. My friend said to me with great earnestness, "If I was to tell you about the miseries of the poor I would keep you here for three-quarters of an hour." But immediately he went on to more entertaining top-ics. He carried a stick which he swung in the manner of a gilded youth, but with more vivacity, and his gait was part slouch, part march, and part swagger. I saw him in Kilkenny afterwards. He was engaged in earn-est and dignified conversation with one of the Civic Guard. "Do you tell me so? First turning to the right? Thank you, officer." Then he went off swinging his stick, an undersized fellow with frowning brows and a fierce moustache.

But, as I have said, he belongs to an order that is well into its decline. Ballad-making and ballad-singing has its great epoch during the national and political excitement of a people who are hardly literate. The few one meets now are the survivals of the ballad-singers who established themselves with "The Peeler and the Goat," "Murty Hynes," and "God Save Ireland." The period of political excitement is now over and the crowd in the country town is literate. They read their newspapers instead of listening to ballad-singers.

The ballads they have went from the city streets to the country roads. They began by being Anglo-Irish, but as they went away from the city they became crossed with Gaelic influences. Here, for example, is a stanza from a street-song that my friend had; it went back to the Franco-Prussian War; the stanza has a Gaelic rhythm:

On the blood-crimsoned plain the Irish Brigade nobly stood;
They fought at Orleans till the streams they ran with their
    blood;
Far away from their homes in the arms of Death they repose;
They died for poor France, and they fell by the hands of her
    foes.

And there are ballads that show that their makers were more familiar with the Gaelic than with the English verse-structure. I often came across a street-song which reproduced, crudely perhaps, the Gaelic system of internal assonances. Here is an example:

I speak in candour, one night in slumber
My mind did wander near to Athlone,
The centre station of the Irish nation,
Where a congregation unto me was shown.

[250]

East and South

Beyond my counting, upon a mountain,
Near to a fountain that clearly ran;
I fell to tremble, I'll not dissemble,
As they assembled for the rights of man.

But in one of the street-ballads is there anything to
match the simplicity and the beauty of Gaelic folk-
song? Their makers were, for the most part, using a
language with which they were not intimate; they were
putting together words that had to be shouted across a
street and addressed to a moving crowd. Personal emotion need not be put into a street-song. Only a few
such songs have any quality of personal emotion. I
was surprised to find that my friend had a song in
which were lines that had as much feeling as these:

O marriage is a holy tie,
Blest by the Lord above;
But woe be to such marriages
Without one spark of love.
Why is it that in our own dear land
Full of warm hearts and true,
They wed for money, not for love,
As other nations do?

Turning from the quays I go through some short
streets to the centre of the town. The type here, especially as shown in the faces of some of the older
women, is distinctive; different from the type one notes
in Cork or Galway. I saw a woman selling something
at a stall, another standing at her doorway, who, it
seemed to me, had the sort of character that George
Borrow has now and again portrayed: perhaps these

types were common in Tipperary and Waterford when Seorsa (to give him his Irish name) was hereabouts. They were gaunt, aloof, prophetic-looking. From what glimpses I had of the younger generations, I thought that the girls of Waterford were exceptionally pretty and vivacious.

I went to the home of the editor of the *Waterford News*, Edmund Downey. I had known Edmund Downey for a long time back as the editor of the definite edition of Charles Lever's novels. Also as Lever's biographer. We discussed Lever's work. It is so voluminous that I could never read all of it again. The editor named the books that it would be profitable to read: they are "Charles O'Malley," "Tom Burke," "Jack Hinton," "The O'Donoghue," "The Knight of Glynn," "Sir Brooke Fosbrooke," "Lord Kilgobbin," "The Bramleys of Bishop's Folly," and "A Day's Ride." I spoke of the vanished Irish life that is recorded in these books and of the fact that the life of a place such as we were in goes unrecorded. How unfamiliar are the lives lived by families who have been in business or the professions here for generations, and have their own outlook, their own traditions. Apart from their businesses and professions, their interests are sporting: there are three or four hunting-clubs in the neighbourhood, four or five golf-courses, and the sea and river fishing is well attended to. These business and professional families have no civic feelings; they exist in hardly any part of Ireland, as the lack of amenities and conveniences in this ancient town show.

Courtesy of The Hackett Galleries

STRAND BY "A. E."

East and South

More and more the agricultural hinterland dominates the city; the distinctive urban life is on the wane.
The Waterford glass that is so treasured by those who
possess any of it has not been made here for generations. Live-stock—pigs and cattle and sheep—butter,
eggs, potatoes, are the staples which the town does business in. Not a vessel of the shipping in the harbour is
of local register, and Waterford was once known as
"Waterford of the Ships."

A Song of Exile

It was when Waterford was known as "Waterford
of the Ships" that a certain vagrom man came down
to these quays and took passage on a ship that was
bound for Newfoundland. He was a "spoiled" priest
and had been a hedge-schoolmaster, and he had come
along the roads from Tipperary with pig-dealers and
cattle-drovers and butter-sellers, and men making the
voyage to Newfoundland, and bringing with them their
provision for their days at sea. Born in Clare and by
name Macnamara, Donnough Roe, or Red Denis Macnamara, he was a poet whose verse was for the audience of the tavern and the roadside.

Teaching in school was my irksome trade
And 'tis known that that is but poorly paid,
But I banished my woes with wenches and wine
Without thought for the morrow each hour that was mine,
And I made no store for the time of need
But the shilling I earned I spent with speed.

Cross Roads in Ireland

One night as I lay on my lonely bed
I thought of the dreary life I led,
How heavy my toil, how light my gains,
And better it would repay the pains
To work for a farmer at shovelling clay
Or guiding horses or driving a dray,
Or, better, to bide in Erin no more
But leave the land for a kinder shore
And embark with the first fair breeze that blew
To try my fortune in pastures new.

I lightly leaped from my bed next day
With the joy of the thought and would make no stay,
I eagerly grasped my stick, a stout ashen,
And a new felt hat with a flap in the fashion,
And I said farewell to each friend and neighbour,
And to some I said it with no great labour,
And the first ship leaving this churlish strand
Should bear me, I swore, to a bounteous land
Where parts and learning would not be spurned,
Where gold was plenty and easily earned.
Be it known to all what the neighbours brought
Of victuals and drink for my support,
And what provision and goods they gave
To pull me through perils of land and wave.

There were seven stone oatmeal and enough
Of scrapings out of the kneading trough,
And a big black chest so long and deep
'Twould answer alike for store or sleep;
A barrel of red potatoes, too,
That many a day would see me through,
A piece of meat of a mighty size,
A crock of butter with salt likewise;
There were seven score eggs of ducks and hens
To carry me to my journey's ends,

And a cask of ale that had sailed from Spain
And might put life in the dead again.[1]

So Denis was well provisioned. In Waterford he got,
for a while, anyway, treatment as befitted a poet:

> And got lodging and board with a maiden bland,
> The loveliest lass in all the land;
> A grace in her gait and a light in her look,
> With lips that smiled or with laughter shook,
> Buxom and blithe and fond of a jest,
> Kind and complacent to every guest;
>
> She was quick to heed and a handy drawer,
> And each tipple you took she'd taste before
> And by word or deed you could no offend—
> At least if she knew you had money to spend.
> The ways of a woman I can't explain,
> But the smile from me made her smile again.
> She powdered my wig like the sparks of the town,
> And dressed me fully from foot to crown,
> And never intruded the cursed account
> But gave me credit to any amount.
> Her stingy mamma was a different tale. . . .

"The Adventures of a Luckless Lad" is not of much
interest to readers who have not a feeling for "its opu-
lent diction and onward-swelling rhythm." However,
this voyager from Waterford has left us one poem
which, translated, can move us, and which has words
that are steeped in a feeling for a life heroic, simple,
and pure-spirited. It is a poem of exile, "Ban-chnuic

[1] "The Adventures of a Luckless Lad," translated by Percy Arland
Ussher.

Cross Roads in Ireland

Eireann Oighe," The Fair Hills of Eirinn O. Both Mangan and Ferguson have made versions of it, but I am not sure that their words go to that moving air to which the song was written, an air which is "supposed to represent, in its soaring and failing cadences, the curves of the Irish hills." I have made a version of two of the stanzas: they can be sung to this cadenced air. An understanding critic of Gaelic poetry has said of "Ban-chnuic Eireann Oighe," "To Donough, good countryman, the noise of the cattle at evening, as men hear it rising from the valley, is sweeter than the music that foreign fingers pluck from the harp; and he recalls the heavy golden grain, the pastures, the race itself, old men and children, in the evening sunlight on the hills." [1] But Donough's poem is a farewell to an Ireland that is already lost in time as well as in distance, to an Ireland in which the people still thought of themselves as being in the long line that was from Heber. The song was made in some place in Europe:

Bear a blessing from my heart to my land far away,
    And the Fair Hills of Eire O,
And to all of Heber's race who in her valleys stay,
    And the Fair Hills of Eire O.
That land of mine delightful where the brown thrush's song,
Through hazel copse and ivy close fills the summer twilight
       long,
Oh, how woeful sounds his music for the downfall of the
       strong,
    On the Fair Hills of Eire O!

[1] The notes upon the poem are from "Gaelic Literature Surveyed," by Aodh de Blacam.

'Tis my lone soul's long sorrow that I must still be far
  From the Fair Hills of Eire O.
Nor watch a maiden coming as through the mist a star
  On the Fair Hills of Eire O!
Oh, the honey in her tree-tops where her oak-woods darkly
    grow,
And the fullness of her cresses where her clear well-waters
    flow,
And the lushness of her meadows where her soft-eyed cattle
    low,
  On the Fair Hills of Eire O!

Ossory

You cross the bridge in Waterford and you are in
the County Kilkenny. You go through little mar-
ket-towns with names that seem to belong to the Handy
Andy period of Irish history—Kilmacow, Mullinavat.
But you can look on a mountain whose name has epic
associations—there is Slievnamon; the name is abbrevi-
ated, and it means "The Mountain of the Fenian
Women."

For this territory is Ossory, the most ancient kingdom of Celtic Ireland. The cycles of stories and poetry
that spread all through Ireland and Gaelic Scotland
had their rise here; they had for their heroes Finn,
Oisin, Oscar. Oscar, that name which now seems German or Scandinavian, is native to this locality and is
derived (as is Oisin) from the root that is in the place
name, "Ossory." The names of all the mountains we
look on recall some poem or some incident out of the

cycle that deals with the lives of the hunters and fighters who were the Fianna of Ireland.

> Three heroes, we, at the hunting,
> The chase on the slope of Slieve Gua,
> Started a stag from an oak-wood
> That was pearly with fresh morning dew—
>
> His like for height and for antlers
> On the height of Slieve Gua never was
> In all the days of my hunting—
> A lithe stag eating young grass!
>
> We loosed them, the dogs for that stag,
> We raced on to pierce him and slay
> But the stag held on and ahead
> Till he reached Slieve Magh, its green brae.
>
> 'Twas there he fell to our spears:
> Oisin, I, and Caolte were there—
> In all the Fian there were not
> Three heroes as good as we were!

A French publicist has related how, while he was here, he came for a brief moment to understand Irish history. "You think you can understand," the Lord of Upper Ossory said to him. "You cannot. But look at my stables. I am the descendant of the Kings of Ossory. My stables are for eighty horses and there are only four in them." The French publicist found it hard to explain why he found this was revealing. When you are in Ossory you see that it is.

East and South

A round tower of a hundred feet; beside it is
the squat turret of the cathedral. The round tower
marks the Celtic foundation around which this mediæval city arose: tower and cathedral are on a height
and a flight of steps goes up to them. The cathedral
bears the name of the Celtic saint whose cell was here;
it is Saint Canice's.

Inside, the walls are of bare grey stone; they
brighten and darken with the changes of light through
the window above the altar, as, every few minutes, the
clouds come and pass. Armoured Ormonds, their swords
carved across their effigies, lie here. I think they have
become the very emblems of mortality. For their effigies are in black marble, and the rings on this sculp-
tored armour, worn down, give a skeleton-like effect—
it is all in blackness, too; the fingers are disjointed and
the noses broken. One earl has his feet resting on a
strange little beast. It is an otter. The bite of the beast
brought about this Ormond's death. He is the ninth
earl, James Butler, and the date given for him is 1546.

I learn that he was not in his own territory when
he met his death. He must have speared many otters
on the banks of his own river, the Nore. . . . A townsman who has been looking at the little beast under
James Butler's feet tells me of an encounter with an
otter hereabouts. He had been wanting an otter-skin
waistcoat for some time. So when he saw one in a garden or yard—the river being flooded the beast had

[259]

come in there—he determined to seize him. He caught him by the tail. Now if ever you do this, you must hold the otter in such a way that he cannot double back and bite you—it must be a ticklish performance. Well, this townsman, holding the otter by the tail, swung him round and round, keeping those teeth away from him. He felt the arms were pulled out of him before he was able to strike the beast against something. He got the otter killed, and now he wears the skin for a waistcoat.

We go through the town, myself and the man with the otter-skin waistcoat. Kilkenny is a mediæval city become an Irish market-town. Fields and hedgerows begin with the last house of a street. On the streets of the town one hears only the rumble of a cart or the jangle of an outside car; there are no trams, no quick-moving traffic, and people's footsteps are always heard. Kilkenny remains the most distinctive of Irish cities: here and there in its streets one comes upon houses with coats-of-arms carved outside and family mottoes in French. I look back on the tower, tall and slender, with the squat grey turret of the cathedral beside it, the steps going up, and beside the steps a house with an opening showing the fire of a blacksmith's forge. One is always coming upon such scenes here; it is a place for an etcher to work.

I was looking for traces of Dame Alice Kyteler, accused of witchcraft. The man with the otter-skin waistcoat knew of "Kyteler's Inn," and brought me to the place that had that name. We came into the courtyard of a house where there was an old well. The house was deserted-looking with probably a few rooms lived in by poor people. But there was one flourishing creature in Kyteler's Inn. This was a black cat that stood on a stairway and arched her back as I went up. I saluted her as the representative of Dame Alice.

Before the picturesque but closed Tholsel a piper was playing. He had on a tam-o'-shanter, and his spectacled face was very whimsical. Was he from Scotland? I asked him. Aye, he was from Bonnie Scotland. He had the strong accent that makes one smile as at a reminiscence of Harry Lauder. He was from Embro, the heart of Midlothian. Had he read the book with that title? Aye, he could talk to me about Sir Walter and give me some rare cracks about Embro, but first he would play "The Cock o' the North" for me. So he marched up and down playing the pipes. He was very "leetery," he said, and he bubbled over when he talked of Burns and Walter Scott. I was greatly entertained by his dry and eager conversation. He was very different from the strollers of our race. With his bookish knowledge, with his spectacles—I was going to say with his wig—he was much farther from the nomads. I shook hands with him as he went away. But in my wanderings through the town I came on him again. He was beside a shelf where some second-hand books were displayed. The one he was perusing had something by or about Robert Burns in it, I imagine, for the little man showed interest and delight.

In that stall I found a book in which there was a

page that gave a picture—an exciting one, it seemed to me—of a happening in mediæval Kilkenny:

The presiding magistrate had ordered his bailiffs to summon the burgesses to the "Butts" or archery grounds. So it was one dense crush of living beings from early morn even unto mid-day, through the Englishtown and Irishtown of the city, out to the Butts Cross. The magistrate now appears on the scene, attended by a group of bowmen and preceded by bailiffs. Already the targets are set in order and the first group of the burgesses are summoned by name to commence the business of the day. The magistrate was evidently delaying the proceedings, for he sent messengers away from his guard constantly and kept riding about anxiously. At length the object of his waiting was rendered evident by the slow and stately approach of some half a dozen military knights (Monks of the Invocation of St. John) mounted on splendid chargers and wearing long black cloaks with a large crimson cross emblazoned upon each of them, and clad from head to foot in complete mail. . . . As the troop of Hospitallers (Monks) rode gravely along through the streets of the old town, after leaving the Butts, their discourse naturally turned upon the day's practice. Now they reached the bridge crossing the Nore. One of the Hospitallers rode forward, and taking a small bent horn from his saddle bow, blew a shrill blast that startled the wild pigeons from the turreted top of the Abbey of St. Francis, and stimulated at once the vigilance of the warder of the Priory of St. John, for as they rode over into the narrow street, they heard their gates unbarring, and the next moment an answering bugle note told them that the way was clear, and the proper attendants in waiting. And so the black-cloaked, red-crossed Priests Militant of the Holy Land slowly entered the cloister walls and the gates closed after them for the day.[1]

[1] "Historical Romance of the Crusades in Ireland," by Dr. Campion.

And there are fragments left of songs in French and English that we know were sung in Kilkenny streets and houses in the early fourteenth century:

> Heu alas pur amour,
> Qy moy myst en taunt dolour.

and

> I am of Ireland,
> And of the holy land
> Of Ireland.
> Good sir, pray I of thee,
> For of Saint Charite,
> Come and dance with me
> In Ireland.[1]

Kilkenny, with the slow river beside it and the serene countryside around it, with its population of Normans, English, and Irish, must have been as gay and colorful as any mediæval city.

Witchcraft: 1324.

It was in a city where such ditties were being sung and under the jurisdiction of a bishop who frowned on the singing of them that a discovery was made that brought to light most heinous practices. A worthy burgess, Sir John le Poer, accused his wife to the bishop. She was Dame Alice Kyteler. Four times she had been married; three of her husbands had died, leaving their property to her eldest son, William Outlawe. Sir John, her fourth husband, had been brought to a strange bodily state: his nails had dropped off, and there was not

[1] "Anglo-Irish Literature, 1200 to 1582," by St. John D. Seymour.

a hair left on his body. A maid-servant had conveyed a warning to him. He had opened chests belonging to his wife and had found in them things of fearful import. His wife was a practitioner of sorceries.

We can see now that Dame Alice and her associates belonged to a cult which had no root in Ireland but which was practised on hillsides and in secret places in England and the Continent, a very ancient and widespread cult; they were a covin with practices that were counter to the practices of the Church. There was a devil's girdle that one wore next one's skin for a year and a day. There was ointment for the greasing of a staff on which one could amble and gallop through thick and thin. There was a brew made up of various dreadful things which they prepared over a fire of oak-logs in a vessel which was the skull of a beheaded criminal. Dame Alice was wont to sacrifice nine red cocks and nine peacocks' eyes to Robin son of Art. Him she received, sometimes as a cat, sometimes as a black dog, sometimes as a strange black man. With this demon two others went; they were taller than he, and one of them carried a rod of iron. Towards twilight Dame Alice used to rake the refuse of the streets towards her son's house, muttering, as she did:

> To the door of William, my son,
> He all the wealth of Kilkenny town.

The covin at certain times denied the Christian faith; they would not hear Mass nor partake of the sacraments.

East and South

We can imagine what sensation was made in the city when it was discovered that influential and highly connected people were engaged in such horrifying practices. The bishop started proceedings against Dame Alice and her associates. But he could not get from the Chancellor of Ireland a warrant for the arrest of the accused persons. He cited Dame Alice to appear before him, but she ignored his summons and left the town.

Dame Alice's connections were highly placed; her son and his relations were bankers, and bankers were no less powerful in those days than they are now. The bishop was arrested and put in the city gaol. Released, he went before the secular power and asked for the arrest of the accused people, repeating his demand in the two languages spoken in Kilkenny at the time, English and French. He heard himself denounced by the seneschal as a "vile, rustic, interloping monk, carrying dirt in his hands." The bishop carried the case to Dublin; he succeeded in getting the secular power to intervene, but it failed to arrest Dame Alice Kyteler; she was able to make an escape.

Ten were arrested and admitted to the practice of sorceries, but declared that Dame Alice had been their mistress in the Black Art. William Outlawe still remained immune, although the bishop had burned in the middle of the town a sackful of the horrid things which had been found in his mother's chests. At last, on his bended knees, William confessed to the charges that were made against him. His punishment was singularly light considering the period, and the horror with which everything that had to do with sorcery was regarded by the people. He was ordered to hear three Masses every day for a twelvemonth, to feed a certain number of paupers, and to cover the roof of the cathedral with lead. The punishment that involved the spending of money he never bore—we note that one of the charges against William was that of usury.

Unfortunately for the memory of the bishop the punishment of the others was not made so light. There was one Petronella of Meath; she was flogged six times until she admitted to her sorceries. Then, when she had publicly refused the sacrament of penance, she was sent to death at the stake. There were other burnings before the affair was closed. Those whose guilt was not considered extreme were marked back and front with a cross; others were solemnly whipped through the market-place and the town; others were banished from the city and diocese; others who had evaded punishment were excommunicated; others fled and were never heard of afterwards. "And thus," writes the chronicler, "that most foul brood were scattered and destroyed."

Catholic Confederation, 1642-1648.

When Kilkenny yielded to Oliver Cromwell, its garrison was permitted to march out with colours flying. But two miles outside the town they laid down their arms, and their next movement was to take ship from Ireland.

East and South

Ireland was already defeated, or, rather, she had frittered away her power to resist irreparable defeat by the time Cromwell had got to Kilkenny. For seven years this city had been the seat of a provisional government that had legislated for the greater part of Ireland; a Council sitting here had handled armies and conducted negotiations with the English king and with European states. This Council was the Executive of the Catholic Confederation that had come into existence in 1642.

Frightened by movements towards new confiscations of Irish lands, landowners of Gaelic stock and Catholic faith in Ulster had gone into revolt. Lands that had been confiscated two generations before and their owners expropriated were claimed again by lords and tillers of the old stock, and the new owners, Protestants, were killed or had to flee for their lives. Their flight in a bitter season was attended by hardships and many cruelties: they were women and children as well as men; they were unprovided with necessaries, and they were encountered by people who had bitter memories of massacre and spoliation and who baffled, stripped, injured, and, in hundreds of cases, killed the fugitives. The Protestant communities in the North of Ireland survived this onslaught, but they survived it with memories that left a tale of terror to their descendants. And the atrocity-mongers of the day were able to describe children with their hands cut off and the rest of it. "A hundred thousand English Protestants massacred by Irish Papists" was how this desperate business was broadcasted in England where the Puritans were making their great push against the monarchy.

The indiscriminatingly anti-Catholic measures taken by the English officials in Ireland forced the landowners of Leinster, a province in which there had been no disturbances, to take side with the Gaelic party of Ulster. This meant a coalition of the Gaelic and Anglo-Irish Catholic nobility, a coalition which some of the Gaelic leaders had been working for. But the Gaelic party had to make themselves subordinate to the Anglo-Irish party, the Lords of the Pale, who had readier access to whatever arms and munitions were in Ireland. The Gaelic party had to make their policy fit in with Anglo-Irish prepossessions. "Why come ye armed into the Pale?" was the formal question that the spokesman for the Anglo-Irish party put to the spokesman of the Gaelic party. "My lords, our suffering has grown too heavy for us to bear. We are the sole subjects in Europe incapable of serving our sovereign in places of honour, profit, and trust. We are obstructed in the ways of learning, so that our children cannot come to speak Latin without renouncing their dependence on the Church and endangering their souls. These things we wished redressed in Parliament, and had they listened to us, or to you, we should have sat down contented. But the Lords Justices are merely bent on ruining our nation, and they involve you in the same distrust with us. . . . We are here to protest in the sight of heaven that we fight the malignant party in Parliament who encroach on the king's prerogative and we invite you to join us in so glorious an under-taking."

The Confederation asked for religious liberty, a free and independent Irish Parliament, and, of course, security in the tenures of their lands. They did not back up their requests by any strong use of their resources, and they had important resources at their disposal. The two parties that made the Confederation never merged, and their differences prevented a unity of military command. From the Irish contingents in the Spanish service they brought over two commanders, and they gave each an important command. "One bad general is worth two good ones," Napoleon declared, but the Confederation that governed from Kilkenny did not have the understanding that is back of this maxim. Either the ordinary Preston who was associated with the Anglo-Irish interest, or the extraordinary O'Neill who was associated with the Gaelic interest, could have won their cause for them. But with two policies, two important military commands, their negotiations and their military operations were feeble.

The Papal Nuncio, Cardinal Rinuccini, came to have a great deal of influence on the Council of the Confederation, for he brought them money and arms. He was an able and a strong man. But it is likely enough that his intervention was unfortunate. After all, he did not represent an Irish interest; he represented a Continental one. He excommunicated the members of the Council who had made an armistice with Ormond. The armistice certainly depressed the Irish interest. But the ban had the effect of separating the Irish leaders. After it had been launched they were not able to bring together enough strength and authority to get terms of any kind. Cromwell did not have to make terms with an opposition that had real strength—that strength had all been frittered away before he came to Ireland —all he had to do was to force detached surrenders.

In the years of war and negotiation that ended in such collapse, one man and one episode stands out for heroic quality: the man is Eoghan O'Neill, the episode is his victory at Benburb. Eoghan O'Neill left a service in which he had been trusted to withstand three marshals of France to serve a cause which was not prosperous and which offered him only the opportunity of giving some measure of protection to his own broken people. The Anglo-Irish element which dominated the Council baulked him continually, and yet he declared that whoever made distinctions between the Gaelic and the Anglo-Irish stocks was no better than a devil. In a war in which Cromwell could excuse massacre by saying that he gave the order in the bitterness and heat of battle—the order that meant the slaughter of women and children and old men as well as combatants in Drogheda—Eoghan O'Neill treated his prisoners with courtesy and consideration. He won Benburb against an army superior to his own in number and possessing artillery, an arm which he did not have; his victory which destroyed an aggressive army was won by high strategy. Eoghan O'Neill held to the knightly traditions of European soldiership. And

Ireland does not know where the bones of this son of hers are laid.

The expenses of the Civil War in England and the campaign in Ireland were to be paid through the sale of Irish lands—that was the resolve of the English Parliament. This meant the expropriation of the native owners of Irish lands on a scale such as had not been attempted by the Tudors or the Stuarts. The grandfathers of men who were in the Confederation had seen in Ulster the first of the great confiscations; they were to see confiscations in Ulster, in Munster, and in the Leinster of the Anglo-Irish nobility; these confiscations meant nation-wide expropriations.

And now an English government was able to bring about something more momentous than the ruin of an aristocracy. It was able to destroy the Irish nation. Generations before governors and generals had realized that if, in the interest of her sea-power, England was to dominate this island of harbours and forests, she would have to do much more than conduct unceasing and ruthless warfare. What stood in the way of complete domination was not a people who fought when they knew they were beaten, but an idea, a tradition—the Irish nation. That idea, that tradition would have to be destroyed. More than two generations before the Cromwellian conquest, Edmund Spenser, informed by governors and generals, had offered a plan for such destruction. The people were to be made to "forgett this Irish nation." And in order that that should be done they were to be separated from their particular locality, from their own leaders; their names were to be curtailed of O and Mac; the Brehon laws, Irish dress, and the Irish language were to be banned. Spenser recommended the organization of wide-spread famine as a way of bringing about this breach with tradition and idea. "The Irish should be constrained first to taste some great extremity, so as to settle them in a more assured and dutiful affection hereafter. . . . Great force must be the instrument, but famine must be the means, for till Ireland be famished it cannot be subdued." Published in 1633, Spenser's was a current work for those who wanted to get an indemnity out of Ireland and avenge on the Philistines and the Canaanites the wrongs that had been inflicted on the people of the Lord. His book was widely read and had great influence.

I remember a conversation I had with a French authority on Irish history, Professor Yann Goblet. Cromwell's agents, this scholar could show, knew what measures were to be taken to make the people "forgett this Irish nation." The nobility who had a sense of responsibility and leadership had identified themselves by joining the Confederation. They were put out of the way. The clergy were knocked on the head. The poets, historians, and such professors of the native law as had survived to that generation were hunted down and despatched in one way or another. And it must be said that the fighting men of the country simplified the job for Cromwell's agents by taking service abroad—34,-000 of them left the country. Then there was the kidnapping of children for labour in the plantations of the Barbadoes. This went on until it was discovered that children of English planters had come into the grip of the kidnappers. "We may be sure," said Professor Goblet, "that these were not the children of paupers although their parents may have been pauperised; it is very likely they were the children of the ruined nobles, of people of the hereditary intellectual classes, children who might grow up to give a new leadership to Ireland. On the other hand, Cromwell was favourably disposed towards the unpossessing, uninstructed classes, and we have many poems in Irish praising him for the protection he had given such persons."

Thus an immemorial order perished at the hands of a man who, on his return from Ireland, was greeted with an ode in which there is this significant verse:

> Though Justice against Fate complain,
> And plead the ancient rights in vain. . . .

The rights that Andrew Marvell had in mind were English—the ancient right of the English people to see themselves reflected in, to feel themselves directed by, a popular monarchy. The ancient rights in Ireland were not allowed to plead; they were hanged out of hand. But that was because there was no body of men in Ireland who possessed the stern insight that is in Marvell's great ode:

> But these do hold or break,
> As men are strong or weak.[1]

[1] "It is characteristic of Irish culture that the privileged classes were not known, as among the majority of Indo-European peoples,

Cross Roads in Ireland

The Ormonds

We can look on the portrait of the Marquis with whom the Confederation made armistice. It is in the gallery of Ormond Castle. He is in armour, magnificently bewigged, a commander's baton in his hand. What swathed-up individuals these seventeenth-century notables were! And here is Charles the First in Van Dyck's painting—a beautiful portrait! One wonders how much of the distinction that is rendered in it was in the king, and how much was in the painter. Charles the First, amongst the rest of the royal personages whose portraits are here, looks like the last of the monarchs—an anointed king. Here, too, is Sir Peter Lely's portrait of Charles the Second: the king looks as cadaverous as a man who has been dug up after burial, and here is James the Second by the same court-painter, looking as if he never had had a vivid moment in his life. Then we have their successors visibly passing from decadent nobility to middle-class commonplaceness.

The Ormonds managed to be always friends of kings. They did not produce vivid personalities as their rivals for lordship in Ireland, the Geraldines, so often

as 'The Nobles,' but as 'The Sacred'—Nemed or Nemeth, and this designation included not merely chiefs and warriors, but poets and craftsmen." So Christopher Dawson writes in his book on early civilizations, "The Age of the Gods," and he traces this peculiarity of the Irish order to Tartassos in Spain, the legendary Atlantis. This ancient and distinctive order was not finally shattered until the Cromwellian conquest.

did. The founder of the family got this place by purchase, buying from Strongbow's heirs the castle that had been built where the King of Ossory had his court. He was made Chief Butler of Ireland by Edward the First, and his heir adopted the name le Botlier, which is our Butler. The office put the family in possession of the Golden Key which is still to be seen in one of the state rooms, and brought them gifts of ivory and gold cups presented by kings and still to be seen in the house of their Chief Butler. And the office had more real rewards. In the early nineteenth century the Crown resumed the prizage of wines but had to pay the Butler of the day over two hundred thousand pounds in compensation. They knew how to gain revenue, these Butlers. The second and last duke had in the eighteenth century an income of eighty thousand pounds a year with thirty titles to grace it. It was no wonder that the Ormonds were spoken of as the richest subjects of any king in Europe.

Their original castle beside the Nore has been remodelled so greatly that only a single tower of the Norman building has been left—it has been made part of the ancient structure. I enter the grounds through a gate in the street: a park with fine trees—the sort of a park one expects to see deer moving through—stretches away, and on the grass, like moving snow-flakes, is a flock of pigeons; they are pure white fantails, the daintiest pigeons I have seen.

Kilkenny should have been a university town; it is a pity a university was not established here, as it is a pity

one was not established in Armagh. There was a famous college here in the seventeenth century, a college
founded and endowed by the Ormond family. Three
great contemporaries took lessons here—Swift, Berkeley, and Congreve. Another dramatist went to the same
college—George Farquhar.

Back to Waterford County

Lismore: I look on limestone roads that go back
into Tipperary and on into Cork County. The town
is a single long street stretching from the entrance to
the castle. On that street, on this day of grace, there is
a single vehicle. It is an ass-cart; it is piled with
freshly caught herrings, and a limping man goes
beside it. His is the only commerce that is being promoted in the town this forenoon. Lismore has a nice
name and is in a lovely situation, but the town to
me, to-day, looks poor and unhopeful. There is an
inn that used to be a good inn and now is not so
good. I get a decent meal in it, and then go to visit
an aunt of a friend of mine.

Tea with the aunt. Then I go into the castle grounds.
As I came along the road from Tipperary this castle on
the height above the river seemed like a castle in a
fairy tale. I wonder will it seem so enchanting when
I go into the grounds. Not much of magnificence has
been left in the castle—it has not the furnishings that
such a place needs. But then it is lived in from time to
time: that owner of many castles, the Duke of Devon-

LE SEAU D'ARGENT BY MARIE HOWET

shire, is sometimes here. I look on the Blackwater from the window of a great room. I look on a fine tree that is growing in a courtyard from another window. I look on mountains in Tipperary from a turret and note the pigeons on roofs below. Never was there a place so full of quietude—a place for a contemplative.

But then I think of the motto written up over an entrance below, "God's Providence is our Inheritance." Something that a saint or a visionary might have whispered to himself after some lonely, hardly endurable struggle, is blazoned down there. The day of judgment by results, of pragmatism, of modernism, had arrived when that could have been so undesperately said.

And here is the portrait of the gentleman who was so complacent about God's providence—Sir Richard Boyle, afterwards Earl of Cork, the great Earl of Cork who estimated his income at fifty pounds a day (and fifty pounds in the Ireland of the time had seven times the value it has to-day). "I arrived out of England into Ireland," he wrote, "where God guided me first hither, bringing with me a taffeta doublet and a pair of velvet breeches, and new suite of laced ffustian, cutt upon taffeta, a bracelet of gold, a diamond ring, and XXVII pounds of money in my purse." Whatever he had in his purse he kept there, we may be sure. He got possession of vast estates; three of his sons were ennobled, and his daughters married into such great houses as that of Kildare. He must have been the most stirring body that ever gave orders about these parts. And he was able to keep on making a stir after his

death. There is a monument to him in St. Patrick's
Cathedral, Dublin. It was once so conspicuously placed
(it had been put up at a great cost, too) that the archbishop complained to the Lord Lieutenant that the
earl's monument had taken the place of God's altar.
The Lord Lieutenant, who happened to be Strafford
(another stirring gentleman), had the monument
moved to another place (where it is at the present
time), but for doing that he was never forgiven by the
Boyles and their supporters: it is said that this affront
to the majesty of the great earl helped to bring about
Strafford's downfall. "He was father to the Ladie
Katherine, Countess of Corke," is an inscription on
one of the sub-divisions of the monument. "She was
mother to the Ladie Katherine, Countess of Corke," is
another. Certainly no one was ever able to give those
who came near him more of a sense of his importance
than the worthy who adopted the motto, "God's Providence is our Inheritance." Is there not another epitaph
somewhere that reads:

> He was brave, just, and God-fearing,
> And second cousin to the Earl of Corke,
> And of such is the Kingdom of Heaven.

Anyway, Richard Boyle came here and took the
place over from the heirs of Sir Walter Raleigh (whom
Raleigh had it from I don't know) and put up a new
building. It has been rebuilt since, but Richard Boyle
is undoubtedly the true establisher of Lismore Castle.
His son Robert (whose portrait is also here) was born

in Lismore. I had read the correspondence that Robert Boyle had his secretary take up with Spinoza, and I can understand how much he did for the organization of research and of scientific knowledge, probably more than any other man of his great epoch. He was the one who forced chemistry to part company with alchemy—or so the historians of science tell us.

In the grounds of the castle there is an avenue of yews: it is by no means beautiful, this avenue, but it is very curious. The trees are immensely old—at least, never did trees seem so ghastly aged: their limbs are paralyzed, their skins are dropping off. The avenue they form is not a long one: about fifty feet, I am told. But when you have walked along it you know that you have been with the very Struldbrugs of trees.

And then I go along the Blackwater, taking the road to Cappoquin—one of the most delightful roads in Ireland. Beside yellowing leaves I see the red coats of men on horses—huntsmen; silent dogs go with them. They turn and cross a bridge, and then suddenly dogs and horses go swiftly. A young priest who is not riding with the hounds, but who evidently likes to keep near the hunt, rides towards me, and then a hunchback farmer well mounted on a big grey horse dashes by.

The Monastery

I hired an outside-car in Cappoquin and was driven up the mountain-side to the monastery. Received by tht guest-master I was immediately brought into the

[279]

refectory where the mid-day dinner was being eaten. We ate silently, myself and about twenty other men, guests of the monastery. A monk in white robes who was seated near the door read to us. The reading— it was about the discovery of the True Cross—was an exercise in humiliation so far as the reader was concerned: not one mind of the twenty was for an instant engaged by it. Our dinner was a good plain one —mountain mutton, splendid potatoes, turnips, with an apple-pie.

Between dinner and vespers was an interval long enough to write one's letters in, or read, or meditate. I walked in the garden in this interval. After vespers comes compline, the last office of the day—the last that we of the guest-house take part in. As we sit in the chapel we can see through the windows the monks and lay-brothers as they come up from the fields, their day's work ended. A bearded lay-brother enters and lights the candles. Then the white-clad monks and the brown-clad lay-brothers come into the chapel. The abbot, bearded and broad-shouldered, and looking as if he should carry the cross-hilted sword of a Crusader, goes into the choir. The monks chant Latin hymns. Outside the light fades, the fields look mournful; within the candles flare, the chant goes on. It is very solemn, this last office of daylight. As we leave the chapel and go upstairs we read the recommendation, "You are expected to respect the silence of the night." It is really night to the monks, although it is only after eight o'clock.

East and South

I have my lamp lighted and am seated at the table in the room that has been given me at eight-thirty. All is silent in the guest-house. Here, say I to myself, is a place where one can read something! Appropriately enough I have Saint Augustine's "City of God" with me: I begin to read the book that saved Europe from defeatism. And then I hear moaning in the corridor. I leave Saint Augustine on the table and go to see what's wrong outside my door. A guest in the room opposite seems to be in a bad way. I go to him. In a minute I realize what's the matter with my neighbour—he is in the D.T.'s A lay-brother comes into the room, and the situation is explained to me.

Amongst the guests are always some who have come to the monastery after a prolonged drinking-bout. They have got frightened; they want to take the pledge with all circumstances of solemnity. At the monastery they get quietude; they get some physical and moral strength back again; they make their religious duties, take the pledge, and return home. The guest-master and the lay-brothers show themselves very long-suffering with such cases. The night before my neighbour went out of his room and rang a bell that awakened the guest-house and the monastery. Guests of this type generally try to bring whiskey in with them—my neighbour had a small bottle hidden in his boot when he came before the guest-master. The liquor is taken from them: if they need any to help them to recover they are given an allowance.

Next morning I got up at 6 A.M. and walked in

the garden until 8.30 when I went to Mass—and it was a High Mass, too. So I was hungry by the time the guests got to breakfast. We sat down to a good meal— good bread, good butter, good eggs, good tea. Everything except the tea is from the monastery's farms. Next day I got up at 8.30, and went to a shorter Mass. The guests who are not Catholics do not go to any of these services, but Catholics are expected to go.

The guests form a community within a community —"the brethren," we have taken to calling ourselves. We, a group belonging to the less transitory guests, sit in the garden and talk of our affairs. Amongst "the brethren" is a priest who was trained in the Irish College in Paris and who has something of the manner of a French abbé; he has read a good deal of out-of-the-way books in Latin, French, and English, and is very good company. He is trying to keep in good spirits a young doctor who may be some relation of his. This medico has fallen into a state of restlessness and depression, and it is the priest's hope that the quiet and quasi-religious life here may get him out of this state. And there is a farmer who is also much depressed. In his case the depression has come through the death of a child—his only son. "He was a little giant," he keeps telling us. "He was known for miles around our place." Then there is a student who, as the farmer tells us, has "come near-handed being priested." He has a dignified walk, wears very white cuffs over his soft hands; he has prominent eyes behind magnifying glasses.

The guest of the room opposite mine is taken in by

"the brethren." His drinking-bout started when he went to Dublin to attend a convention. He sent his ticket in to the convention and went to the races at Punchestown instead. There he lost all bets and started drinking. Next day he went to Leopardstown races. There he backed five winners out of six. A horse was running with the name "Leave-well-enough-alone." He thought advice was being given him instead of the name of a horse being told him, and he desisted from betting that day. Next day, Sunday, he went to Phœnix Park races —"to Nancy Ann's." He won at these races, too. He had been drinking all the time, and now he started for home. He got to Sligo. It took him four days to get from Sligo to Tubbercurry where he was to take the train for Mayo. When he realized he was still in the County Sligo after four days' travelling he decided to start for the monastery. He is going home in a day or so with a pledge that he is to keep for five years.

Our abbot has gone to Dublin. "He'll be there for the races; I hope he'll back a good thing," says one of "the brethren" seriously. We all laugh. We are very easily amused, but still the idea of our abbot becoming a race-track character is an entertaining one. The medico and I get permission to take a walk on the mountain-side. I hadn't been outside walls for a week, and so I started up the mountain-side with quite a sense of adventure. It suddenly came over me that the women we saw on the roadway or standing at their doors were surprising creatures. We didn't speak to anyone, for the medico had the notion that we should keep guest-house discipline. The walk was grand: the Knockmael-down Mountains in Tipperary are near; as we come down the hillside we see the monks working in the fields.

They get to the fields about noon and go back to the monastery about six o'clock. But before their field-labours they have had a day. They rise at 2 A.M. on week-days and 1 A.M. on Sundays. At 6 A.M. they break their fast. They engage in devotions until 11.30. At noon they take the meal of the day, and then go to the fields, returning to their devotions from time to time. At 6 P.M. they take a meal and at 8 P.M. they go to rest. It is now nearly a hundred years since these monks of the Cistercian Order—they are the same as the Trappists—came to Ireland from France. They took the side of this mountain, and they have turned its bareness into woods and farms. The hillsides here are, next to the Forestry Department's plantations on the Wicklow hillsides, the best bits of re-afforestation that has been done in Ireland. Their farms are model ones, and they take young men students who work under their direction. The monks have all taken the vow of silence: as the man who drove me said, "They have to make tokens with their fingers when friends come to see them." Some are dispensed from this silence from time to time—the guest-master, who holds office for a year, converses; so does the abbot who, with farms and schools and the business of a great house-hold to manage, has many transactions with the world. To stay at the monastery's guest-house is to have an experience that makes real a period in history: a Roman house must have been like this, a great mediæval house must have been like this in the fact that it is self-contained; everything, or nearly everything, that the household needs it produces itself. The wheat is grown and milled here; the bread that we eat is baked here.

When I got back I discovered that the sole of my boot was broken. The medico took me to the lay-brother who is shoemaker for the monastery and he fixed it for me very neatly. Afterwards he took me to the dairy and introduced me to the lay-brother in charge. He is a man whose acquaintance is well worth making. He gave me a great measure of buttermilk. Afterwards, whenever I felt I had need of refreshment, I went to him and he handed me this splendid beverage. This lay-brother is a poet of a kind. He makes little poems in Irish about the saints. I get him to repeat one to me while I drink his buttermilk. But he says them in such a low voice that I get only words here and there. Our community has it that this lay-brother was a publican's assistant who got tired of handing pints of porter and glasses of whiskey across the counter, and left the topers and the licensed premises one day and came to the monastery. He was given the brown habit then, and put in charge of the dairy. This account of our buttermilk-dispenser may be—it probably is—true.

The abbot, when he came back, was good enough to ask to see me. I spent a pleasant and profitable half-hour in his reception-room. Such magnificent physique as he has is surely a testimonial to the benefit of a strictly regulated life. Also vegetarianism, I suppose. The monks do not eat meat. In this very different climate they keep to the regimen of the French foundation, and use olive-oil instead of butter. The milk they drink is skimmed. The abbot tells me that the trouble that makes it most difficult to enter the Cistercians is insomnia. Any of their postulants who cannot take their full rest at the proper times cannot enter the order. The little sleep the monks permit themselves would, of course, be entirely inadequate for one who could not go to sleep at once and sleep continuously.

A day came when I sat at table for the last time. The reader entered, looking like a great bird in his white fluttering robe. He took his seat. The reading was an account of the angels, and I was reminded of Yeats's plays, "The Countess Cathleen" and "The Hour Glass." Once again the reader accepted the humiliation of our complete disregard. I said good-bye to the guest-master and took an outside-car back to Cappoquin. I was quite a long bit on my way before I realized that I had left no offering for anything that the Order takes an interest in. Not that it is ever made apparent to any guest that any offering is expected: indeed, the whole idea of a return for service and hospitality leaves one's mind while one is a guest here. I turned back; I came before the guest-master again, and left a little offering with him. As I went on to the town I noted with surprise and interest the world become secular again. "We are all well here, and trying, anyhow, to be very good," said a card that came to me a week later from one of "the brethren." "The medico has left—he was in somewhat better spirits towards the end of his stay. Father Benedict was gratified by your remembrance of him. The abbot spoke to me yesterday about you and joked about your becoming a Cistercian." With these remembrances from the little—and the great—community I bring this note on a profitable sojourn to an end.

Story: The Death of the Rich Man

It was a road as shelterless and as bare as any road in Munster. On one side there was a far-reaching bog, on the other side little fields, cold with tracts of water. You faced the Comeragh hills, bleak and treeless, with little streams across them like threads of steel. There was a solitary figure on the road, a woman with bare feet and ragged clothes. She was bent and used a stick; but she carried herself swiftly, and had something of a challenge in her face. Her toothless mouth was tightly closed, her chin protruded, wisps of hair fell about her distrustful eyes. She was an isolated individual, and it would be hard to communicate the sensations and facts that made up her life.

Irish speakers would call the woman a "shuler." The word is literally the same as "tramp," but it carries no anti-social suggestion. None of the lonely cabins about would refuse her hospitality; she would get shelter for the night in any one of them—the sack of chaff beside the smouldering fire, the share in the household bit.

But though she slept by their fires and ate their potatoes and salt, this woman was apart from them, and
apart from all those who lived in houses, who tilled
their fields, and reared up sons and daughters; she had
been moulded by unkind forces—the silence of the
roads, the bitterness of the winds, the long hours of
hunger. She moved swiftly along the shelterless roads,
muttering to herself, for the appetite was complaining
within her. There was on her way a certain village,
but before going through it she would give herself a
while of contentment. She took a short pipe out of her
pocket and sought the sheltered side of a bush. Then
she drew her feet under her clothes and sucked in the
satisfaction of tobacco.

You may be sure the shuler saw through the village, though her gaze was across the road. Midway on
the village street there was a great house; it was two
stories above the cottages, and a story higher than the
shops. It was set high above its neighbours, but to
many its height represented effort, ability, discipline.
It was the house of Michael Gilsenin, farmer, shop-
keeper, local councillor. "Gilsenin, the Gombeen man,"
the shuler muttered, and she spat out. Now the phrase
"Gombeen man" would signify a grasping peasant
dealer, who squeezed riches out of the poverty of his
class, and few people spoke of Michael Gilsenin as a
Gombeen man; but his townsmen and the peasants
around would tell you that Michael Gilsenin had the
open hand for the poor, and that he never denied them
the bag of meal, nor the sack of seed-potatoes; no, nor

the few pounds that would bring a boy or girl the prosperity of America. To the woman on the ditch Michael Gilsenin was the very embodiment of worldly prosperity. It was said, and the shuler exclaimed on Heaven at the thought, that Michael's two daughters would receive dowries of a thousand pounds each. Michael had furnished the new chapel at a cost of five hundred pounds; he had bought recently a great stock of horses and cattle; he had built sheds and stables behind his shop. And Michael Gilsenin had created all his good fortune by his own effort. The shuler wondered what bad luck eternal justice would send on his household to balance this prosperity. And in her backward-reaching mind, the shuler could rake out only one thing to Michael's discredit. This was his treatment of Thady, his elder brother. It was Thady who had owned the cabin and the farm on which the Gilsenins had begun their lives. Michael had reduced his grasping and slow-witted brother to subordination, and he had used his brother's inheritance to forward himself. In forwarding himself Michael had forwarded the family, Thady included, and now, instead of life in a cabin, Thady had a place in a great house. Michael was old now, the shuler mused, he was nearly as old as herself. It was well for those who would come after him. His daughters had dowries that made them the talk of the county, and his son would succeed to stock, farms, and shop. The shuler stretched out her neck and looked down the road and on to the village street. She saw the tall grey building, the house of stone with the slated roof and the many windows. And she saw a man hobbling out of the village. He had two sticks under him, for he was bent with the pains. The man was Thady Gilsenin, Michael's brother.

Thady Gilsenin was grudging and hard-fisted to the beggars, but he always stayed to have speech with them. His affinities were with these people of the roads. By his hardness and meanness, by his isolation and his ailments, he was kin to the shuler and her like. She quenched the pipe, hid it under her clothes, and waited for Thady Gilsenin.

. . . . . .

He stood before her, a grey figure leaning on two sticks. His hands were swollen with the pains, their joints were raised and shining.

"Well, ma'am," said Thady, "you're round this way again, I see."

"My coming won't be any loss to you, Thady Gilsenin," the shuler returned.

Thady turned round and looked back at the big house.

"And how is the decent man, your brother?" asked the shuler, "and how are his daughters, the fine growing girls?"

"His fine daughters are well enough," said Thady, turning round.

"There will be a great marriage here some day," said the shuler, "I'm living on the thought of that marriage."

"It's not marriage that's on our minds," Thady said, in a resigned way.

The shuler was quick to detect something in his tone. "Is it death?" she asked.

"Ay, ma'am, death," said Thady. "Death comes to us all."

"And is it Michael that is likely to die?"

"Michael himself," said Thady.

This to the tramp was as news of revolution to men of desperate fortune. The death of Michael Gilsenin would be a revolution with spoils and without danger. She was thrilled with expectancy, and she said aloud: "O God, receive the prayers of the poor, and be merciful to Michael Gilsenin this day and this night! May angels watch over him! May he receive a portion of the bed of heaven! May he reign in splendour through eternity! Amen, amen, amen!" And crying out this she rose to her feet. "I'm going to his house," she said. "I'll go down on my two knees and I'll pray for the soul of Michael Gilsenin, the man who was good to the poor." She went towards the village, striking her breast and muttering cries. Thady stood for a moment, looking after her; then he began to hobble forward on his two sticks. They were like a pair of old crows, hopping down the village, towards the house of Michael Gilsenin.

.   .   .   .

She could never have imagined such comforts and conveniences as she saw now in the chamber of the dying man. There was the bed, large enough to hold three people, with its stiff hanging and its stiff counterpane, its fine sheets, its blankets and quilt, its heap of soft pillows. There was the carpet warm under her own feet, and then the curtains to the window that shut out the noise and the glare. A small table with fruit and wine was by the bed, and a red lamp burnt perpetually before the image of the Sacred Heart, and so the wasting body and the awakening soul had their comfort and their solace. Michael's two daughters were in the room. They stood there broken and listless; they had just come out of the convent and this was their novitiate in grief. The shuler noted how rich was the stuff in their black dresses, and noted, too, their white hands, and the clever shape of their dresses. As for the dying man, she gave no heed to him after the first encounter. He was near his hour, and she had looked too often upon the coming of death.

They gave her a bed in the loft, and she lay that night above the stable that was back of the great house. She had warmed herself by the kitchen fire, and had taken her fill of tea, and now she smoked and mused, well satisfied with herself. "This night I'm better off than the man in the wide bed," she said to herself. "I'm better off than you this night, Michael Gilsenin, for all your lands and shops and well-dressed daughters. I'm better off than you this night, Michael Gilsenin, for all your stock and riches. Faith, I can hear your cattle stir in the sheds, and in a while you won't even hear the rain on the grass. You have children to come after you, Michael Gilsenin, but that's not much, after all, for they'll forget you when they've come from the burial. Ay, they will in troth. I've forgotten the man that lay beside me, and the child that I carried in my arms." She pulled a sack over her feet and knees and up to the waist, and sleep came to her on the straw. But she was awake and felt the tremor through the house, when Death came and took his dues. From then onward her sleep was broken, for people had come and horses were being brought out of the stable. Once old Thady came out, and the shuler heard him mutter about the loss in hay and oats.

When she came down to the yard she saw a well-dressed young man tending his horse. One of Michael's daughters came and stood with the young man, and the two talked earnestly together. The shuler knelt down on a flag and began sobbing and clapping her hands. She was working up to a paroxysm, but gradually, for she wanted to attract the attention of the pair without distressing them overmuch. The girl went indoors and the young man followed her. The shuler saw two empty bottles; they were worth a penny. She hid them under her dress and went into the house. She made her way to the front door, passing by many. People of importance were coming, and in such an assembly something surely would be gained. She stood by the street door and watched the great people come—priests, doctors, lawyers, shopkeepers, and councillors. She stood there like an old carrion bird. Her eyes were keen with greed, and her outstretched hand was shaking. She heard old

Thady saying, "Now, thank God, we can be clear for the day of the fair. I was thinking that he would still be with us on the fair day, and we would have to close the shop, and that would be a great loss to us. Now we can have everything cleared off in time. God be good to Michael's soul."

PART VI

The South

Youghal

I WENT the water-way to Youghal from Cappo-quin—straight down the Blackwater. Arriving in Youghal I went into the garden where potatoes were first planted and the first pipe of tobacco was smoked in Ireland. The good Elizabethan house that Sir Walter Raleigh lived in is still here—the house in which he entertained Edmund Spenser. I suppose canto after canto of "The Faërie Queen" was read here, and I suppose that as morning and afternoon hours went by in the reading, the poet and his auditor were drawn away from wars and burnings and massacres in Ireland and court-intrigues in England:

> Nepenthe is a drink of sovereign grace
> Devisèd by the gods for to assuage
> Heart's grief, and bitter gall away to chase
> Which stirs up anguish and contentious rage;
> Instead thereof sweet peace and quiet age
> It doth establish in the troubled mind.
> Few men but such as sober are and sage
> Are by the gods to drink thereof assigned;
> But such as drink, eternal happiness do find.

I walked up narrow laneways towards the hills, and then walked back to the strand. Fishermen were standing around their nets and their catches representing (although they made nothing at all of the fact) a more ancient life than the monuments of the Elizabethan age in Ireland. Along the beach, seaside lodging-houses had taken the place of fishermen's cabins. Going into them and coming out of them were seaside visitors: their voices had the surprising intonation that belongs to the inhabitants of Cork city—an intonation that can only be rendered by musical notation. I was now in Cork County.

Seated before a house and regarding the sea in a professional manner were three petty-officers from a British battleship. For some reason a couple of ancient men, natives, had attached themselves to the Britishers. "You have a pleasant face, mister," one said, "will you raise us a harmony?" Evidently these Youghalers thought that the right way to entertain distinguished visitors was to get them to express themselves in song. Neither the gentleman with the pleasant face nor his fellows concerned themselves at all with the invitation. "I'll rise one myself," said the ancient to the ancient, "but these are officiated gentlemen, and it's only manners to ask them first." The other signified his approbation. The officiated gentlemen took no more notice of the words than if they had been in a speech so unintelligible that there was no point in giving any attention to what was being said. But the resolute entertainer, encouraged by his crony and possibly by his own sense of public duty, laid his stick against the wall and began to sing a ballad that was as doleful and as rambling as any I have ever heard. I didn't wait for the end of it. The officiated gentlemen continued to regard the sea with professional interest.

I asked a young man whom I met upon the bridge and who seemed to be knowledgable about Cork and its resources where I could procure an ass and cart when I went to that city. He said:

"There are good she-asses in Corney Barry's stables in Featherbed Lane, or in Larry Broderick's in the Marsh, but Duggan's Yard on the Western Road is the surest place for you. You'll strike it on the day that the ass-owners of the district are bringing the mares to the stallions, but you needn't mind that. And there's Desmond's Stables in Winthrop Street where you could get a hardy ass if I know anything about the breed. And where there are asses there are carts: You'll be easily able to get both in Cork."

Cork

There are many distinctive things about the town and the people of Cork, and the most distinctive is the way of speaking that the proper Cork inhabitant has. He or she speaks with a gesture that is far more abundant and far more appropriate than that used in any other part of Ireland. "Are you going out fishing to-night?"—the sentence is spoken with a rising stress. The women keep the musical pattern better than the men; I listen with great interest to the way in which young girls talk to their younger charges. One must distinguish between the Cork intonation and the Cork grammar. Many who speak with this intonation use their words grammatically, but there are odd lapses in grammar. Sitting in a public-house I hear a man say, "Tom Fitzmaurice have got a new car." The girl whom I heard talking to her young charges had said, "I'll never get marry—I've such a surfeit of kids." In this speech of the public-house there are lapses that remind me of the eighteenth-century caricature of Irish speech. 'Th' becomes 'd'— "wid de excitement he lose de train."

I hear it, but I know that this sort of speech is already archaic. Cork is changing. In a few years it will have ceased to be the old-fashioned provincial Cork where this kind of dawdling popular speech can be heard and will be a modernized and industrialized city. The change is being brought about by Henry Ford, the descendant of a Cork emigrant. "We could get 100,-000 Irishmen any time we wanted them. And speaking of Irishmen, they are mighty good workmen," he said recently. His estimate of the Irish workmen's quality was based on the labour organization he has formed in Cork.

He has established a plant in Cork which is manufacturing tractors for the European market. Already he has between five and six thousand men employed there, the biggest labour unit that Cork has ever had. The high wages paid in the Ford factory have already changed the standard of living in the place. And the handling of tangible things, the necessity for technical mastery, the premium placed upon skilled work, the emergence of executive ability, are bound to change the mentality of this city.

The Ford plant in Cork is turning out at the present time 800 tractors a week. The works are to be enlarged; other industries will grow up beside the Ford factories; the Shannon will supply Cork with abundant electrical power. Cork will become an industrial and commercial centre. . . . I heard this prophesied, and then I heard this prophecy being denounced. The people would be turned into robots by Ford and the modern industrialists. The national distinction would be lost and with it the possibility of creating a co-operative commonwealth. We would have the ill of capitalism added to our other ills. The workers would be highly paid, but what use would that be when they would have nothing inside themselves? . . .

But who was he who was standing in the corner of the bar?—listening to what was being said, a mocking smile on his face. It was the young man whom I had met on the bridge at Youghal—the same who had told me where to procure an ass and cart—an ass and cart which, I had just decided, I did not want. He had that ambiguous appearance—the look of one who is half a worthy and half an outcast—which in the Irish countryside we associated with a "spoiled priest." He said:

"You talk as if you did not know that the vast majority of the people of Cork live in hovels or in Jew-shop furnished villas, having never known, or long since forgotten, what the social life means. Don't you know that there is neither town life nor city life where we are—there is only the life of back-kitchens and front-parlours (locked from 11 A.M. to 7 P.M.)? Nobody in Cork has sixpence to throw at a beggar except the priests. There is no threshold, except the threshold of the poor, that I would not rather cross outwards than inwards." Having said this, he took up somebody else's glass, drained it, and crossed the threshold outwards before any of the townsmen could frame the answer to what he had said.

As for me, I went into the picturesque grounds of the University College and looked at the interesting buildings there. I discovered, or was discovered by, one of the college staff. It was Long Vacation, and there were no students about: like Galway, Cork is a constituent College of the National University, but I gathered from what the member of the staff told me that Cork has independent ideas, and will probably develop as a separate university—the University of Munster. Even now, more than any other Irish-learned institution, it strives to influence the life of its city; it is bringing together Irish scholars who have a special interest in the rich Munster poetry. And the philosophy through which, as I believe, Ireland could form her intellectual life, the Thomistic philosophy, has a representative here.

The time to walk through Cork is in the twilight: then the little capital and the country town are blended; the bridges, the odd steeples and turrets, the little stalls by the river, the houses lighted by candles in the narrow side-streets, become traditional so that one thinks they can be related back to Saint Finnbarr and his wattled house on the island of the river Lee. Then I think that a writer like Hans Christian Andersen, a writer who could feel the folk-life that is within the harness-maker's shop, at the blacksmith's forge, or that end house in the lane with its half-door on which a tame jackdaw perches, might come out of Cork; I never feel that a writer of this kind could come out of Dublin. A fiddle is being played in a room behind the shop that sells sugar-sticks; the girls who pass with shawls across their heads say, "Good-night, neighbours," in a friendly way.

Belfast, Dublin, and Cork has each its record of ordinary life in St. John Ervine's "Mrs. Martin's Man," James Stephen's "Mary Makebelieve," and Daniel Corkery's "The Threshold of Quiet." Dublin has also its epic portrayal in James Joyce's "Ulysses" and a presentation that is distinctly personal in "Portrait of the Artist as a Young Man." I leave these two masterly books aside for the reason that they do not reflect the life of Dublin's average people. "Mrs. Martin's Man," "Mary Makebelieve," "The Threshold of Quiet" seem to me to reflect the life of Belfast's, Dublin's and Cork's average.

Each of the three is a book by a young man. I think that "The Threshold of Quiet" is the most mature of the three: it is about an inner life and it is by a writer who has made terms with life. And the people in this book are the people who give its tone to the public life of Ireland, to the Ireland that is outside the Ulster counties; their aspirations are Irish aspirations, their inhibitions are Irish inhibitions. The characters in the book seem to have been picked casually: there is Martin Cloyne, a clerk who is also a student; Stevie Galvin, an artisan, "a sophisticated carpenter," Ned Connell, a clerk who is also an athlete; then there is Lily Bresnan, her younger brother Finnbarr, and her friend Minnie Ryan, and a few outside characters. And there are two important people who never appear bodily in the story—Lily Bresnan's brother, Frank, who is found drowned as the story opens, and Stevie Galvin's younger brother, Phil, who is sailing the seas.

In a sense, "The Threshold of Quiet" is the story of a quest for a brother, for a fulfillment through love of and service to a brother. Stevie Galvin has in a moment of temper flung his brother Phil out of the house, and he is now living for the time when Phil's sailing-ship, *The Pinestar*, will put into the port of Cork.

Martin Cloyne loves Lily Bresnan: he has been awakened to a consciousness of his love for her through brooding upon the events that may have brought her brother Frank to suicide; amongst these events is his own failure to have kept intimate with him.

It is a book about quiet people, about lonely people, about people who have a sense of their own past. Martin Cloyne's land of heart's desire, as he recognizes, "is under a very quiet, pale star indeed." But for all its quietness this story about Cork has passages which vi-

QUIET INTERIOR BY LEO WHELAN

brate with emotion. Lily, in obedience to the discovered wish of her brother, enters a convent as a nun. Stevie's brother never comes home to him; *The Pinestar* is wrecked on the rocks of Kinsale. Martin Cloyne and Stevie Galvin are left to face that "quiet desperation" which, according to the line of Thoreau's quoted as a motto, is the lot of the mass of men:

The room was filled with quietness; not with the quietness of peace, it may be, but then it is not the quietness of peace that leaves men's souls gentle and deep and rich, even if just a little, a very little, pensive, not to say bitter. Bitter! but when such souls quit our company it is the sweetness of their quiet spirits that remains like a fragrance in the air.

"The Threshold of Quiet" is a book of sustained writing, in which, in spite of sparseness of character and incident, there is a rich life. When we have read it we know a great deal about Cork, that "sunken city," with its crowded bridges, its miserable back-streets and lanes, its far-sounding bells, its river, its neighbouring lake, the sea beside it that gives dreams to its young men, its convents and monasteries on the hills, its long days of rain, and its nights of wind and rain. In the prologue we are given a lay-out of the city:

Leaving us, the summer visitor says in his good-humoured way that Cork is quite a busy place, considering how small it is. And he really thinks so, because whatever little we have of pastors, postmen, urchins, beggars; of squares, streets, lanes, markets; of wagons, motors, tram-cars, ships; of spires, turrets, domes, towers; of bells, horns, meetings, cries; concert-halls, theatres, shops—whatever little we have of all these as humdrum a collection of odds-and-ends as ever went by the name of a city—are flung higgledy-piggledy together into a narrow, double-streamed, many-bridged river valley, jostled and jostling, so compacted that the mass throws up a froth and flurry that confuses the stray visitor, unless indeed he is set on getting at the true size and worth of things. For him this is Cork. But for us it is only the "flat of the city." What of the hillsides? Go but three steps up any of those old-time, wide-sweeping, treeless, cloud-shadowed hills and you find yourself even at mid-day in a silence that grows on you. You have scarce left the city, yet you raise your eyes, you look around and notice little gable-ends that finish in little crosses of stone, or arched gateways of sandstone or limestone or both, or far-stretching garden walls that are marked with tablets of brass on which are cut holy emblems and sacred letters—and as you look the silence seems to grow deeper and deeper; indeed you have come on the very fruitage of the spirit of contemplation—convents, monasteries, chapels, hospitals, houses of refuge. And to us these quiet hillsides also are Cork. Perhaps they are the quieter for the noise in the valley; perhaps, too, that little stir and bustle is quickened for those long slopes of quiet sunshine and peace. But both are Cork, hillsides and city marsh.

There are bits of description that make part of the city come to the eye:

Morrison's Quay at night is a deserted spot. The river is narrow and sunken, a black pool if the tide is low. In the scanty light of the far-scattered gas lamps, the chain-stones of the edge of the quay gleam against the darkness beyond; they seem to protect night travellers from that as much as from the river. The narrowness of the quay itself and the great height of the houses, the upper stories seeming to gaze into the black depths, add to the gloom. The doorways and windows are deep-cut in the reserved, old-fashioned way; bidding defiance to lamp-light, to star-light, they catch a glimmer as rarely as the sunken eye of an old man. They keep their secrets.

The opposite side is just as dark and deserted. The stores that run along the quayside there are of all sizes and shapes, the windows mostly shuttered; and the odd house that stands among these unlighted buildings, where the rats must make so free, looks as if only some back room or garret was lived in, for there is never the gleam of candle or lamp in two windows at a time. From this quay a few wide old streets branch off, trafficless and ill-lighted. They seem to lead to places still more silent, still more deserted. A small schooner was lying against the opposite quay, her deck some distance below its level. Masts, spars, cordage, hull, it was unvaried black except where, in the little cabin-house aft, a dull light glimmered on a panel from which the paint had bleached off, just a gleam. There was no light on the deck or in the rigging.

As he climbed up Barrack Street, nearing home, he heard a boisterous tramp, tramp, tramp of feet, and the loud, coarse music of a melodeon coming towards him. At the steepest and narrowest part of the old hillside street they swung by him, a crowd of young men and women, two by two, boy and girl, and every girl had stretched her shawl about her companion's neck. And amongst them was a crutch, which stubbed the ground, all out of tune with the rhythmic music and feet. Rapidly, boisterously they swung down the hill; he saw their raised heads and laughing lips in the light of a gas lamp; and he knew that he would never forget their high-spirited, careless features. His senses had suddenly become all activity. He felt that the coarse, free expression on the bright faces, as they went by, were being seared on his memory; yet as they went on and their music came fainter and fainter up from among the walls of the sunken city, he gave them pity rather than blame—there was not one of them but would be quiet enough yet! And farther up the hill he came on the lane that had sent them forth: a wedding was evidently in progress; there was singing and music, a sense of merry excitement. The processionists were an offshoot of it, a rocket, rather; they would encircle the city with their tramping music, they would wake up the sleepy heads, and come back with great tales of where they had gone.

The rain had ceased, but the winds were still moist; it was not an unpleasant wind, not cold; without stinging, it whipped the blood up into people's cheeks, and they became as merry as their looks. Hardly a person entered the office without a bright word. One said the city after its drenching was the colour of an owl; it was certainly not sunny-looking. Another said the river had become so "big in itself" that the bridges across it looked like straps on the point of breaking.

Blarney Castle

The best way to get to Blarney Castle is to walk there—to walk there, I mean, from the town of Cork. You will go to Patrick's Bridge. You will walk along the quays. You will pass Shandon Church whose bells a poet has made famous. You will come to a second bridge. Then you will turn up Blarney Street. You will go on until you come to a place named Clougheen. And the valley which Blarney Castle dominated is then before you.

But you should stay for a while upon Patrick's Bridge and take in the scene and the people. Across the way is Shandon Church with its turret.

> White and brown is Shandon's steeple,
> Parti-coloured like the people.

The South

Two sides of the turret are of white stone, two of brown stone. The white stone is used again in the embankment of the river; the Lee flows along quays built of limestone. This, the central part of Cork, is a very little way from the countryside. Turn off the bridge along the quayside and the ass-cart filled with cabbages, the country cart loaded with peat, are the vehicles you see. Gulls are flying over the river. And the people who give Ireland her journalists, schoolmasters, and civil-servants are passing by.

They are a merchant-folk primarily—ready of tongue, shrewd of mind, good at bargaining. They have soft and rippling speech and are ready to engage in long conversations with one another. Lots of young men seem to be detached from any employments—strolling about, or pushing barrows, or carrying baskets. Several monks pass, brown-garbed and with sandals on their feet. Sometimes one sees an old woman who has on the voluminous hooded cloak that was worn everywhere in Munster a century ago. The girls look as if they all had personality—a fresh, clear, but unvivid personality; the younger they are the prettier they are; the girls seem to be at their prettiest around fourteen. But when you go along the quaysides and come to the second bridge you see more of the folk-life of Cork. They are real types, these old women who are selling gooseberries, apples, blackthorn-sticks. I went to buy withered apples from one of them. Both she and her charming grand-daughter were so eager to serve that I bought gooseberries, too; they measured them out for me in a

Cross Roads in Ireland

pewter mug, and I'm sure they gave me an extra ha'-penny worth for good measure. And so, eating gooseberries, I turned up Blarney Street.

'Tis a long street that begins in an undistinguished part of the town and ends as a lane. But then I am out of the town and in the county of Cork. Clougheen—"the little stones"—is not a village; there is a church there, a few houses, a pump, and that is all. And the road to Blarney is before me.

I go to Blarney by fields that are the greenest of all the green fields of Eirinn. Yonder field is a green mirror for the clouds to make shadows upon. And I pass a field that has yellow dandelions and grass so soft and smooth that I think that only the cattle of a king have any right to graze there—no other cattle would be worthy of such a sward. Passing these fields I come to Blarney village with its factory, a dull little place. And then I go through the gate and enter the grounds of Blarney's old castle, grounds overgrown with shrubs.

Near the gate, under the trees with a shawl over her head for shelter from the showers, is a simple-faced old woman. She returns my salutation, and I go over to talk to her. She has a simple and rambling mind. She tells me that her husband was employed on this property, and that she has permission to come here and sit under the trees. She likes the air here and she likes to watch the flowing water. She does not say it to me, but I gather from her rambling allusions that she nurses the hope that some of the visitors will make her some sort of offering—something that would give her an allowance of tea, or snuff, or tobacco. There are wild children in the house she lives in; there are bad neighbours all around her; she does not sleep. So she likes being here, within the gate and under the trees. And over and over again she tells me that she likes to watch the flowing water from where she sits. There are handsome trout in that stream that never were caught and that never can be caught. She tells me a legend of the castle that has as much to recommend its authenticity as any of the half-dozen legends that are current. And as I go away from her she says, "May God carry you every road safe."

The keep is built on a shelf of the rock that dominates the valley. I get to the top, about a hundred feet up. And there I come on a group who are not ordinary visitors: a personage whom I take to be an Indian prince is kissing the stone by proxy—a servitor is hanging down the wall to lip it. From the top of the keep I look on the green lawns that are all around— Blarney has nothing to show better than them.

Except, perhaps, a yew-tree that grows out of a tier of the rock on which the castle is built. It bends outward and some of its branches grow towards the ground: these are bare. The branches that are lifted up have constant movement like waves—dark-green, feathery branches waving against rock and wall. There it grows, blended somehow with rock and ruin, like some unused image that has come spontaneously into a poet's verse.

Cross Roads in Ireland

The legend of the castle that my old woman told me had to do with water and a fairy woman, and, although the woman in it is old, not young, is, I imagine a fragment of a Melusina story. The King of Munster saved an old woman who was about to drown in the lake. She had nothing to give him by way of reward. She told him, however, that if he would mount the topmost wall of his castle, and kiss a stone which she described to him, he would gain a speech that would win friend or foe to him, man or woman. There is a lake that might well be the scene for an encounter with a Melusina: it is about a mile from the castle.

But, as the friend who meets me here, a poet and a scholar, reminds me, Blarney was famous for its groves before its stone and its lake were ever heard of. The place-name itself means "groves." And it is for its groves that Blarney is celebrated in what is the most diverting of Irish poems. As we walk amongst the trees, my poet-friend from Cork, Frank O'Connor, repeats the poem and comments upon it. Imitations of Gaelic verse, he holds, should not be intentional; there should be no striving for the effect of Gaelicism—it should come indeliberately. He instances "The Bells of Shandon," written by a Latin scholar who wrote for the sake of mystification, and "The Groves of Blarney" which was made up to parody a song made in school-master's English. The structure and the sound of Gaelic poetry are reproduced in it: the "a" sound of "Blarney" is woven through every stanza,

The South

but every word that has the sound seems to have gone
into its place smilingly:

The groves of Blarney, they are so charming
Down by the purling of sweet silent streams,
Being banked with posies that spontaneous grow there,
Planted in order by the sweet rock close.
'Tis there the daisy and the sweet carnation,
The blooming pink and the rose so fair,
The daffydowndilly, likewise the lily,
All flowers that scent the sweet fragrant air.

There's gravel walks there for speculation
And conversation in sweet solitude;
'Tis there the lover may hear the dove, or
The gentle plover in the afternoon;
And if a lady would be so engaging
As to walk alone in these shady bowers,
'Tis there the courtier he may transport her
Into some fort or all underground.

For 'tis there's a cave where no daylight enters,
But cats and badgers are for ever bred;
Being mossed by nature that makes it sweeter
Than a coach and six or a feather bed.
'Tis there the lake is, well stored with perches
And comely eels in the verdant mud;
Besides the leeches, and groves of beeches
Standing in order for to guard the flood.

There's statues gracing this noble place in—
All heathen gods and nymphs so fair.
Bold Neptune, Plutarch, and Nicodemus,
All standing naked in the open air!
So now to finish this brief narration,
Which my poor genius could not entwine;

Cross Roads in Ireland

But were I Homer, or Nebuchadnezzar,
'Tis every feature I would make it twine.

This is the poem which James Stephens, as he told me once, would rather have written than anything else in an Irish anthology.

Glengarriff

An excursion-boat brought me from Cork Harbour to Bantry Bay—a considerable stretch of the coast of Cork. I landed at Glengarriff. To navalists, the bay is one of the best in Europe, sheltered, with deep water, without dangerous rocks or shoals—a bay in which a great fleet could be secure. Mountains close in the sea's long inlet, and an astonishing profusion of vegetation shows itself along the shore. It is a lonely place, too. No town rises beside the bay; no fisherman's boat is on the water; one knows that glens and rough defiles are features of the country that opens to the mountains around.

To this bay, around Christmas-time in 1798, came the French ships that were to bring men and munitions as aid to the Irish insurgents. After a long waiting and a great effort the high-spirited and persistent Wolfe Tone had prevailed upon the Directory to give such aid. The ships got here, but not a man, not a gun, not a cartridge got landed. And Wolfe Tone looked from the ship he was on to this land in a suspense that was saved from being agonizing by an unflagging spirit. "It is curious," he wrote in his journal,

WEST OF IRELAND SCENE BY PAUL HENRY

"to see how things are managed in this best of all possible worlds. We are here, sixteen sail, great and small, scattered up and down in a noble bay, and so dispersed that there are no two together in any spot, save one, and these are now so close, that if it blows to-night as it did last night, they will inevitably run foul of each other, unless one of them prefers driving on shore." The next day there was prospect of their landing, and Wolfe Tone and the French officers were as gay as larks. "It is altogether an enterprise truly unique, we have not one guinea; we have not a tent; we have not a horse to draw our four pieces of artillery; the general-in-chief marches on foot; we leave all our baggage behind us; we have nothing but the arms in our hands, the clothes on our backs, and good courage. But that is sufficient." Still the wind would not relent, and on December 29th failure was acknowledged. "At four this morning the commodore made the signal to steer for France; so there is an end to our expedition for the present; perhaps for ever." But Wolfe Tone was doomed to make another attempt to get French arms and French soldiers into Ireland.

Glengarriff and the way thence into Kerry is magnificent for scenery of mountain and glen. Around Bantry an enchantment is added to this magnificence: trees and flowers and plants find the atmosphere so kindly that they flourish surprisingly. It looks as if the bounds of gardens had been broken, so much of rare and flowering kind grow amid rocks and by the wayside. This is the place to see that native, the arbutus, with its shining green leaves and its bunches of red berries. The fuchsia has gone native: one has never seen fuchsias unless one has seen them growing around Bantry Bay.

It was the happy thought of a lady living here to make one of the islets off Glengarriff, Garinish, into a garden. This happy thought has been realized in a way that recalls Edgar Allan Poe's "Landor's Cottage." Mrs. Annan Bryce has now spent many years collecting and cultivating flowers, trees, and plants that can grow here—and any sub-tropical species can grow here. And she has made her island-garden part of the landscape: one looks down a vista of ilexes to the Kerry Mountains. One walks down an avenue of blooming Mediterranean shrubs to the water of this Irish bay. One sees fantastic orchids close to rocks on which the native heather has been left to flourish. Garinish has been made into a garden of gardens. And it is not merely an enchanting botanic display. There is a home amidst this profusion of trees and plants and flowers—the friendly home of Mrs. Annan Bryce. Painters and writers have been made welcome here. Here is the lovely little house in which Bernard Shaw worked at "Saint Joan."

The Outer Places

But we should be deceived if we thought that the flourishing vegetation that we see around the bay indicates a rich countryside. This is one of the poorest districts in Ireland—it is the southern limit of the resourceless, overcrowded lands officially known as the Congested Districts that stretch with some breaks from Donegal down through Kerry. When we pass the fronts of the hotels with their fine gardens and country-seats with their demesnes we come upon most poverty-stricken places. Glengarriff itself is a miserable village. But there are more miserable places around it, as I was to discover in a day or two.

I was in the dining-room of a hotel. The maid had brought in a lamp, and MacKinstry, the official from the Land Department, had finished dinner. He had been through the country on his motor-cycle, and he was relating his experience and his views in his staccato Ulster voice. "You should have seen the places where I was to-day. I wonder in the world how people can live in them. In one place the whole of the land occupied by seventeen families wouldn't make one economic holding. What's the total valuation, do you think?"

I told him I hadn't any idea.

"Forty pounds—total valuation, mind you, and there are seventeen families trying to make a living on it. I don't know what's to be done for them. Their miserable holdings are even compact—the fields are all through each other. James Moriarity has a ridge on Michael O'Sullivan's two-acre field, and O'Sullivan has a patch about the size of this table on Mary O'Driscoll's ground. Economic holdings, how are ye! I tell ye that the whole of the land owned by the seventeen families wouldn't make one economic holding."

I asked him did the curious distribution of their pieces of ground lead to disputes amongst these neighbours.

"No, then," he said. "They're agreeable enough to each other. You see, their customs are long established and well known. But how to settle them on a fair piece of ground—that's the problem."

There was a hesitating knock at the door, and MacKinstry called out, "Come in." No one entered; the knock was repeated, still more hesitatingly. I went and opened the door. There was a man standing just outside it. He wore no overcoat, but, as a kind of protection against the wild weather, he had a handkerchief rolled around his neck and he wore mittens on his wrists. Rain-drops fell from the worn brim of his hat. The man was about forty; he had a sunken face, red-lidded eyes, and that spiritlessness that comes from a long strain. "I was told," he said, "that I might come here and ask for the doctor." MacKinstry recognized the man, and addressed him as Mangan. He was from the uneconomic land that he had just been talking about.

"What's the matter, Mangan?" MacKinstry asked.

"The wife's very bad, sir."

"What is it?"

"They say it's fever, sir."

I told Mangan that the doctor wasn't in the room, but that I knew where to find him. Gilroy, the *locum tenens*, was staying in the hotel, and I thought that I could find him in the smoking-room. Mangan came with me. He was amazed at the comforts that the hotel displayed. "Sure, Mr. MacKinstry, it is heaven here," he said longingly. Then he saw the Commercial Room, with the fire of coal piled high, and the table covered with a cloth, lighted with lamps, and laid for dinner. He said, "I never thought there was a place the like of this in our parts." In the Smoking Room, the leather-covered chairs and the wide lights over the billiard-table made him exclaim in wonderment. Here he was given a glass of whiskey, and Dr. Gilroy, who was in his own room, was sent for. Mangan drank his whiskey slowly, with his eyes fixed on the red ball on the table. He was still gazing at it when Gilroy came in. "The wife is bad with fever, sir," he said, "and they want you to go to her to-night."

"Where do you live?"

"Templepatrick, seven miles from here, sir. Up the mountain it is. You leave the car at the commencement of the hill, and there will be a man to guide you across the fields."

I asked the doctor to let me go with them. He agreed. After a few minutes he had his bag in his hand and was ready for the road. We drove along an empty and hedgeless road. At the commencement of the hill a man was waiting for us. Here the county road stopped, and the arm of the mountain-road lifted itself abruptly. Bogs were each side of it. The car-man was told to wait for us, and Mangan and the doctor, the stranger and myself turned into a laneway. The stranger was Mangan's brother-in-law. He caught my arm and held me back for some confidences. At first I thought he was overcome with emotion, and then I realized that he was intoxicated with illicitly distilled mountain whiskey. The doctor and Mangan got far ahead of us. My guide brought me across a wall of loose stones, and then dragged me into a shough of water. He kept me standing at the other side while he went on with apologies and confidences. Then I got him to make a start again.

We came on a piece of building that I thought was a low wall of loose stones, but which turned out to be the back of one of the cabins. We passed the gable-end of a lightless house, and then we saw Mangan's cabin to the right of us. The doctor was in the room with the woman when we entered. The only light in the house was the candle placed near the sick woman's bed. On the kitchen hearth some sticks were lighted. Before them sat three children with a woman who, I imagine, was their grandmother. There was nothing in the kitchen except a dresser, a table, some stools, turf, and a settle-bed. "Will I live or die, doctor?" the woman in the bed was saying. "We always want people to live. Now tell me, what did you have to-day? Did you take gruel?" "Yes, doctor, I took a little gruel." "That's right. And was the priest to see you?" "He was, doctor. I was anointed, but the people said that didn't mean . . ." "Yes, of course, people are anointed if there's the least danger. They say they get better after seeing the priest. They're easier in their minds. Isn't that so?" "Yes, doctor." "I'll leave you something to take." And so the conversation in the room went on, the woman eager, terrified, but trusting; the doctor, professional, kind, and soothing; the husband sometimes putting in a word. The children sat together and were very quiet. The old woman rocked herself and repeated phrases in Irish. I thought she was praying, but I caught words of a charm against fever.

The doctor came down looking as vital and efficient as ever, and the man of the house followed him like a dog. "Send the children up to their mother and come outside with me," the doctor said. The children went into the room quietly, the grandmother remained shaking her head and swaying herself, and the doctor, Mangan, and myself went outside. When we were some distance from the house, the doctor faced Mangan and told him that his wife would not live—she had no reserve of vitality. By this time the brother-in-law had come up with us, and Gilroy took him along for guide. The three of us went on. When I turned round I saw Mangan walking back to his desolate house.

To Limerick

Kerry, Clare, Galway, Mayo, Sligo—the counties of the west coast were before me, each one with its own distinctive interest. I had made up my mind, however, not to go into Kerry or the Connacht counties. I should go to Limerick now. The Shannon enters an inlet there, and as I had already (this will be told) come down the Shannon from Cavan, I could round off my travels by standing on the bridge across it in Limerick town. So from Bantry Bay I went to Macroom, and from Macroom to Mallow (all in West Cork) and from Mallow to Limerick.

Michael Collins

We were on the road to Macroom and going to Bandon when the driver of the outside car turned around and said to me, "You knew Michael Collins?" I said "No," and told him that I had never seen Michael until after his death—until I looked upon him lying in state in Dublin. We were on the road on which he had been killed in an ambush in August 1922. The man who was driving me became silent, and we went on for a long space without speaking to one another.

I was thinking what a legend-invested figure he was, this man whom the man driving me had known, whose death happened when he was thirty-one, and whose public career was a matter of only three years. He was born and brought up just a little south of where we were; often, as a boy, he must have been on the road we were travelling, the road he was killed on, and this, too, I thought, was in keeping with that legend-invested life. I recalled the portrait of him that I had seen in the room in Leinster House in which the Executive Council of the Free State has its sittings. The portrait of Robert Emmet is beside it. Emmet, unlike the representations of him in simple Irish households, does not look a romantic figure in this authentic portrait: what one remembers is the narrowed eyes, the tightened mouth—a man, one would say, not primarily of vision, but of doctrine and decision. Boyish, alert, responsive, the face of Michael Collins makes a contrast to that of the earlier insurrectionary leader. Emmet is the eighteenth-century European; Michael Collins is the Irishman of the resurgence, native for that blue-black hair in the "glibbe" across his forehead and his wide grey eyes, native for the round and soft contour of the face that yet holds something extraordinarily dynamic. Michael Collins was the most racial of all the men who have given leadership to Ireland— as racial as Daniel O'Connell.

The O'Coileain or Collins are plentiful in this their native district, and have been to the fore here since the time of the Munster principalities. Michael's father was a West Cork farmer who at the age of sixty married a girl of twenty—a girl of the district. There were eight children in the family and all survive except the one who was killed here. Michael, the youngest, was born when his father was seventy-five. A vigorous stock! His father had the sort of culture that befitted a Munster man whose youth was back in the time of the hedge-schools and the wandering teachers of the classics. He spoke Irish and English and he had a knowledge of Latin and Greek. Michael went to London as a youth and got some sort of clerical appointment there. He came over to Dublin in 1916 as a member of an Irish Volunteer company to take part in the insurrection. His chief was Joseph Plunkett. "He retreated with his dying chief to Moore Street, and was among the surrendered prisoners of Head-quarters Staff." Such was his entrance into Irish revolution. Six years after that he is commander of the army which has had its origin in the insurrection, and he is killed when the armoured car in which he is making a tour of inspection runs into an ambush of Irregulars.

He would have been in a European army a great chief of staff, and in American business an efficiency expert who would have filled his office with go-getters. When he was killed he was head of the Provisional Government of Ireland, he was commander of the military forces at the disposal of that government, and he was Minister of Finance. He was more than all this. I once asked one of the ministers of the Provisional Government if they had to form an inner cabinet. "Michael was the inner cabinet," he said. "He made the decisions and gave the instructions." But it was as chief of the intelligence department of an outlawed and proscribed legislature that he did the work that counted in the last Irish struggle. He helped to destroy the British Government in Ireland by depriving it of its eyes. He got more spies and better spies than Dublin Castle got or could get; he made it dangerous to be informative in the precincts of the castle. He realized how essential an intelligence service was to the revolutionary movement and to its enemies. "Spies," he wrote, "are not so ready to step into the shoes of their departed confederates as are soldiers to fill up the front line in honourable battle. And even when the new spy stepped into the shoes of the old one, he could not step into the old one's knowledge. . . . We struck at individuals, and by doing so we cut the lines of communication, and we shook their morale." He was always seeking for information, for data, and he was seeking beyond the battle-line. While the turmoil of the civil struggle was still on he wrote to a colleague in London, "Would you please go to the Swiss Ambassador, and inform him you are acting for the Irish Government, who are wishful of sending a party of four experienced officers to make a report on the Swiss Army system for the Irish Government." The information he gained he was able to make part of himself. The English sculptor to whom he gave sittings told me that he noticed that Collins' understanding of sculpture grew from day to day.

He was an extraordinarily energized man. A scholar-friend of mine who saw him at the Griffith funeral said that he radiated power, that one felt that by touching him one would gain in vitality. For over two years there was hardly a day, hardly a night, in which he was not in danger of meeting a violent end. This was when people were becoming aware that in the partially smothered warfare that was being waged with the British power he was the most notable of the champions. At the time only a very small part of the Dublin public had ever looked upon him. When the truce with the British came and when Dail Eireann was able to go into public sessions, "crowds fought with one another to obtain a glimpse of the mysterious man who, through two years of war and terror, had been a legend in Ireland. . . . Many were surprised to find a cheery-looking, smiling, unassuming young Irishman in place of the romantic figure they had pictured to themselves." [1] Arthur Griffith said of him, "He was the man who made the situation. . . . He was the man whose matchless energy and indomitable will carried Ireland through the terrible crisis; and though I have not now, and never had, an ambition about either political affairs or history, if my name is to go down in history, I want it associated with the name of Michael Collins."

According to Lord Balfour this last Irish revolutionary effort was "steady, systematic, and ruthless." Its steadiness was due to Arthur Griffith's Sinn Fein programme; its system was largely due to Michael Collins. Others in that and in previous revolutionary efforts had qualities of fearlessness, devotion, singleness of purpose. Collins had all these qualities and he had another quality which made him an exceptional figure in an Irish revolutionary movement—an interest in and a mastery over detail. But this spirited and amazingly energized young man was, as one who was very close to him told me, often a sorrowful person. Probably he foresaw the breach with old comrades, the

[1] Piaras Beaslai: "Michael Collins and the Making of a New Ireland."

The South

condemnation that an Ireland that carries so much slavery of mind is likely to visit on leaders who have to make decisions, the doubt about the value of what has been achieved that comes after a time of violence; probably he foresaw the end that awaited him. As he came along this road he said to General Dalton, the soldier who was with him, "I don't suppose I'll be ambushed in my own county." He said it pensively. His car was ambushed. Instead of keeping within its armour he jumped out to attack the attackers. The bullet that killed him, President Cosgrave told me, bounded from the armour of the car; it struck him at the back of the head. "Then," said General Dalton in his report of the happening, "O'Connell now knelt beside the dying but still conscious chief, whose eyes were wide open and normal, and he whispered into the ear of the fast-sinking man the words of the Act of Contrition. For this he was rewarded by a slight pressure of the hand. . . . Then, with my heart torn with sorrow and despair, I ran to the chief's side. Very gently I raised his head on my knee and tried to bandage the wound, but, owing to the awful size of it, this proved very difficult."

Michael Collins was praised by prophecy. In the end of "The Green Helmet," Yeats' heroic farce, when Curoi picks Cuchullain for the championship because he alone of the heroes is ready to lay his head on the headsman's block while the axe was held above him, we have a projection of an heroic figure which was realized in this young champion:

Cross Roads in Ireland

I'm the Rector of this land,
And with my spitting cat-heads, my frenzied moon-bred band,
Age after age I sift it, and choose for its champion-ship
The man who hits my fancy.
And I choose the laughing lip
That shall not turn from laughing whatever rise or fall,
The heart that grows no bitterer although betrayed by all;
The hand that loves to scatter; the life like a gambler's throw;
And these things I make prosper, till a day come that I know,
When heart and mind shall darken that the weak may end the strong,
And the long-remembering harpers have matter for their song.

The Shannon

In Land-under-Wave—that is, in the Country of the Immortals—there was a well that was called Connla's Well. Seven streams issued from it, and over it grew the sacred hazels; "that is, the hazels of the science of poetry, and in the same hour their fruit and their blossom and their foliage break forth, and then fall upon the Well in the same shower, which raises upon the water a royal surge of purple." In the Well was the Salmon that fed upon the fruit of the hazels— the Salmon of Knowledge.

Now Sinend, the grand-daughter of Ler, went to the Well, and, hoping to gain knowledge, she followed one of the streams. But, although she was of the Divine Race, all that she did was done without due rite or preparation. The fountain itself pursued and overwhelmed her. It swept her lifeless body into the world of mortals, and made a stream that has kept the rash goddess's name, Sionnain— the Shannon.

But now if we go to where the Shannon has its rise we will be made think that none of the world's great rivers make so unsensational an appearance. In a farmer's field in the County Cavan there is a pool of an irregular oval shape and about the size of a kitchen floor in one of the cottages. Out of this pool issues a stream which one could easily leap across; this stream is the Shannon on its first appearance. Higher up are the low Quilca hills: waters gather there, flow underground, and then, through a fault in the limestone rock, rise into this pool. The water is still and peaty-brown; a few bog-myrtles grow across the pool. There is no hazel dropping its nuts of knowledge into the water, no rowan or mountain-ash showing its scarlet berries in the peaty water. And the legend that connects the rise of the Shannon with violation of the rites in the approach to science and art is not remembered hereabouts.

The stream in which the Shannon begins has bog-myrtles growing across it and reeds growing into the middle of it. It flows on; it widens; a large stream flows into it; it widens still more and flows through a lake—Loch Allen. The lake is so shallow as to be unnavigable; the Shannon flowing out of it is shallow and unnavigable. A canal running alongside the river makes it possible to take a boat from Loch Allen to the second of the Shannon lakes, Loch Ree. Loch Ree has wide and deep water, and it is down Loch Ree that we travel now.

This is a highway upon which the traveller need feel no sense of being alien from early or even legendary times. One sees no towns nor villages as one travels down this part of the Shannon; there are fields tilled and untilled; the wild duck rises to fly in threes; cormorants sit like sentinels upon rocks and hasten away as one goes by. This expansive and peaty-brown water belongs to times undated and legendary, and even the noise of the motor which drives the boat cannot distract one from the sense of the past; this river is as it was when the coracles of saints went up and down it in search of more perfect solitudes, and the boats of marauding Norsemen came up it to plunder the monasteries.

There are islets on Loch Ree and we land on one of them, on Hare Island. Here are trees with ivies growing thickly around trunks and branches. Ivies cover the ground. Hollies grow beside the ivy-covered trees. There are banks of brackens. All is green, but sombre green—the green of an enclosure, not of open places. Here and there a low-sized mountain-ash holds up bunches of berries that have the red of flowers. There is no song of birds; now and again a wren flits silently from the ivies of one branch to the ivies of another. But the islet, as soon appears, is not the sanctuary which it seemed to be. We meet an angry man who is the steward attached to the one house on the island. He is going to be up and watching all night; fellows have been coming to the island and stealing trees. A night's work here gets several trees down and away in boats. The Civic Guards have not been able to trace the timber stolen, but it is suspected that the depredations are being done by fishermen from a village down the river. They cut up the timber and use it to make or repair their boats; one can't identify it and claim it in their yards or sheds. He was a suspicious steward, and he was not sure but that we were associated with the raiders. Leaving the islet and going down the river we come in sight of the bridge and castle of Athlone.

Athlone

On the bridge of Athlone there was a man and he was ringing a bell. The jangle he made was to announce something quite up to date—a Charlie Chaplin show in one of the two cinemas the town possesses. Nevertheless this bell-ringer (Jack Stirabout is his name) was practising an hereditary calling; his father, his grandfather, and his great-grandfather were bell-ringers and watchmen to the town of Athlone. So they tell me, the girls who are taking me to the cinema. And afterwards to a bridge-party, they say. But I say no. Nora can go to her bridge-party, and Cathleen, if she wants to, but Brighid has won a silver medal at the Feis, and it is fitting that she should bring me back to the house and let me hear the prize-winning song. We cross the bridge; we go into the cinema and sit with the young soldiers from the barracks, and watch

"The Gold Rush." Outside I hear the hereditary bell-ringer.

Athlone is at the very centre of Ireland. Cross the bridge over the Shannon in one direction and you are half-way to Dublin; cross it in the other direction and you are half-way to Galway. The place had always military importance; here was the ford and here was the bridge across the Shannon; armies going into or coming out of Connacht had to cross the river here. It is an uncared-for town. Its old graveyards are the most nettle-covered of all the graveyards of Ireland (and that's saying a good deal). There is a huddle of high walls along a crooked, narrow street that looks grim at night—like Spanish convents and fortresses. And when one has come down that street one can stand on the bridge and watch the darkened river. In the day-time the best of Athlone is the levelled redoubts and forts which give something of a park to the town: the ground is hillocky; hawthorns are in the hedges and a bush or a clump of bushes stand up here and there in the open. When they are in blossom it is pleasant to walk here. These dismantled fortifications are more of a common than a park. Goats and children and donkeys are all over the place.

One morning I stand under the remains of the old bridge of Athlone. A builder was making or repairing boats under the fragmentary arch, and a Franciscan friar in a robe with wide sleeves was standing there. Out of the hanging sleeves of his robe he produced

Estella F. Solomons

THE BUSY MILL

The South

manuscripts that told of happenings in old days in Athlone.

But I got very little of what Father Angelus told; for he began by mentioning that a Franciscan house was established in Athlone by King Cathal. Now of all the kings of Ireland that O'Connor king is the one whom I have least desire to know about. Is he not named King Cathal More of the Wine-red Hand, and can any record of battles or treaties add any interest to one who was so named? Surely not. To have got himself named Cathal More of the Wine-red Hand was achievement enough for any king of any Irish state. Not even the poets could add any interest to that title. Mangan tried. But he cannot substantiate the vision of magnificence that comes to us with the mere name; after the first stanza, in spite of the chiming verse, there is a fading away, and the effect that remains is due to the reiteration of the name:

> I walked entranced
> Through a land of morn;
> The sun, with wondrous excess of light
> Shone down and glanced
> Over seas of corn
> And lustrous gardens a-left and right.
> Even in the clime
> Of resplendent Spain,
> Beams no such sun upon such a land.
> But it was the time
> 'Twas in the reign
> Of Cathal More of the Wine-red Hand.

[331]

Cross Roads in Ireland

As I repeated the name to myself I lost Father Angelus's tale of early happenings in Athlone.

After their defeat at the Boyne (1690) the Franco-Irish forces held the line of the Shannon, Athlone and Limerick being the commanding positions. The first attacks on both places were beaten off. Then came the second attack on Athlone: it was under the command of Ginckle, a Dutch general; the defence was under a French general, St. Ruth. The struggle for Athlone became a hand-to-hand combat, the attackers taking the bridge across the Shannon arch by arch: on the 26th of June, with the exception of the arch on the Connacht side which the defenders had broken down, the bridge of Athlone was theirs. Now they laid timbers across the break and prepared to rush over them. On the defending side volunteers were called for: men with axes were required to hack through the planks and clear them away; as the attackers had artillery they would be exposed to a deadly fire. The first volunteers were from a Scottish regiment, and when they advanced with their axes there was breathlessness on both sides. Then cannon and muskets went off, and when the smoke cleared the first batch of volunteers were lying dead across the timbers. Other volunteers came forward. Plank after plank was torn up under fire and flung into the Shannon, and that arch might not be crossed.

St. Ruth was over-sanguine. He neglected the defence of a ford lower down the river: under German

officers Ginckle's forces made a crossing. They forced
the garrison out of Athlone. Patrick Sarsfield, an enter-
prising and successful Irish officer who was subordinate to St. Ruth, tried to induce the command to fall
back on guerilla operations. St. Ruth declined to adapt
his European tactics to Irish conditions, and offered
battle at Aughrim, a place eighteen miles west of Athlone. He was killed by a cannon-ball which took his
head off, and Aughrim was lost to the Williamite
forces.

At the end of the war the forces in the field came
under Irish control. St. Ruth was dead; Lauzon, who
had charge of the defence of Limerick, left the place,
saying, "It is not necessary for the English to bring
cannon against such a place as this. What you call
ramparts might be battered down with roasted apples."
But the defence of Limerick by Sarsfield was to give
a flash of gallantry to the war that established a Protestant succession in England and Catholic solidarity
in Europe. After the capitulation of Limerick the
fighting men, as after the Cromwell campaign, took
service abroad, leaving the land without defenders.

Aughrim looms in Irish tradition as the great historical disaster. It was the last stand of an organized
Irish army in the field. Afterwards what fighting there
was was by undirected and untrained insurgents. I look
on the place, a dreary flatness of grey field and brown
bog. From a rise of the ground a sightseer surveyed
this field three days after the battle when many of
the slain had been buried: he saw naked bodies of men

and they looked to him like flocks of sheep dotted over the pastures and the bog.

Lissoy

A few miles down the Shannon is Clonmacnoise, a place of the greatest interest. But it happens that I have written about Clonmacnoise in another book, and so I cannot take a reader there with me. But if I go a little way northeast of Athlone I can come to the place where Goldsmith's father lived when Oliver was a growing boy. Here is Lissoy. The walls of the house in which Noll Goldsmith was reared still stand, but they form a barn for the farmer who lives in the house next it. Farm-carts are in front of the old house; geese are lying on the ground before the door. At the other side of the road is the grassy rise—"the little mount before Lishoy gate" from which Oliver thought he could take in "the most pleasing horizon in nature."

The place has not been preserved as it should have been. The front wall of the house is standing; there is an arched door and two windows on the level of the door, and the remains of three windows above. Inside there is a zinc-roofed shed where a farmer has his carts. To the right is the farm-house, and to the left a few beech-trees. Geese are digging into the grass which is before the door.

Young Goldsmith

He took up a journal left there by his brother-in-law, and read "At the New Room an Assembly will

Estella F. Solomons

"THE DECENT CHURCH THAT TOPT THE NEIGHB'RING HILL"

be held on Tuesday and so continue on the second Tuesday in each month for the future, and as it is to subsist under proper Regulations and a proper person appointed for each Night to put them into Execution, it is hoped that the Meeting will prove agreeable to those who think it proper to attend." He had been at such an Assembly the night before. The young ladies had left him very much alone. No mama, after having drawn him to her chair, had remarked, "Lydia looks well at the harpsichord, does she not, Mr. Goldsmith?"

Now he looks at himself in the glass opposite. He is short in figure and shambling; in his shabby clothes he knows that it is possible to mistake him for a journeyman-tailor. He knows, too, that he is spluttering and hesitating in his speech. In his face he notes flabbiness and rusticity that are from the protruding upper lip, the unclosed mouth, the chin which, although defined, falls away from the lower lip. His face is badly pock-marked. His brow, his eyes, and his nose are good features: the brow very full and prominent, the nose forceful, the eyes well-fixed and seeing. Seeing what figure he makes he walks up and down the room in perturbation. "An ugly and a poor man is a society to himself; and such a society the world lets me enjoy in great abundance." He was to write that sentence while he was still twenty-four; he was away from his country and his own people when he wrote it, but he had not been long away. Now he began to know that he was destined to have such usage from the world.

Cross Roads in Ireland

As a boy living in these parts the world had treated him handsomely enough. From the time he was seven he made verses which were praised by his father and his uncles; they set him up for a prodigy and they delighted in showing him off. He was conscious of a circle around him who were ready to applaud his wit, his learning, and his drollery. His mother favoured this second son of hers who favoured her own side of the house. She insisted on his being given an education that would fit him for a profession. In the society to which they belonged education and prospect of the kind were claimed only for the elder son. So this second boy with the pock-marked face was kept very much forward. In his boyhood his appearance had not affected his spirits. But in the university at which he had spent a long time, his ungracefulness, his tongue-tiedness, his pauperism, his frequent blunders had created a circle of another kind around him—a jeering, unfriendly circle.

His isolation had not left him saturnine. He had taken to playing the flute. Isolation had helped him to reflection, to ordered thought, even though it had left him awkward, bashful, blundering. His escape from humiliation was in the turn that he has for vagrancy. "I love a straggling life above all things in the world; sometimes good, sometimes bad; to be warm to-day and cold to-morrow; to eat when one can get it, and to drink when it stands before one." He is speaking through a character when he says it, but by that time he had known vagrancy and its penalties, and he spoke without any bitterness. He had the sanguine spirit that goes so well with vagrancy. "No person had ever a better knack of hoping than I."

He had come on a visit to this house in which he had been reared: here his father and mother had lived, and here he had been brought up with his three brothers and his two sisters. His father had been passing rich, not on forty pounds a year, but on something more considerable—two hundred pounds a year, a good stipend in those days and in that part of the country. His father is dead now, his mother is living in a cottage in a near-by village; his sister Catherine and his brother-in-law, Dan Hodson, are the occupants of Lissoy. And he is back from Dublin with a bachelor's degree and the reputation of being only "a fair Idle Scholar."

When Catherine brings him to the tea-table, and when Dan Hodson, coming in from the farm, welcomes him to the house, he tells stories of his student escapades, knowing that what he tells will be re-told and will lose nothing in Catherine's re-telling. He stands at the door of the house and sees the dairymaid, Peggy Golden, coming from the fields; he waits for her, and she, in great delight, presses the hands of Master Noll. Now he will walk back to his mother's cottage in Ballymahon.

But he first goes up on the grassy eminence that is opposite Lissoy. Often he had sat there, looking over the countryside. It is wide and flat and nearly empty. Furze and broom are blossoming near him, and a blackbird is singing from ivy-covered wall. A pinnacle in the distance marks the centre of Ireland. There are houses like his father's with orchards beside them and trees around them, there are many miserable cabins, and there are walls that were once the walls of cottages. Once again as he sits on that eminence he feels the pensive influence of that landscape.

Now he takes the road. He hears the sound of a flute. It is being played in a cabin by the roadway; always he is charmed by an Irish tune, and he stops to listen to this one. He goes within. The chimney in that cabin is one hole and the window is another; the furniture is a table, a few chairs with seats of hayrope, some rickety stools, a pot, a cradle. He is welcomed and brought to the fire of peat that is upon the hearth-stone. The man who has been playing stretches a hand out to him. The household is speaking Irish; he speaks Irish, too, as he comes in. And now he listens to stories that he has listened to before—stories about the champions who had wreaked vengeance on the oppressors of the people forty years before. Someone, a stranger, whispers something about him. Is he not the son of the clergyman of the church to whom they had to pay tithes? But the man who whispered is silenced, for those in the house know and trust this young man. He knows what has been whispered about him. And he knows that he is no upholder of the pious, glorious, and immortal revolution that King William consummated on the plain beyond the river, in the Battle of Aughrim that is a disaster in the stories told at this cabin fireside. The man who whispered is silent now, and Galloping O'Hogan and Baldearg O'Donnell make their raids and take their last stands. Then the "collegian," Oliver Goldsmith, takes the flute and plays on it a tune he had learnt in Dublin.

Now the day is almost gone; it will be candle-light by the time he is at his mother's cottage. He takes farewell of those in the cabin and starts down the road. As he goes along he remembers a cheerful house that stood hereabouts. The general who was landlord had cleared away his tenants to give space for a park that was being laid out. How dispiriting was the vacancy in which the house had once stood! The cheerful tune that was in Noll's head went from it, and something that was full of sadness took its place. He stood and looked around him. An old woman, lone and shrinking, was carrying into a ruined and unlighted house a bunch of cresses she had gathered from the stopped stream. Now she was a trespasser on the place that had once been the garden of her house. He went within. Beside the huddled and silent figure of the woman he left one of the two or three coins he had had in his pocket.

He stayed on the roadway a little while, pausing and then going slowly along. There was in the landscape some influence that was reaching to him. The country was not quite flat: it went in little rises around him; there were sheep in the grey fields. Over a mere the twilight was coming slowly. The sunset over the Shannon left a few bars of light, and except for these the sky was colourless and toneless. There were ash-trees and beech-trees along his way; they were becoming chilled and lonely as if something was withdrawing from them. The trees, the sky, the mere, he thought, were showing themselves to him as tokens of a forsaken land. Deserted!

He lived at his mother's, but such centre as his life had was at his uncle's house. The Rev. Thomas Contarine was a thoughtful and learned man, and when he was with him Oliver felt he could talk as one scholar with another. His uncle had always had an interest in him; now that his father was dead he was prepared to help him to enter one of the professions. On his advice Oliver went on with his French studies. In the neighbourhood there were several Catholic priests who had been educated in Paris, who spoke French and had collections of French books. Young Goldsmith went diligently to one and another of them, and in a short time he had better command of French than any of the students who had left Dublin University in his time. To one of the priests he would often say that if all else failed him he would take the friar's cord.

Meanwhile he went on errands for his mother and had his solace in playing the flute.

His uncle claimed descent from the Contarini of Venice, and Oliver always thought there was something high-bred and noble about him. To him he would go, not as Noll, but as Oliver, putting off his vagrancy, his happy-go-lucky ways. They would talk about the university. Oliver would tell his uncle that he had not been good at the mathematics, but that no one had proved better at turning an ode of Horace's into English verse than he. He can show him that he knows Latin well and that he is beginning to know French exceptionally well. He lets him see that he makes good verses. And his uncle has always been able to recognize that he writes perspicacious English. He listens to his uncle's reminiscence of his days at the university.

Young Thomas Contarine had been the friend of young George Berkeley. He had heard as the most dramatic event in his life the expounding of the new system of philosophy; Berkeley's thought in Berkeley's delivery had been one of the influences on his life. In his book-room were all the books that the philosophic bishop had written at all the stages of his career. What was said about the immateriality of objects in the universe had never been grasped by him. But the parts of Berkeley's philosophy that dealt with politics and economy had made an impression upon the Rev. Thomas Contarine's mind; he often read to his nephew passages that dealt with such topics: that the countryside was the proper scene of human activity; that the merchant was to be distrusted; that wealth based on commerce was illusory; that all that was distant was dangerous, and that our activities have the happiest results when they are confined in small areas. Such discourse delivered under the sanction of the great bishop were readily accepted by young Oliver Goldsmith.

Cross Roads in Ireland

From Emlaghmore, his uncle's house, he would go to Kilmore where his uncle's daughter and her husband lived. He would find some of the grace of atmosphere that belonged to his uncle's in that house. He had always known Jane Lawder. Although she was much older than he—she was a married woman while he was still a child—he and she could banter each other and be merry together. So with deep content he would find himself at her tea-table, and afterwards he would join his flute to her harpsichord.

For his own brothers and sisters he had varying degrees of affection and intimacy. The family, indeed, was in irregular order: there were Henry and himself and his two sisters—they made a family to themselves; then, when it had been thought for some time that there would be no more children in the Goldsmith household, Charles and then Maurice were born. After another long space there was another child, Jack; he was now about seven, an ailing child.

Good-nature and dignity had belonged to their daily life in the house at Lissoy; they belonged, in a smaller measure, to the daily life of the family in the cottage at Ballymahon. His mother, Noll discovered, was an altered woman; she showed herself now as managing, strict, and exacting.

And why should there not be this change in her temper? She had lost one whose life had kept her in good hope. She had come down in the world; she was threatened, moreover, with the loss of a property she had fallen back on. Her family, she was beginning to think, had not many members who would prove themselves a credit to herself and their father. Henry, the eldest, was in holy orders; he had succeeded to his father's living and was respected and respectable. But, marrying young and of his own choice, he had broken his career at the university without making himself the scholar that it was expected he would be. Catherine, married to Dan Hodson, had not done badly for herself. But Jennie, foolishly taken in, had married beneath her. Maurice and Charles were grown men now, but neither had wit nor education enough to rise in the world; they would have to become tradesmen unless their friends and relations could help them to something better. Then there was little Jack. He was not likely to survive, and his mother had herself to blame for his sickliness. And now Oliver was back to her. She had liked him better than any of the others, but what was he going to do with himself now? He was unsteady. And he had an annoying trait—he was fond of making up and of telling stories; this had been encouraged in him as a child, but it was apt, she saw now, to put him astray. It was no wonder, taking the widow's anxieties into account, that the cottage had much less of an atmosphere of dignity and good-nature than Lissoy had had.

Oliver joins himself with Henry, his elder by about seven or eight years; he teaches in the village-school for his parson-brother. But will he become a parson himself? He does not relish the prospect, for his inclination is towards a roaming life. His uncle, however, is directing him towards a parsonage.

So Noll Goldsmith reads for holy orders. There are to be no more delays in calling on the bishop in Elphin —the bishop to whom his uncle has written and who has such good memories of his father. "But I must have a good coat on my back, Mother, if I am to call on His Grace." "Your uncle, several times, left money to outfit you." "I lost that money, Mother." Money will be left for an outfit, but not left in a place where Oliver can get hold of it. It will be left with the tailor.

He rides away and gets measured for a coat, and rides away another day and comes back with the coat in a package. He dresses himself in an uncle's house in Elphin and makes ready to call on the bishop. "Mr. Goldsmith, Your Grace." "But this fellow is wearing a scarlet coat. I cannot, I shall not present him." Then Noll goes back to Ballymahon. "But I should have to wear a drab coat, Mother, and how could I do that?" It was not altogether the livery he appeared in that prevented Noll Goldsmith's being entered for the church: the bishop had a relative whom he wanted the living to go to.

And now his cousin, Bob Bryanton, who had been with him at the university, going there later, was back in Ballymahon. Times were more lively in the village now. The house that had Bob back in it, and that had Betty and Peggy in charge of its tea-table, was often visited by Noll. Bob had brought back a liking for deeper potations than had satisfied him before. He was often in the taverns now. One of them became his headquarters; he formed a club that met in it. And at that club's meetings, Noll Goldsmith was a favourite entertainer.

He would sing street-songs he had made. He would tell how he made one now and again, and got five shillings for it from those who provided the ballad-singers with their sheaves; he would tell how he would slip out of bounds and stand at the street-corners to hear his ballad sung. Often, especially before those who have regard for his father's memory, he will bring in the names of the heirs to this and that great property hereabouts when he tells of his life in the university. But he will laugh a little after he has talked of such folk, remembering that as sizar he paid nothing for his food and tuition in the college and little for his lodging, and that he had to do menial services in return, such as sweeping up the court, carrying dinner to the Fellows' tables, changing plates, and pouring out ale; remembering, too, the garret which he had shared with another student, one who had the same sort of broken boots, the same sort of out-at-elbows clothes which he had himself; remembering how he was satirized openly by the professors to the glee of the young bucks and bloods who were around, moved more and more to laughter by his embarrassments and blunders. Perhaps he can remember himself on a bench in the college grounds, with such thoughts in his mind as made his own society not so intolerable, after all, or walking down a back street and listening pitifully to some tale so distressing that it had to be told even to a ragged student.

His uncle got him a place: he became tutor in the house of one of the gentry of the neighbourhood. It was not a house that could be hospitable to Goldsmith the scholar; it could not offer him any impression of grace or fineness. "Most of the bucks and bloods whom I left hunting and drinking and getting bastards I find are dead. Poor devils, they kick'd the world before them. I wonder what the devil they kick now?" Such was the impression that the Irish gentry of his generation left upon Oliver Goldsmith. They were not interested in his French prose writers and his Latin poets. "There has been more money spent in the encouragement of the Padareen mare there one season, than given in rewards to learned men since the times of Usher." The response to what teaching he could give was not encouraging. And away from the influence of his uncle and the sharp glances of his mother he, too, began to live the life of the young squireen. He played cards in the tavern and the country-house; he amused the company by singing rollicking songs of his own composition. In the tavern or in one of the houses he visited he met a bold maid who looked him full in his pock-marked face when he asked her to take him upstairs to see her handiwork.

Vagrancy grew on him. He wandered around the countryside, and attended many a dance and was in many a wake-house. Often, riding back at night, he

The South

would hear that sound that so deeply impressed him, a sound characteristic of that part of the country with its rivers and lakes—the booming of the bittern. "Those who have walked in the evening by the sedgy sides of unfrequented rivers must remember a variety of notes from different water-fowl: the loud scream of the wild goose; the croaking of the mallard; the whining of the lap-wing, and the tremulous neighing of the jack-snipe. But of all these sounds, there is none so dismally hollow as the booming of the bittern. It is impossible for words to give those who have not heard this evening call an adequate idea of its solemnity. It is like the interrupted bellowing of a bull, but hollower and louder, and is heard at a mile's distance, as if issuing from some formidable being that resides at the bottom of the waters." Along those unfrequented river-sides he hunted the otter.

Sometimes, as he rounded up his charges and turned them to their dog-eared primers, a sickness of spirit would come upon him. Why did he stay here? Would it not be better for him to be in a garret in London, living four pairs of stairs high, and writing for his bread, than to endure this tedium and emptiness? God's curse! who were the people at whose beck and call he was? Did they know who he was? He'd tell the cubs, although they would not be able to comprehend what he was telling them! "Do you know whom you have offended? A man whose character may one of these days be mentioned with profound respect in a German comment or a Dutch dictionary; whose

name you will probably hear ushered in by a Doctissi-
mus Doctissimorum, or heel-pieced with a long Latin
termination. Think how Goldsmithius, or Gubblegur-
chius, or some such sound, as rough as a nutmeg-grater,
will become me?" "You're not teaching us very well
this morning, and papa says you are not a good tutor."

Then something happens over cards—Oliver wins
too much, or he loses with a bad grace, or he loses
more than he possesses. He has to leave the house. He
walks down the avenue, his head bent, a wine stain on
the coat that had been bought for him when he entered
upon his tutoring career. He walks out of the domain,
and the lodge-keeper closes the gate upon him.

He is back in Ballymahon. Now he talks about a
ship sailing for America in six weeks' time in which he
will take passage and land himself a better position
than he can get in Ireland. His uncle shows his disappointment in him and intimates that he has lost the
hope of seeing in his nephew the worthy scholar that
it had been his hope to see. But his other relatives are
willing to have Noll leave the country. Money is made
up for him, a sum of thirty pounds. A handsome horse,
too, is provided to carry him from Ballymahon to
Cork, a distance of one hundred and thirty miles. He
is to sell the horse when he gets to Cork, and add the
price to his capital.

He has a good suit on his back and he carries shirts
which his mother and his sister Catherine have made
for him. He makes a round of farewells, and early

one morning he starts off, his brother Charles going some of the way with him. Charles often has a notion of going to foreign parts himself, and he urges Noll to be sure to write and give him all information about prospects in Boston or Pennsylvania, or whatever the place is that he is to land in. . . . Six weeks later Noll is home. The handsome horse which he had under him when he rode south has disappeared; in its place is a sorry beast that looks just worth the price given at the knacker's yard—eighteen shillings.

Noll Goldsmith is home again! The tidings go through the village and the neighbourhood, and great is the anticipation of a prime tale of adventure. Relatives gather to his mother's cottage to hear the account the rambler will give of himself. He tells how he converted his handsome horse into cash, and how he paid the captain of the ship for his passage. "But the wind did not answer for three weeks, and you know, Mother, that I cannot command the elements." When it did answer he was not near at hand, and the ship sailed from Cork without him. He had to give himself some entertainment to get over his disappointment; he stayed in the town and gave himself up to what pastimes he was led to. Then he bought this Fiddleback of a nag for a few guineas and started for home. He had adventures on the way. There was a woman who was in such distress that he had to give her a share of the money he had left in his pocket. A stingy acquaintance declined to give him assistance; a generous stranger entertained him, and let him have the loan of the three half-guineas that had enabled him to get back to his mother and his good friends—to get back on Fiddleback, the substitute for the horse they had presented him with.

"And now, dear Mother," he says, "since I have struggled so hard to come home, why are you not better pleased to see me?" "Pray now," says she, "have you written a letter of thanks to the dear good man who helped you?" "I have not." "Then," says she, "you are an ungrateful monster, a savage." He laughs at that, and coolly informs her and the assembled family that the story told has just been made up to amuse them. Thereupon they all upbraid him for being so unprincipled as to squander the money they had made up for him and to come back with a lying story in his mouth. Afterwards he tells his sister Catherine that the story was not all made up; there was some truth in it.

The family resolve to show Noll that they are through with him. Uncle Contarine will not see him nor speak to him; this is a matter of real distress to Oliver. His mother shows him that she does not want him in the cottage. Dan Hodson and his sister take him in, and he goes to live at Lissoy. Jane Lawder remains his friend, and she strives to bring about a reconciliation between Cousin Noll and her father.

He appears at Bob Bryanton's club, and for the cronies there he makes a longer and a better story out of his journey to Cork. His reputation as a humorous fellow grows, but less and less is thought of him as a scholarly man. When some of his sayings and doings are reported there are hearty laughs in the tavern by the roadside. "It's the very stamp of Noll," acquaintances say. At last Cousin Jane's efforts lead to a reconciliation: good Uncle Contarine sees him. He will help him once more. . . .

Edward Mills, Oliver's cousin, was going to study law; Oliver should do likewise. So between Uncle Contarine and some other relations a sum of fifty pounds was raised; once more Noll was given an equipment, and once more he went from mother and uncle, from brothers, sisters, and cousins.

He reached Dublin. There he renewed acquaintance with fellow-students who were now being trained for the legal business. He goes back to the college; with cronies he goes into the garret where he had lodged; he looks at the name he had scratched on the window there, and he talks of the time when that name will represent a great legal luminary. Money is shown. There is a visit to a gambling-house. Then another visit. And after a third visit there is no money left on which to make an entrance into the profession. Once more Noll Goldsmith rides back to Ballymahon.

But he is a different Noll Goldsmith from the one who had appeared in the village at any other time. No longer was there anything rollicking about him. He is so dejected as to appear broken-hearted. He makes no rounds with Bob Bryanton; his place at the club knows him no longer. In his sister Hodson's he takes refuge; there he sits and broods or else writes for hours at a stretch. He no longer plays the flute, but he often sits at the fire-place in the old kitchen, and has Peggy Golden sing to him.

And so it goes on until his good uncle once again comes to his relief. Jane Lawder asks him what he wants to do with himself: he has tried to enter the Church and the Law and evidently has no heart for either. He is to say what he wants to do, and his uncle for the last time will help him towards what he wants. Even as his cousin says this to him Oliver Goldsmith knows what profession he fain would enter.

For he remembered how he had looked on this man and that man walking down the street of a city, a gold-headed cane in his hand. A doctor! Yes, that was the profession for him. Medicine that was not drab like the Law or the Church, and that would not separate him from people but put him amongst them. Medicine! He would be a doctor and carry a gold-headed cane. So overjoyed was he at the prospect that he saw before him that, for the first time in months, he joined his flute to his cousin's harpsichord.

Uncle Contarine considered the proposal. Oliver thought of Edinburgh, and the name of Munro—he had heard it from students in Dublin—became a talisman for him. " 'Tis he, I venture to say, that draws such a number of students from most parts of the world, even from Russia." His uncle agreed to bear the expenses, or most of the expenses, seeing that Medicine had power to arouse such enthusiasm in the man who lately was so dejected.

THE TIPPERARY HURLER BY SEAN KEATING

The South

An elation that had not been part of the feelings he had had, the expectations he had formed before any of his other departures, now possessed young Oliver Goldsmith. He was leaving an effortless, a spiritless life behind him. Already in his mind there were plans and projects. Edinburgh was a capital which Dublin was not: he would meet there men who would recognize something in him and help to form it. And he would not be one of the obscure of Edinburgh, either; the Duchess of Hamilton was there, Betty Gunning, with whom he could claim kin. He would visit her, and the beautiful duchess would not be inactive in advancing his fortunes. London was not remote from Edinburgh; the fortunes that Swift and Steel had attained to there might be attained to by another.

Things were made ready for his going—hats and boots, shirts and suits. He would bring money with him and draw on his uncle as necessities arose, necessities that would be necessities indeed. A little of the money was now in his pocket. It was fair day in Ballymahon, and with Cousin Bob he went into one or two of the taverns and paid scores that had long been due. He counselled Bob against the deep potations that he was now getting the habit of indulging in. Everywhere Noll Goldsmith was received as a man who had the prestige of departure already upon him. Cordial were the good-byes that were given him at the club. Townspeople, bringing his father's name into everything they said to him, wished him the height of good fortune. Well, by the time he was back amongst them

Cross Roads in Ireland

George Conway would have his sign put up, Tom Allen would have his new wig, but there would still be the same pleasant people to meet in Ballymahon.

The young men were throwing the hammer in a place off the fair-green. They called to him as he came along. He stood amongst them and watched them mark the place of the farthest throw. Then, taking off his coat, he laid his hands on the hammer's handle. He threw it; it passed the farthest mark. A cheer went up for Noll Goldsmith. The prize was handed him; he went with the young men to this and that tavern, and drams were handed round and taken.

Henry, his brother, paternal as ever, came to the cottage: Charles and Maurice were there. Charles attentive as always when foreign places were being talked of. Little Jack Goldsmith had no talk about his complaint. His mother made Oliver listen to exhortations, but she spoke them in a hopeful tone. Bob Bryanton came in with his sisters Betty and Peggy; the girls kissed Noll and lamented his going to such distant parts.

And then Uncle Contarine and Cousin Jane and Cousin Jane's husband came in. Oliver looked upon them all, mother and brothers, uncle and cousins, taking notice of one and all, and feeling what happiness it would be to be back amongst them, skilful, learned, and famous, wearing a bloom-coloured coat and carrying a gold-headed cane. Then, in his uncle's face he would see a look of approval, and not, as now, the look of a man who was conscious of doing a charity.

The South

Pity and charity! They were great virtues, but pity
'twas to have always to look for them. "His pity gave
ere charity began," he said to himself as he thought
of his father's quick identification of himself with
hunger and beggary as he relieved some distress. And
now his uncle was passing over letters and money for
the journey and initial expenses in Edinburgh. The
look he gave him made Oliver spring up and put his
hand in the old man's hand. "You are the philosopher
who carries all his goods with him," Uncle Contarine
says to him. "Let me acknowledge the humility of the
station in which you found me," Oliver responds, "let
me tell how I was despised by most, and hateful to
myself. Poverty, hopeless poverty, was my lot, and
Melancholy was beginning to make me her own." It
was a solemn occasion; little Jack Goldsmith, however,
made a distraction by bursting into tears.

He will start from Lissoy, and that evening he goes
back there. To Dan Hodson he speaks very readily of
the prospects before him. He will combine poetry and
medicine; he will be the philosopher of medicine. He
tells him and his sister Catherine that he wants to take
farewell, not only of them who are the nearest and
dearest to him, but of the whole countryside. Once
again he climbs the eminence and looks across the
countryside with its little rises, its long mere. He remembers a night in summer when he stood here and
saw lovers seated under the hawthorns around, and
old men discoursing in a group, or seated upon a bench.
Voices came up to him; they come back to him now.

Cross Roads in Ireland

He feels in the scene something Virgillian—*sunt lacrimæ rerum et mentam mortalia tangunt*. In a house near by someone plays a fiddle. The door of the house he was brought up in is open. Peggy Golden stands there and sings. And once again Noll Goldsmith listens to "Johnny Armstrong's Good-Night."

The Holy Island of Iniscealtra

The next day we are in the third, the last, and the largest of the Shannon lakes.

It is a great expanse of water lying between three counties—Galway, Clare, and Tipperary. From the Clare side our eyes search in vain for the brown Shannon stream—in that expanse the entrance and egress of the great river cannot be marked. The peaty colour of the Shannon has left no trace on the lake; in this August sunlight the lake is flashing as though flakes of fire were dropping on its waters; the ripples take the sun and break forward in lustre.

In Loch Derg, about eight miles from Killaloe in Clare, is the island of Iniscealtra. There are ruins on Iniscealtra which belong to the very earliest period of Christian history in Ireland, the period of the emergence from Paganism. . . . Those early saints, one must think, had a different outlook from the saints who founded the later monasteries. These put their establishments on the trading and travelling routes, and had an eye for good pasturage and good tillage-land. The earlier saints seem to have chosen places for one thing only—fairness of scene. And there could be no fairer scene in Ireland than the one that is to be had across the water from this fifty-acre island:

Fresh in wild holiness over
Each glittering mile,
And green with the blessings of Cellach,
There lies an isle,
Foundered on its own shadow
Of brambles and grass—
Its selvage of brambles still bending
Where saints sang the Mass;
Yet healing of sleep and the quiet
Of wells still are there,
With cold rushes telling their beads
On stones of dumb prayer!

I was able to say these lines by F. R. Higgins, a poet who has written often and beautifully of these lake-island retreats.

I had been here before and in a company of which one was the noted archeologist, Professor R. A. S. MacAlister. Professor MacAlister gave me afterwards his notes upon the early dwellers upon this island—a saint named Colum was the first of them.

Now on the day of the arrival of holy Colum at Iniscealtra, the Lord made for him a supper. For there was on that island a tree by the name *tilia*, whose juice distilling filled a vessel; and the liquor had the flavour of honey and the headiness of wine. And with that best of liquors were holy Colum and his followers filled. Now Colum lived in Iniscealtra for a long time, and the birds of heaven were wont to have friendly intercourse with him, and to sport fluttering about his face. Then

Nadcuimius, his pupil, said to him, "Master, wherefore do the birds not flee from thee, whereas us they avoid?" To him, Colum answered, "Wherefore should birds flee from a bird? For as a bird flieth, my mind never ceaseth to fly up to heaven?" . . . After this, holy Colum, not enduring the vexations of men visiting him, and shunning earthly pomps, left Iniscealtra for an island of that sea which is called Luimnech, and there held Iniseirc."

This saint was not the first occupant of the island, Professor MacAlister surmises. We hear of a woman who lived here; legend has it that the round tower on the island was left unfinished because of her scoffing at the builder. He came down from the top of the tower and struck her with his hammer, metamorphosing her into a figure of stone. And there she remained with the mark of the hammer upon her, and there the tower stood unfinished. She was a Fairy Hag, says the folk-tale. Professor MacAlister thinks she was a Druidess and the original custodian of the island's sacred tree. She cursed the saint who came to take the tree from her.

One would vastly like to know something more about this Fairy Hag, but neither tradition nor what has been written in the books has anything more to say about her. In the folk-tale about the struggle between her and the builder of the tower Professor MacAlister sees "a dim recollection of the early struggle between Christianity and Paganism on the island." [1] He concludes that the saint was not completely victorious,

[1] Proceedings of the Royal Irish Academy, Vol. XXXIII, Section C, No. 6.

and that the statement about his "not enduring the vexations of men visiting him" was an excuse. The first saint had to leave Iniscealtra.

But, of course, Paganism and its Druidesses could not long possess such an island-retreat as Iniscealtra against the enterprise of the saints of the sixth century. They came and they left a long succession; their legends are in books, and the names of a few of them are on inscribed stones which are still to be seen here.

A Prayer for the Chief Elder of Ireland, for Cathasach.
A Prayer for Tórnóc, who made the cross.

And then, after a thousand years, the faith which the saints had taught to people around the lake became proscribed itself. "At a place called Minahinshe . . . and at another place called Inishgaltraghe in Connaught, an island near the Shannon side, there was gathered together in each place to the number of at least 15,000 persons and some say there were many more," reports an English Deputy to the Privy Council. And what had these persons gathered for? To hear "the Jesuits and priests from abroad . . . the most eager and stirring of them usually come and go hence with the swallow, making a yearly revenue here of poor and rich, with their indulgences, pardons, and other Romish illusions. . . . There is not one of them, from the murderer of his brother to him that steals a goat, but believes in them, and flocks to them, and will make a conscience to cherish and protect them from officers, if any be so honest and dutiful as to offer to attach them."

The round tower associated with the early saints still stands; it is topless, and it has always been topless, the archeologists say. A round tower is always strange-looking and impressive: it stands isolated in time and place, and yet its stones have associations with fifteen hundred years of Irish history. Here, the mortar has dropped from between, and yet the stones remain together, grey stone topping grey stone. The tower is eighty feet high, and it stands beside a ninth-century chapel. The proximity of tower and chapel is like some scenic arrangement, a device for evoking the feelings and associations which we have for Celtic life. The little chapel has the bareness of the stones and the significance of the stones: the doorway is its only architectural feature, and the order of the doorway seems to have come less from the conquest of the stones than from some co-operation between the builder and his material; the decoration seems to have been made by simple-minded men who were used to working in hard materials.

In the chapel, on the ground or against the walls, are stone monuments; they show inscriptions, crosses, circles, elaborate Celtic patterns, all cut in stone. In the monks' burial place, as we pass along, we see varied designs of cross and circle and interlaced pattern upon stones. The garden enclosure is still marked and the postern to the garden remains. There is a chapel with a doorway intact; there is another chapel, a late one, in which there is an altar of stone; a broken figure has been set upon it. In this roofless building the altar looks wide and archaic, a Druid's altar.

And then, in the middle of the island, there is a cell, perhaps the cell of the first anchoret of the island; there are great ramparts around, earth-works now become grassy circles. Standing within the inner circle one can survey the whole island. Iniscealtra is like a green mound; a few trees are scattered across the green, and a thick clump of ash and hawthorn is near the landing-place. The island must be very fair when all that hawthorn is in bloom. At present the beauty of the island is in its setting in the blue water. The tower dominates the island. It was the citadel of the monastery: the stones could not be fired; the building could not be undermined; there was no cornerstone the removal of which would make a break in the tower; the door was covered with plates of iron. The treasures of the monastery and its books could be put into the tower when marauders appeared.

Amongst the bushes we discover another relic of monastic life. Here are four upright stones with a wider cell before them. I remember that the archeologist thought that the island's anchoret had had himself walled up between the upright stones, and that the cell in front was for the use of those who came to him for confession or instruction. A little below this cell there is a single slab; it may mark the grave of the anchoret. I leave the island thinking about him, and about the Daughters of Fergus whose feast used to be celebrated here. No one can tell us anything about them, but I think it no harm to repeat an aspiration in which they are mentioned—"The women-children of Fergus I beseech, the chaste ones without an evil course."

Clare and Limerick

Below Lough Derg is Killaloe. I stood on the long bridge across the Shannon there and looked towards the hills of Clare that were near me—the bloom of heather was distinct upon them; I got the impression of a region of strange colour and strange formations. And this impression of Clare has stayed with me, although at that moment there was a good deal going on to take from that romantic impression. A very ordinary regatta was being held on that part of the Shannon on that day and hour. Very ordinary people had come from the Clare side and the Limerick side to look at the boat-races and the rest of what goes on at regattas. A drizzle of rain came on, and the feats on the water became, as far as one spectator was concerned, less and less inspiring. There was a piper there —he had come south from Galway, I imagine—an upstanding man whose music I should like to have heard. But he got no encouragement to pipe for us. And there was an Italian ice-cream vendor. The vehicle he drove had gay stripes and bright pictures upon it; it had bells, too, and the vendor himself had a bugle on which he blew. He certainly made a stir at Killaloe. He

GALWAY BY MICHAEL MACLIAMMOIR

drove across the bridge and went towards the purple-mantled hills that looked so enchanting.

"In a wrinkle of these hills," said my friend, Hugh O'Brien, to me, "there is the oddest little village I ever was in—I have just come from it. It contains nine houses, all set at different angles, with no street—except in the purest Gaelic sense. The village is hidden until you turn a corner and come into it. I think I got to know the householders by heart. There is James Molloy and James Mellody, and the representative of Pat Mellody, James Mellody Con and James Mellody Michael, Con Mellody James, Con Mellody John, Mary Molloy and Nora Molloy. One of them is descended from a famous inventor: a stream flows through the village over a little water-fall, and the people draw their water from it. The invention was a piece of eave-shoot which, being laid down in the water-fall, greatly facilitated the filling of vessels therefrom. The inventor's descendant, James Mellody, is always distinguished by the title that has come to him from this ancestor—he is 'James of the Spout.' I have a feeling that the village was originally and essentially a nest of brigands; anyway, I can't imagine a more suitable nest. But the inhabitants are now all small farmers, and pay their annuities to the state most respectably."

Beside Killaloe is the site of a stronghold famous in Irish history and poetry, Kincora. But no trace of a stronghold now remains. Kincora was the stronghold of a king who, basing his power on the control of the

Shannon and taking pattern by Charlemagne, strove to work out a policy which would have made the high-kingship a reality. The king was Brian Boru—the only one of the Irish dynasts whose wars and policy we can recognize as having a national significance. Brian was an old man when he was killed at the close of a battle in which he had been victorious; had he survived that day he probably could have added little to what he had already done—disclosed an idea, formed a few instruments that could be used in the making of a state. No, Brian's death at seventy should not have been a disaster. The disaster was in the fact that he left no successor politic enough to get on with the work.

As one goes from Killaloe to the town of Limerick, one sees that fresh embankments have been given to the river and that areas of ground have been cleared. And then one sees high structures that have the shaft-like lines that express modern reach and power. They are power-house, piers, walls of locks. Built of concrete, they look as if they were thrust up out of the earth. These structures are surprising here, for they are not only modern but ultra-modern: they are representative of the latest phase of contemporary engineering. Inside the great power-house the walls have the grey of a battleship's hull; even the great pieces of machinery that are there have room to spare for their functioning, so spacious is the enclosure. This speckless, shadowless place is like a temple of modern power.

The South

In a room where there are small instruments and big charts I speak to some intent-looking men. "A crow can't strike against a wire in Kildare without our knowing about it here," one of them says as he makes an observation from an instrument. Here is concentration of practically all the hydro-electrical power the Irish Free State possesses, and concentration, too, of almost all the technical accomplishment of that area. And now the Shannon has begun to pour into the great turbine outside the power-house; with the use of that volume of water Ireland begins to redress the balance that has been against her industrially owing to her scanty coal supplies. Ninety thousand horse-power energy is now available; it can be brought up to one hundred and eighty thousand.

The Shannon as it nears Limerick has a drop in its level of about a hundred feet. This drop is in a series of falls, none of which are steep. The first stage in the enterprise was the making of a canal nine miles long which leads fifty per cent of the Shannon's water to a point at its lowest level. This is the place. The water has a fall of about a hundred feet into the turbines. These structures, the release of energy which they bring about, is the first manifestation of national vision, national direction. The work was undertaken immediately the Free State had any organization. And nothing that the Government could have embarked upon in the way of industrializing the country could have made such appeal to the imagination of the people as the harnessing of the river that is so famous in legend and history.

Limerick

Limerick has a wide principal street with massive Georgian houses—fine houses and a fine street. It has character through this street—rather a vacant street, it must be said—and the river that here shows itself as a river indeed. Intellectually, the town doesn't exist; I don't know a single book that has anything to say of Limerick since Gerald Griffin's "Collegians." The town hasn't a theatre or a picture-gallery. The people seem to be a distinctive folk. The children have plenty of character; they crowd the little, unkempt park that is here, red-haired, black-haired, yellow-haired children, all full of life; the good, clear faces of the children show that there is sturdy life around Limerick.

The Shannon is copious here. I watch a boat sailing down it; it is a very worn boat; it has two sails; with much creaking of tackle they are raised—sails as black as crape. As the boat goes towards the sunset, as the wind fills them, the sails look like sheets of iron; the boat seems heathen to me as its blackness comes between me and the verdure of the other bank of the river. But the four old men who are on that black-sailed boat are Christian men, for, as the angelus bell rings out, they cross themselves, stand still, and pray. And then I find out that there is nothing heathen

Courtesy of The Hackett Galleries

NIGHT'S CANDLES ARE BURNT OUT BY SEAN KEATING

in this black boat at all; it is only a peat-carrier coming from Clare.

The satirist of Trinity College, Mahaffy, once said of Limerick that it was the one city in Western Europe where, in the middle of the principal street, at the busiest hour of the day, a bittern might be observed standing on one leg. How odd that it is in a town of which this could be said that one most readily detects that positive outlook which will be the main ingredient in the new leadership of the country. The principal street is still rather vacant even at the busiest hour of the day. But one can meet groups of young men whose minds have the positive quality that is in the shaftlike modern buildings with their shadowless interiors that are a little way up the river. A new epoch begins in Ireland; the scene of its beginning is around Limerick.

Shannon Saga: Brian's Battle

Their defeat by the king whose dominion was at this end of the Shannon seemed portentous to the Northern rovers whose swords and axes had hewed out victories from Iceland to Normandy and from Caithness to Constantinople. They related that defeat in the Njal Saga with every weird circumstance. Earl Sigurd had such foreboding that for long he was steadfast against obeying King Sigtrygg's summons: he went to Ireland at last, but it was against the will of his followers. And after another earl, Brodir, had resolved to go, a shower of boiling blood fell upon him and his men; their axes and spears fought of themselves; ravens flew at the men and pressed them so hard that they had to keep them off with sword and shield. In Iceland, on the day of battle, blood came on the priest's stole. In the Orkneys a chieftain saw the apparition of Earl Sigurd and rode forward to meet it—"men saw that they met and rode under a brae, but they never were seen again." In the Southern Islands Earl Gilli dreamt that a man came to him from Ireland and sang runes about the battle. In Caithness a man saw folk riding twelve together to a bower; he looked through the window slit and saw women weaving: men's heads were the weights of the looms, men's entrails were the warp and woof, a sword was the shuttle, the reeds were arrows. And as they wove the women chanted a lament for "the sword-bearing rovers" which the man who watched learned by heart. These rovers considered the battle which King Brian offered them at Dublin as a battle for a kingdom.

This king's people were Southern; compared to the Northern dynasts they had such little importance that the literati who made up the pre-Christian history of Ireland and distributed shadowy high-kingships amongst the ruling families, did not trouble to give them a representative at Tara. But they became important when two brothers, Mahon and Brian, defeated a Norse and Irish force in their native territory. The Norse had been raiding into Ireland since the year

800. They built fortresses, Dublin being their first. But they made no conquests—only a dozen place-names in Ireland are of Norse origin. Their settlements were trading centres: there was one at Limerick. They fought amongst themselves, made alliances with the Irish, married Irish women. The mother of the Norse king of Dublin, Sigtrygg, was an Irish woman; Earl Sigurd, too, had an Irish mother.

A few years after the victory that had raised the prestige of the little state at the end of the Shannon, Brian came to the headship of his people, and took a title that had prestige attached to it—he was now King of Cashel. For the next twenty-five years he occupied himself with affairs at this end of Ireland. In 980 a prince in whose family the rule of Tara adhered became high-king; he was Maelseachlainn whose name is often written Malachi. He had defeated the Norse at Tara; he had taken their stronghold of Dublin, and, liberating captives there, had brought away two famous trophies, the sword of Carlus and the torque of Tomar. He and Brian divided Ireland between them, Malachi taking the northern half as his sphere, and Brian the southern half.

But Leinster, included in the southern half, made an alliance with the Norse of Dublin, and declared war. Brian, with the support of Malachi, defeated the Leinstermen and the Norse; he took Dublin and plundered it. Then he made an alliance with the Norse. Gathering all his forces he marched on Tara and demanded that Malachi acknowledge him as high-king.

A month was given for preparation for the contest. Malachi's poets appealed to all the race of Niall to support their kinsman against Brian. Malachi himself offered to surrender the high-kingship to the northern kindred if they would defend it. But when he found them more inclined to bargain with him than to defend their dynastic privileges, he went into Brian's camp and accepted gifts from him—a token of submission. Malachi seems to have been free of that military vanity which in its nobles was the curse of the Gaelic polity.

In the year 1002 Brian became King of Ireland. In the Northern metropolis, Armagh, his secretary wrote his title in words which can still be read, "Imperator Scotorum." He was consciously taking pattern by Charlemagne, and the title he assumed seems to show that he wanted to establish in Ireland something like Roman authority. He claimed possession of all the Southern fortresses. He attempted to weaken the Northern dynasts by recognizing the petty kingdoms from which they drew tribute. His alliance with the Norse of Dublin gave him an army that was detached from any particular Irish state. But in striving to create a dominating state in Ireland Brian had a more difficult task than an able and ambitious dynast in any other part of Western Europe would have had. The whole constitution of society was opposed to centralized authority. And Ireland had not been disintegrated by conquest after conquest in the European states where a central authority was being established: society here was at once vital and conservative, and if it recognized any right to titular high-kingship it recognized it in the descendants of Niall, the Northern kindred.

Twelve years after he had declared himself high-king he had to face an invasion of Ireland. The Norse and the Irish accounts show a woman working to bring about the war. She was Gormlai, the sister of the King of Leinster, the mother of Sigtrygg, the Norse king of Dublin: she is called Kormlada in the Njal Saga. Gormlai brought about a new alliance between the Norse and the Leinstermen. She prevailed upon her son to gather forces that would be great enough to overthrow Brian's. And when Sigtrygg told her he had secured the help of Earl Sigurd with the promise of the kingdom of Ireland and herself for his wife, "she was well pleased, but said they must gather greater forces still." And so with Earl Sigurd he summoned Earl Brodir.

The Norse of Dublin with the Leinstermen and the Vikings from overseas made a force of about twenty thousand men—a great force for those days. Brian had the men of Munster and Connacht; he had the support of Malachi with the men of Meath; and he had Scottish allies, Domnall, Steward of Mar, with the men of Mar and Lennox. He was old now, and at the actual battle he remained in a "shieldburg" outside the line. The fighting took place in what is now covered by the northern streets of Dublin city: the Viking ships lay at Clontarf, and the retreat to them was across a weir. In Irish history the battle is "The Battle of Clontarf," in the Norse saga it is "The Battle of Dublin."

Earl Brodir's mail-clad men were greatly dreaded by the Irish who still fought in their tunics. They were the right wing of the Norse army with Earl Sigurd and the Orkney and Shetland men. Murchadh, Brian's son, led the wing opposed to this powerful force: he had the home-forces, the men of the Shannon side, and he was supported by the Scottish allies. The Norse centre was made up of the men of Leinster and other Irish forces, and it was opposed by Munster forces. The Norse left was made up of the men of Dublin, and was opposed by the Connacht forces. The battle opened with a single combat in which both champions were killed.

Then Brian's centre was broken by the men of Leinster: his forces were saved by the arrival of Malachi with the men of Meath. The battle went on. Murchadh's onslaught on the Norse right wing was so vigorous that the mail-clad fighters were dispersed. Brodir was forced into a near-by wood. Tordelbach, Brian's grandson, who is named Kerthialfad in the Njal Saga, opposed Earl Sigurd.

Earl Sigurd, had he won this battle and set himself up as King of Ireland, could have claimed kindred with a dynastic family, for his mother was Eithne, daughter of a King of Ossory. It was she who wove the magic banner that he carried. The earl's Saga tells how he went to his mother for advice about a battle he was going into, saying to her that there would be no less odds against him than seven to one. She answered, "I had reared thee up long in my wool-bag had I known that thou wouldst like to live for ever. . . . Better it is to die with honour than to live with shame. Take thou here hold of this banner which I have made for thee with all my cunning, and I ween it will bring victory to those before whom it is borne, but speedy death to him who bears it." Now Brian's grandson, a youth of fifteen, came against him, the Njal Saga tells, "so fast that he laid low all who were in the front rank, and he broke the array of Earl Sigurd right up to his banner, and slew the banner-bearer."

"Then he got another man to bear the banner, and there was a hard fight. Kerthialfad smote this man to his death-blow at once, and so on, one after the other, all who stood near him."

"Then Earl Sigurd called on Thorstein, the son of Hall of the Side, to bear the banner, and Thorstein was just about to lift the banner, but Asmund the White said, 'Don't bear the banner! For all who bear it get their death!' 'Hafrn the Red,' called the earl, 'bear the banner.' 'Bear thine own devil thyself,' answered Hafrn. Then the earl said, ' 'Tis fittest that the beggar should bear the bag,' and with that he took the banner from the staff and put it under his cloak."

Seeing that the battle was going against him, Sigurd formed the design of capturing or killing Brian. He drew Brodir from the near-by wood to join with him. Breaking through the lines they slew the king's guards.

His son and grandson hurried to where Brian was. Sigurd with his banner was killed. But Brodir, breaking into the shieldburg, had slain the king. Now, surrounded by foemen, Brodir was slain by an unknown hand.

The battle was over; the King of Ireland had won over the Norse and their Irish allies; the Vikings had retreated to their ships. But Brian was dead in the shieldburg. His son Murchadh, engaging in single combat with a Viking, lost his life, and Tordelbach, his grandson, was slain in the water beside the Viking ships. Possibly an Irish defeat by Earl Sigurd would have been less disastrous than a victory with the deaths of Brian, Murchadh, Tordelbach, and the weakening of the Southern power. Malachi resumed the high-kingship. But after his time all who claimed it were written of as "Kings of Ireland with opposition." The old sanction for the high-kingship, descent from Niall, was gone, and before a new sanction could grow up the Normans had come into the land. The song which is given in the Njal Saga, the song which Darraud had heard the weird women sing, was prophetic for Ireland:

> Now new-coming nations
> That island shall rule,
> Who on outlying headlands
> Abode ere the fight;
> I say that king mighty
> To death now is done,
> Now low before spear-point
> That earl bows his head.

The South

Soon over all Ersemen
Sharp sorrow shall fall,
That woe to those warriors
Shall wane nevermore;
Our woof now is woven,
Now battlefield waste,
O'er land and o'er water
War tidings shall leap.